COCHRAN

COCHRAN

JAMES HARDING

Methuen · London

First published in Great Britain in 1988
by Methuen London,
Michelin House, 81 Fulham Road, London sw 3 6 rb
and distributed in the USA by HEB Inc,
70 Cork St., Portsmouth, New Hampshire 03801
Copyright © James Harding 1988
Photoset by Rowland Phototypesetting Ltd
Bury St Edmunds, Suffolk
Printed in Great Britain
by Mackays of Chatham plc
Chatham, Kent

British Library Cataloguing in Publication Data

Harding, James, *1929*–
Cochran.—(A Methuen dramabook).
1. Great Britain. Theatre. Production.
Cochran, C. B. (Charles Blake), 1872–1951
I. Title
792'.0232'0924

ISBN 0-413-15350-9

To the memory of
Douglas Byng
– his favourite comedian
and mine

CONTENTS

LIST OF ILLUSTRATIONS

1. Charles Blake Cochran at the age of seven.
2. Cochran the young impresario sets up a deal on the telephone.
3. Mrs Cochran, nee Evelyn Dade, at the time of her marriage.
4. Cochran as the promoter of Hagenbeck's zoo.
5. Mr and Mrs Cochran at a garden party.
6. Cochran the wrestling match impresario.
7. Cochran behind the scenes at Olympia. *Photo*: BBC Hulton Picture Library.
8. A scene from Sacha Guitry's *Mozart*: Sacha Guitry with Yvonne Printemps as Mozart.
9. Augustus John's design for the second act of O'Casey's *The Silver Tassie*.
10. Cochran with Noël Coward and some of the 'Young Ladies' on board ship at Southampton. *Photo*: BBC Hulton Picture Library.
11. Poster for *Bless the Bride*.
12. Cochran sizing up a dress for *Bless the Bride*. *Photo*: BBC Hulton Picture Library.
13. Cochran with Jessie Matthews. *Photo*: BBC Hulton Picture Library.
14. Tilly Losch in one of her speciality dances. *Photo*: BBC Hulton Picture Library.
15. Cochran seen by 'Autori' at the height of his London Pavilion successes.
16. Valerie Frazer.
17. The seaside tableau in *Cavalcade*.
18. Cochran and Yvonne Printemps in Paris.
19. Cochran discusses a point with Wendy Toye. *Photo*: Popperfoto
20. Cochran at rehearsal. *Photo*: BBC Hulton Picture Library.
21. Noël Coward at the time of *Cavalcade*.

ACKNOWLEDGEMENTS

Although the late Douglas Byng in common with other nonagenarians could not remember events of the day before yesterday, he had until his lamented death aged ninety-four a clear memory of his years with Charles B. Cochran in London Pavilion revues and elsewhere. I am grateful to him for the reminiscences he told in his characteristically dry and witty manner. My thanks are also due to Miss Evelyn Laye CBE and to Miss Dorothy Dickson for their recollections. Mr Billy Milton kindly produced a wealth of documentation. Miss Valerie Frazer (Mrs C. S. Martin) gave me invaluable details about Mr Cochran's Young Ladies, the Trocadero shows and the revues of the late nineteen-thirties. Mr Dennis Van Thal of London Management and Sir Peter Saunders drew generously on their personal recollections, as did Miss Oriel Ross (Lady Poulett). I must also record my gratitude to Miss Anne Marie Koller, Mr Frank Churchett, Mr Ion Trewin, Mr Lee Menzies, and Mr Patrick Newley. As always it is a pleasure to acknowledge the secretarial skills of Mrs Lynda Saunders.

FOREWORD

Few weeks go by without reports by that excellent paper *The Stage* of anguished pleas from toilers in the subsidised theatre. If, they claim, more and still more money is not forthcoming from the tax-payer, then Britain will become an arid waste, a desert of Philistinism where the arts have withered and perished. Such appeals would have astonished Cochran, or Charles B. Cochran as he liked to be known. During his fifty years and more of showmanship he mounted about a hundred and thirty productions which he financed himself or with backing from others. He could always raise money for new shows when he wanted it. Such was his charm and such his confidence that hard-faced businessmen readily pledged large sums without even knowing what Cochran wanted them for: it could have been a heavyweight boxing championship or a season of Eleanora Duse, a rodeo or a play by Rostand, a skating competition or experimental drama by Pirandello.

Cochran is usually remembered as the genius of revue, a mixture of wit and satirical comment, of popular song and pointed sketches. It depended for success on the skill with which it was blended and the sequence the individual items followed. The audience were not allowed time to be bored. Each number was carefully placed to increase the excitement and lead on with the promise of even greater things to come. No-one was more adept at mixing this delicate brew than Cochran. He did so with flair and panache. His chorus girls were more beautiful than anyone else's, his costumes and settings were more lavish, his stars more famous. His revues were a by-word for glittering excellence and his name alone an assurance of glamour. He did everything in the grand manner. Once he organized a giant cabaret at Grosvenor House. His electricians told him it was impossible to accommodate the three stages and the circus ring he wanted because the roof was too low. 'Very well,' he answered without a pause, 'take the roof off.'

He was everything to be expected of a master showman. The bonnet of his Rolls-Royce carried his personal mascot, a crowing cock. His cigars rivalled in size those of Lew Grade. His suits were immaculate, his shirts a miracle of crisp purity. His collection of modern French paintings was one of the finest in private hands. He knew that to be successful you must give the appearance of success. The poorer you were the more important it was to have a suite at the Ritz, and the bigger your overdraft the greater the sums of money you should ask for. He made the equivalent of today's millions, lost them all and left a meagre twenty thousand pounds. Money did not interest him except as a means of creating lovely stage pictures. He was a gambler who played the game because he loved it and not to enrich himself. Twice he went bankrupt. On the second occasion his creditors were so impressed by his arguments that they ended the court proceedings by bursting spontaneously into a chorus of 'For he's a jolly good fellow!'

As he himself was to say, he would not have lasted so long in the cruel world of the theatre had he not possessed enduring optimism and toughness. The only critic whose opinion he respected was the box-office. When bookings started to falter he readily cut his losses and moved on to another of the many projects he always had in reserve. He was disappointed that the public might not have shared his enthusiasm for a given play but he did not repine. Even if a show was playing to full houses he would sometimes take it off because he was bored with it and confident that his next production would be just as triumphant. His energy was limitless. During his career he ran, at one time or another, thirteen of London's most famous theatres. There were occasions when he managed half a dozen of them simultaneously. To operate one theatre successfully and to stock it with profitable entertainment is an achievement in itself. To do so with six at the same time is virtuosity. Although closely associated with revue he was a man of wide cultural taste. It is often forgotten that his very first production in 1897 was Ibsen's *John Gabriel Borkman*. He brought to London Sacha Guitry, the Pitoëffs, the Chauve-Souris, Eleanora Duse, Sarah Bernhardt,

Katina Paxinou and Diaghilev's Russian Ballet. On all of them he lost money yet considered it well spent for the sake of the pleasure they gave to him and to a select portion of the public. O'Casey, Brieux, Rostand, O'Neill, Pirandello and Barrie's last difficult play were other objects of his disinterested benevolence. The connoisseur of women's legs was also a connoisseur of the avant-garde.

His gift for publicity was unerring. An example is his invention of 'Mr Cochran's Young Ladies.' He manipulated journalists adroitly and was a master at building up public expectation. Many artists owed their initial progress to his astute grooming, among them Alice Delysia, Binnie Hale, Evelyn Laye, Florence Desmond, Jessie Matthews and Elisabeth Bergner. The famous partnership with Noël Coward was to end in bitterness and, on the latter's part, recrimination. In later years, without Cochran to guide and advise, none of Coward's musical plays ever equalled the success of *On With The Dance*, *This Year of Grace* or *Bitter Sweet*.

Although he was short, stocky and red-faced, Cochran dominated with a mixture of charm, persuasiveness and cool authority. He spoke in quiet tones and hardly ever raised his voice. Delegation was one of the secrets that enabled him to achieve so much, and he gathered around him a team of experts whom he could rely on for technical perfection. Another was the intuition that seized on a bare idea and immediately visualized it as a complete stage spectacle. Like all great impresarios he had a flair for choosing the right talents, unexpected though they might at first appear, of bringing them together and of creating the conditions in which something unique was born. He knew a lot about everything, – music, lighting, design, acting, costume – but it was his gift for the whole that ensured success. Through his lieutenants he imposed an unmistakeable hallmark on each show he produced and supervised every detail down to the type of silk from which his chorus girls' knickers were made. To achieve this personal control he needed absolute independence. Committees he loathed, shareholders he despised, limited companies he abhorred. Total freedom meant total responsibility, and he took on his own shoulders, and his alone, the triumph or failure that resulted. As a showman, a title he gloried in, he was ready to give the public what he thought it wanted: rodeos, performing fleas, midgets, circuses, boxing matches, plays, musical comedies, operettas, revues, pantomimes or pageants. The English Diaghilev may have been wrong as many times as he was right, but he never gave up trying in spite of failure, bankruptcy and the crippling arthritis which was to cause, indirectly, his horrible death.

Chapter One
CHARLIE COCHRAN

'Many times I have said with absolute sincerity
that I would rather see a good juggler than
a bad Hamlet, a good clown than a bad
King Lear.'

Charles B. Cochran

---

i
AUBREY BEARDSLEY AND PEPPER'S GHOST

'From my earliest days I have been a hero-worshipper and I see
nothing to regret in the fact. To me a genuine enthusiasm is the
salt of life . . .'

CHARLES B. COCHRAN

The Christmas pantomime for 1879 at the Brighton Theatre
Royal and Opera House was *Sindbad The Sailor*. This 'grand
operatic fairy spectacular' as the posters described it had been
produced under the personal supervision of Mrs H. Nye Chart,
proprietor and manageress. Mrs Chart, widowed at an early
age, had inherited from her late husband a theatre sunk in
decrepitude and near-bankruptcy. Over the years that followed
she restored its fortune and made it into one of the most
successful on the provincial circuit. Brighton knew her as a
leading personality and as the embodiment of the Theatre Royal
where her influence, back-stage and front of house, dominated
everything. At the end of each performance it was Mrs Chart's
habit to sweep on stage and take a solo curtain all to herself.
Gentlemen in the audience eagerly looked forward to this

traditional event since she was a large woman of handsome proportions who always wore a very low-cut dress and who always bowed very deeply. One evening a stage-hand much in liquor from celebrating Christmas rushed on at the moment when her bow was at its deepest and impiously grasped what she so generously revealed. 'Now,' he shouted, staggering back into the wings, a lifetime's ambition achieved, 'sack me!'

It was typical of Mrs Chart's flair that for *Sindbad The Sailor* she should have engaged Arthur Roberts, at the time England's most famous comedian. His special talent was impromptu 'business'. None of his performances was ever the same, although, a true professional, however exuberant his improvisations he scrupulously refrained from upsetting his fellow players' exits and entrances. In *Sindbad The Sailor*, playing the part of Tinbad the Tailor – 'a snip of the old block,' said the programme, 'whose soul being above his shears, from *sheer* necessity, *sheers* off' – he could gag to his heart's content, for the loose conventions of pantomime gave him the broadest of licence. Off-stage, too, he was continually inventive. One of his favourite jokes was to embark on a long and rambling narrative to a friend which, as others drifted up to hear, he would embroider with all sorts of preposterous twists and turns designed to confuse and bamboozle. This he called 'spoof', and, in his autobiography *Fifty Years of Spoof*, he gave a new word to the English language.

Among the audience at a performance of *Sindbad The Sailor* was a schoolboy of seven called Charles Blake Cochran. It was his first visit to the theatre, and his memory of it stayed with him for the rest of his life. He never forgot the red and gold curtain swishing up to reveal the port of Baghdad and the ship 'Tubberino' waiting at the quay. (That it was, according to the programme, 'bound for Shoreham', constituted an adult joke he did not realize). The good ship took Sindbad on a journey to adventures with Tornado the Storm King, the fabulous Roc, Queen Quipsankranky, the gorgeous Princess Pretty Pearl and a villainous gang of wreckers. On the enchanted isle there were fairies in spangled costumes to dazzle the eye and the mellow gleam of gas and lime to shed a soft radiance of mystery. The transformation scene blazed into a magnificence he remembered until he died. Above all he was fascinated by the big rolling eyes and india-rubber mouth of Arthur Roberts, the drollery of his manner and the torrent of laughter he could evoke with the slightest gesture, often no more than the arching of an eyebrow or the flick of a finger. There was no doubt about it: when Charlie Cochran grew up, he decided there and then, he would become a funny man like Arthur Roberts.

One Sunday while fashionable churchgoers paraded on Brighton front he saw his hero in person.

'So,' Arthur Roberts was saying to a friend, 'I got up and had a splash in a pie-dish!'

The boy, intrigued by this shred of conversation, walked straight ahead and cannoned into him. He mumbled an apology and Roberts made some kindly remark. A little while later Charlie's father took his son back-stage at the Theatre Royal and introduced him to Roberts himself in the presence of Mrs Nye Chart. Cochran senior already knew Mrs Chart and had met Roberts before. They laughed affectionately at the little boy and his awe on finding himself confronted with a god and goddess. Forty years later, when Cochran had become a famous impresario, Roberts's glory was eclipsed. Younger men like Dan Leno and George Robey had overtaken him and he was no longer a star. Cochran, remembering the old days, gave him employment in his London Pavilion revues. Although the veteran comedian was by then shaky and ailing, once in front of an audience he could still make them laugh with his irrepressible capers. The whirligig of time proved that Cochran's memory had been justified by inspired clowning which neither public indifference nor the passing of years were unable to dim.

Even as a child of seven Cochran was excited by feminine beauty, and another member of the *Sindbad The Sailor* cast impressed him, though in a different way from Arthur Roberts. The part of Jinbad the Jailer was taken by Dolly Tester, the daughter of a very humble family who had once worked for his grandmother. Dolly married, as actresses often did at the time, into the peerage, though her choice of husband was lamentable. This was the Marquess of Ailesbury, known as 'Ducks', who squandered his fortune and aspired, before all else, to be taken for a bookmaker, a coachman or a costermonger rather than a nobleman. His mastery of rhyming slang was unequalled. When a groom he was about to sack for drunkenness protested that he'd been 'very steady lately,' Lord 'Ducks' interjected: 'Steady be damned! You ain't been first of October for a bubble-and-squeak!'* Cochran often saw him on the front at Brighton. His Marchioness wore furs and sables. His Lordship favoured loud checks, a top-coat with buttons large as saucers, and flourished a riding whip. His command of language other than rhyming was Homeric.

Lord 'Ducks' was only one of many picturesque figures whom Cochran used to see on the front. Society had not yet acquired the habit of foreign holidays, and Brighton was where everyone spent the weekends and long vacations. Here came famous journalists like the red-nosed George Augustus Sala – when introduced socially to a well-known pawnbroker he grunted: 'Good morning. It's the first time I've seen your legs' – and George R. Sims, author of *Christmas Day In The Workhouse* and numerous blood-boltered melodramas. On Brighton front were to be seen millionaires, jockeys, trainers, judges, musical comedy stars and even the sly shade of Henry Irving. It was here, against a background of wedding-cake hotel façades and dashing broughams and cabriolets, that Cochran acquired what was to be a lifelong appetite for talent of every sort, for achievement and for unusual personalities.

His father, James Elphinston Cochran, owned a wholesale tea and cigar importing business at 49 North Street. It was, in the early days at least, a prosperous affair. He married a pretty girl named Matilda Walton, daughter of a Merchant Navy officer, a Londoner born in Fleet Street. Widowed before the age of twenty-one, she was the relict of a Mr Arnold by whom she already had a son called Bert. Mr Arnold possessed absorbing literary tastes. One evening, so family tradition had it, he came home but could not get in because the front door was locked. He calmly sat down on the step and, in the light from a nearby lamp-post, read a book of poems. So engrossed was he that he did not feel the increasing cold of a chilly night which

*   Sober for a week

eventually brought on the pneumonia that caused his early death.

When Mr Cochran wedded his Matilda he also took on Bert as his stepson. Over the years that followed Bert was joined, with a celerity typical of Victorian times, by five sisters and four brothers. There were Minnie, Alice, Tilly, Louisa and Edie, and Charlie, Alec, Frank and Arthur. Their mother gave further proof of robustness by surviving until 1929 when she died at the age of ninety-one, still wearing to the end a voluminous black hat secured with a vast bow of the sort favoured by the late Queen Victoria. She had long outlived her husband who succumbed to an attack of typhoid fever after his sixtieth birthday in 1900.

The daughters, as time passed, found husbands. Of the boys, Alec lived on into his nineties after running a public house at Bexley Heath and, later, a catering establishment at Whipsnade Zoo. Frank went into the music-hall and became a juggler-cyclist in a troupe known as The Westwood Brothers, after which he settled down as a photographer in Cambridgeshire. Arthur was a casualty of the 1914–18 war. And Charlie? At the age of seven he wanted to follow a multiplicity of callings. We have seen that one of his ambitions was to be a comedian like Arthur Roberts. For a time, inspired by his father's interest in racing, he saw himself in the mould of a famous jockey like Fred Archer whom he glimpsed on the steps of the Old Ship Hotel in Brighton. The novels of Charles Dickens instilled a brief resolve to learn shorthand and take up the career of a parliamentary reporter as their author had done. He day-dreamed, too, of romantic ancestors. May he not have been a descendant of Admiral Cochrane the great naval commander, hero of many sea battles and eventually buried in Westminster Abbey? Could he have been related to the historic family of Baron Elphinstone, as his father's second Christian name might suggest? He preferred to overlook the obtrusive 'e' which both these more famous patronymics carried.

From kindergarten at Lewes Charlie was sent with his younger brother Alec to a college at Eastbourne. There, one Guy Fawkes night, he and some other boys played truant to see the fireworks. Charlie was expelled. He next went to Brighton

Grammar School and, on his first day there, entered on a close friendship with a thin, red-haired boy. This boy, who in profile revealed a large beak of a nose such as might have belonged to some exotic bird, had long slender hands and tapering fingers. He talked excitedly and gesticulated with nervous motions. His name was Aubrey Beardsley and he already had a mania for filling sheets of paper with odd, spidery drawings. The two friends shared a room and, with Beardsley's encouragement, Charlie developed an interest in acting. Under his new friend's guidance he read the classic plays, Elizabethan and Restoration, eighteenth-century tragedy and comedy, and modern pieces as well. Beardsley, he was later to say, had a great influence on his life.

The headmaster of Brighton Grammar School was a pedagogue with original ideas. He taught Latin grammar by means of rhymed drills and instructed his pupils in English history with the aid of verse. At Christmas the boys were all expected to contribute to and take part in seasonal entertainments. The 'book' was written by a master and illustrated by Beardsley. One of these performances took place at the Dome and recounted the adventures of *The Pied Piper*. From the nearby Corn Exchange, used as a Green Room, Charlie Cochran and Beardsley led the boys in their flamboyant costumes and marshalled them on the platform of the Dome. A year or so later the two boys collaborated on a play given at the Brighton Pavilion. The programme, headed '*A Brown Study*. A one-act play by Aubrey V. Beardsley,' features the name of Charles Cochran in the cast. It is the only known play Beardsley ever wrote.

Beardsley's fantasy overflowed into his private life as well. He and Cochran once travelled to the college which had been the scene of the Guy Fawkes escapade for the purpose of scoring a cricket match. It was Beardsley's suggestion to dress up as an old man, to call on the headmaster and to pass himself off as an uncle of two boys there. 'I am Jasper Rayner', announced a venerable and bearded apparition at the headmaster's door. He went on to explain that he had made his fortune in California and that he wished to take the boys out for tea. The headmaster, impressed by the elderly gentleman's rugged but honest demeanour, gave his permission. Mr Rayner took the lads with him, stuffed his beard in his pockets and, at the Albion Hotel, entertained them to crumpets with Charlie.

The Cochran family spent their holidays with grandparents at the White Cottages on Lindfield Common. Charlie loved the countryside there, although it cannot have pleased him that, some years afterward, Lindfield was the birthplace of Hannen Swaffer, the acidulous drama critic and journalist with whom he was later to have sharp disagreements.

So great was Charlie's attachment to Lindfield that, in books of reference, he always claimed to have been born there. His place of birth was, however, the family home at 15, Prestonville Road, Brighton, where he first saw the light of day on the 25 September, 1872. Yet Lindfield he regarded as his spiritual home. If the Brighton Theatre Royal had given him a passion for the stage, Lindfield inspired him with his love of fairs and circuses. Here, on Lindfield Common, he delighted in the garishly rouged men and women who paraded before the side-shows urging crowds of gaping rustics to enter and wonder at the bearded ladies and midgets and giants and two-headed babies that lurked within. When darkness fell and naphtha lights spluttered and winked, the colours flickered on the sweaty faces of voluble showmen and turned the scene into a bizarre kaleidoscope. Among the ancient tricks of illusion he learned from the fairground was that of 'Pepper's Ghost', a device used in the chilling climax of *The Mistletoe Bough*, a Victorian poem long a favourite with parlour reciters. The corpse of an unhappy bride was placed in an old oak and chest and the lid firmly clamped down. At the end the body materialised and rose ghost-like from the chest. As Charlie was to realize, there are few theatrical illusions that cannot be created with the aid of black cloth or black paint.

The most glamorous event of the season was the circus procession. From a first-floor window Charlie saw Britannia, a lion at her feet, borne through the streets on a lofty golden chariot embellished with a riot of allegory and drawn by four high-stepping horses. Liveried grooms and a loud brass band plonking out jingoistic tunes went before her accompanied by clowns swaying on high stilts and peering impudently into bedroom windows. Then came elephants snatching with their trunks at buns held out by daring urchins. They were followed by cages of roaring lions and tigers presided over by a nonchalant trainer in sparkling uniform. And at last came the great man himself, 'Lord' George Sanger, husband of the lady who impersonated Britannia. He rode, top-hatted and upright, in a grand carriage harnessed to six pairs of horses and escorted by postilions and outriders. He had no real claim to his lordly title. In a dispute with the rival showman Buffalo Bill the latter had been described by counsel as 'The Honourable Mr Cody.' Outraged at the presumption, Sanger declared: 'If he's an Honourable I'm a Lord!' From then on he was known as Lord George Sanger. At the first of many royal command performances Queen Victoria asked him for an explanation of his self-ennoblement. When Lord George told her she observed: 'Most amusing'.

In later life, whenever he glimpsed a circus tent in a field, Cochran would always break his journey and go on a visit there to make new friends. He learned to appreciate the freemasonry of circus folk, their generosity to each other and the strict discipline that governed their professional lives. The smell of sawdust was magic to him, and the sound of hoofs padding softly around the ring became music in his ears. As a boy he fell in love with dainty Miss Ginnett who jumped through hoops from a broad-backed horse. He was no less enamoured of music-hall stars such as Marie Lloyd whom he admired for her pertness and brilliant timing. He could even remember Charlie Chaplin's father as a singer of pathetic ballads. The old Oxford at Brighton was the first music-hall he ever entered, although his elders deplored it as one of the gates to hell. Enticed by a singer billed as 'The Man Who Goes The Whole Hog', he sat in the gallery quivering with illicit expectation, only to be disappointed by a lachrymose rendering of 'Poor Old Joe'. Much more exciting was a Chinese juggler who, having swallowed a sword, would then strap a cannon to his head and fire it off. 'Now put your heads down!' he would scream before detonating the infernal machine. One evening an adventurous youth, anxious to see how the trick was done, popped his head up and received the paper wad in his brain. The juggler was tried for manslaughter but acquitted. Ever afterward he billed himself on posters as 'The Man Who Blew The Boy's Brains Out At Brighton.'

ii
'A DISMAL FAILURE' GOES TO AMERICA

'As I have said before, all those connected with the theatre, from stage-hands to producers, are stage-struck; if they were not they would not choose the theatre as a means of livelihood.'

CHARLES B. COCHRAN

Charlie and his friend Aubrey Beardsley were reluctant members of the classroom. 'Neither of us,' the former once recalled, 'did a great deal of work at Brighton Grammar School.' Beardsley had a quick mind which, as exams approached, enabled him to put on a sudden spurt and, with concentrated study, to make up for months of laziness. Charlie was not so sharp but somehow managed to struggle on. Nearly every week, encouraged by a master fond of the theatre, he and Beardsley took part in a play. Once it was a popular farce called *Ici On Parle Français* in which Beardsley, naturally a fast talker and much given to gesticulation, played a Frenchman, and Charlie took the part made famous by the well-known comedian J. L. Toole. They did melodramas, too, and gave recitations at which Beardsley thrilled his audience with 'The Dream of Eugène Aram', Thomas Hood's eerie murder story. Charlie was delighted to read that one of his own performances was described in *The Sussex Daily News* as 'quite professional.'

As he grew older he was allowed occasional visits to London. Here, in 1888, he saw the première of *The Yeomen of The Guard*. The most abiding impression of those years was made by Henry Irving at the Lyceum. Irving was unique, a phenomenon unrivalled by any other player. In later years, feeling that perhaps his youthful fervour had misled him, Charlie asked contemporaries what they had thought of Irving: he found that their opinions were the same as his and that their recollections were equally vivid. As Robert Macaire, Irving conveyed depths of villainy which were frightening, and Charlie discovered that everyone else thought the same. He decided that play-goers who had not waited for the green baize curtain to rise at the Lyceum in Irving's day had never fully enjoyed the exquisite delights of anticipation. There was nothing to rival the glory of Irving's reign. Charlie regretted that he was five years old when Irving last played Hamlet and had thus been unable to see the actor in one of his most famous rôles. It was no great consolation to realize, at the end of his life, that he had witnessed over eighty different actors as Hamlet, for he had missed the greatest of them all.

His first Hamlet he saw at the Brighton Theatre Royal. This was Edmund Tearle, uncle of Godfrey, who declaimed the verse in a rich rolling voice. Another and greater star of the time was Madge Kendal whose acquaintance Charlie also made at Brighton. Her technique struck him as the acme of simplicity and her method as supremely natural. An actor at a crucial point upstaged her through sheer nerves – something one just did not do to Mrs Kendal, for she was a notorious tyrant – and he apologized humbly. For once she did not fly into a rage. 'My dear,' she told him, 'I don't care two pins where you are! I should be ashamed of myself if I couldn't convey my feelings through my shoulder or my back as well as my face! Every bit of you has got to act if you can act at all!'

Charlie's father shared his son's interest in the theatre. Mr Cochran also enjoyed the excitements of the race-course, and, so long as his tea business flourished, was able to cut something of a figure on the turf. He kept his large family in reasonable comfort and employed a nurse, a cook and a maid. Hunting gave him as much pleasure as racing. Driving was another recreation, and he owned a good stable of horses. In fashionable clubs he was known as an amiable sportsman and a *bon vivant*. By 1888, however, when Charlie was sixteen, Mr Cochran had lost, rather speedily, considerable sums of money. He would come home later and later in the evening and was seen less and less around the house. Eventually the business was sold to pay his debts. The elder sisters were put out to work in a laundry and another was thankfully married off. Charlie, not without a certain relief, found himself taken away from school and placed as an office-boy with an estate agent. He soon realized that he had exchanged one type of boredom for another, and with the added disadvantage that the hours were longer.

In his scant leisure time the reluctant office worker became aware of a new pastime which he soon discovered to be as absorbing as the theatre. Boxing matches were then often held near his home, and one of the principal figures was a heavyweight called Jem Smith. As Smith's later career showed, he was a dirty fighter who specialised in hitting low and in back-heeling. Charlie, then an innocent hero worshipper, did not realize this and looked on Smith with admiration as the devious puncher slugged his way through bloodied combats. Although gloves were by now obligatory in England, Smith fought a number of bare-fist engagements abroad, once sustaining a hundred and six rounds in two and a half hours. The result was a draw. Charlie followed newspaper accounts of these epic affairs with gloating excitement and, wherever possible, went to see his hero Smith in person. As well as theatre magazines and plays, his favourite reading now included *The Licensed Victuallers' Gazette* and *The Police News* with its pictures of scintillating diamond belts and of chunky boxers warily circling around each other.

Boxing, theatre, music-hall, circuses: these were the topics which enthused him, not the surveyors' reports and rent-books that clouded his days in the Brighton estate agents' office. For nearly two years he struggled with the boredom of posting letters, running errands for the partners, making tea and sweeping floors. He only really came to life on expeditions to the prize ring and the theatre. In the summer of 1890 he travelled to London with Aubrey Beardsley, thin and fidgety as ever, his long bony fingers itching to scribble the caricatures which, at his drawing desk, he threw off by the dozen. Beardsley's pretty sister Mabel came with them and they saw *As You Like It* in which Ada Rehan, the greatest American actress of her time, was then dazzling the town. Such interludes were unsettling. They reminded Charlie of the brilliant world he longed to join and, by contrast, of the dreariness that was currently his lot. He thought again of Arthur Roberts and decided that he would try his luck as a comic singer.

At a Brighton music hall, the Alhambra, he made the acquaintance of a stage-manager called Lonsdale who had written that popular song 'Tommy Make Room For Your Father' and other numbers. Charlie began performing some of them at smoking concerts with a pianist by the name of Wilson. Both these men were, in Charlie's eyes, veterans of the stage, and he listened eagerly to their conversation. Wilson later took a post at the Royal Clarence music-hall in Dover and invited him for a week's engagement to sing his comic songs there. Charlie arrived full of confidence and pleasantly surprised with himself at not feeling the slightest bit nervous. He bounced on stage and sang three items in complete silence. When he made his exit the silence continued without a hint of applause. In a letter to his mother he wrote: 'I was a DISMAL FAILURE.'

The proprietor dismissed him for incompetence and refused even to pay him. 'All that life seemed to me worth living for (FAME and popularity) had vanished and I felt that I cared for nothing.' Charlie wrote. At Brighton smoking concerts he had sung with a piano accompaniment to a gathering of boozy friends anxious to applaud him. In the music hall, performing unrehearsed with a band, he confronted an audience of strangers who would make no such concession.

Next morning after breakfast he strolled on the pier and battled within himself. He had to face the fact that one of the great questions in his life had been answered. 'Was I to be a music-hall singer?' The verdict was no. Even so he could not help feeling that if he had the money to buy a good song from one of the leading composers the result would have been different. He agonised to his mother: 'You who know not the sweets of applause cannot imagine the blow I received after having been sought after so much in Brighton and received as though I were a genius . . .'

At least, he consoled himself, he had tried, and although the effort had left him in debt he would never have settled to anything while still cherishing the illusion that money and popularity awaited him at the stage door. The week's holiday he had taken from the office was up and time came for him to return. He could not face it. A new idea was already flowering in his mind. At school he knew a boy called Scotson Clark, son of the composer who wrote the *Marche aux Flambeaux*, a Victorian best-seller much thrummed on drawing-room pianos. Clark was a 'strange impressive youth', Charlie remembered, handsome and intelligently opinionated about art and literature. He had a talent for drawing and, eventually, became a successful art editor. 'Let's go to America,' Charlie suggested. 'I will earn my living on the stage; you will become a painter.'

Clark agreed to the proposal. How, though, was Charlie to get there? His father was penniless, there remained nothing to pawn, and an office-boy's wage only provided enough, with stringent economy, to travel as far as Dover. The answer was simple: Charlie abstracted the money from his employers. With the aid of this deft embezzlement he took the boat from Newhaven.*

The two boys crossed the Channel in high spirits and arrived at Dieppe. They decided, as there might not be another opportunity, to visit Paris. Charlie's first acquaintance with a city he was to know very well indeed led them to the Divan Japonais where he saw Toulouse-Lautrec, a strange, almost terrifying apparition with a mouth that looked like a gash, an inky black beard, and a body of normal proportions stuck on the legs of a shambling dwarf. From there Charlie and Clark went on to the Moulin Rouge to take a drink in the garden beside the huge plaster elephant and to hear the young and unknown Yvette Guilbert sing one of her 'shocking' songs. She was dressed as a governess, but although she used a comic English accent Charlie could not understand the words that sent the audience into screams of laughter. When she had finished her number the skeletal Valentin led the boisterous quadrille of frenzied dancers whom Toulouse Lautrec recreated in his famous pictures. Another of the painter's subjects was Little Tich in his 'Spanish dancer' turn. At the Folies-Bergère Charlie saw him sweep on stage dressed as a grand lady. '*Je m'appelle Clarice!*' chortled little Tich in a thick Birmingham accent. 'I've just

* Forty years on, when Cochran had made his name, his former boss recognized the one-time office-boy and good-naturedly reproached him for absconding. Cochran replied by sending him tickets to all his first nights.

come from the court ball – what a *succès fou! – beaucoup de succès!* – very nice!' The audience, who loved him more than the English did and looked on him as a Dickensian reincarnation of mediaeval dwarf jesters, roared back: 'Very nice!'

After this taste of the life Charlie longed for, a life unknown to office boys and estate agents, the money began to run out. From Boulogne he and his friend hastened to sail steerage in the company of wretched fellow-travellers whose squalid habits drove them up on deck to sleep near the funnels. Some of the crew took pity on them, allowed them to doss down in their bunks when they were on duty, and shared their own food with them as a relief from the uneatable gruel served in steerage. They came to New York with less than five pounds in their pockets.

That city, Charlie noted with surprise, still had a colonial atmosphere. Tramcars drawn by sauntering mules grated through dusty streets. On either side stood ramshackle one-storey shops and houses. In the bars and taverns roistered millionaires come from the West to spend their money and to enjoy a good time in New York. They wore huge sombreros and, as tie-pins, gold nuggets set with diamonds. Charlie and his friend, now almost penniless, set about finding a job.

At an audition for a new play they walked on stage among a crowd of extras. The producer's glance fell on Charlie. 'I want ladies and gentlemen,' he complained, 'not children. What's that child doing there?' Charlie's plump face turned red and he made his way out. Scotson Clark, despite being the same age, was lucky enough to win acceptance, and the dollar he was paid for each performance had for the time being to support both himself and his friend. He bought himself a top hat and flowing Inverness cape, and, posing as Charlie's manager, sought to convince theatre managers that he represented a comic singer of great talent. No-one believed him.

For a while Charlie helped a champagne representative on his rounds. After a plate of porridge for breakfast he existed for the rest of the day on champagne, since at each house of call the salesman, naturally, would order a bottle of his own firm's manufacture. At least, Charlie thought, he was learning to find his capacity for drink. Then he picked up a singing engagement at a museum of freaks opposite Tammanay Hall. Eight times a day, with as neighbours the dog-faced boy, the fat lady, the skeleton dude and the tattooed man, he sang his comic songs to gaping visitors. After a week or so his voice gave out.

A chance to play old-man parts in a repertory tour of *Our Boys*, that classic English hit comedy, took him out of New York and as quickly brought him back again, for no-one felt like paying to see it. One very hot day he travelled across New York to audition for *Around The World In Eighty Days* at Niblo's Garden, a long way from his theatrical digs. Since he had only a few cents left he decided to walk. At one point the sole of his right shoe fell off, and, having managed to stick it back on again, he slithered along laboriously for the rest of the journey. He was rewarded with seven parts to play, among them an Indian, a sailor, a waiter and a policeman. Despite a heatwave of 90 degrees in the shade the production did well and set off on tour. It ended at Cincinnati where the company broke up. Some of them, Charlie included, struggled on to St Louis where he was obliged to double up even more parts. Finally the despairing backer threw in his hand and offered to pay the fares of the remaining cast back to where they came from or to Chicago. Charlie opted for Chicago.

Snow was falling as he descended from the train at Chicago with twenty-five cents in his pocket. Through a friend who appeared with him in *Around The World In Eighty Days* he obtained an engagement to play in Ohio. For a few weeks he enjoyed a regular salary touring Michigan, Wisconsin, the Lakes, wherever the production could be fitted up in bars, saloons and lumberjack camps. In Eau Clair the tour fell apart and he was a vagabond again. Somebody stole his watch. When he had made his way painfully back to Chicago an unknown thief relieved him of his only suit and even a bundle of dirty washing. He was destitute.

For a while he was sustained by the charity of an actor friend. This benefactor soon, however, had spent all his money as well. A lucky session at roulette won him thirty-five dollars, more cash then Charlie had seen for weeks. He ignored Charlie's anxious plea to give up while the going was good and, with steady fingers, picked up ten dollars and left twenty-five on the winning number. To everyone's astonishment it came up again, and again, and again. When he decided to stop his winnings amounted to eight hundred and seventy-five dollars.

They went out to a restaurant and treated themselves to cocktails, vast porterhouse steaks and big cigars. Afterwards they visited the World's Fair then being held in Chicago and marvelled at the splendour of it all. That night they spent a hundred dollars. Next morning Charlie awoke to see that his friend had vanished. In the afternoon he came back. He had been playing roulette again and, this time, had lost everything.

Desperately they looked for employment. At Jersey City Cochran worked as stooge in a medicine show. The company played a brisk little drama in the booth as prelude to a hard-selling speech by 'Dr' Greenberg flamboyantly praising his ointment. Charlie and his fellow players then circulated among the audience and sold bottles of the nauseating stuff. He earned twenty-five dollars a week plus commission on the amount he persuaded the gullible audience to buy.

Another tour came up. Everyone in the cast was expected to play a musical instrument and Charlie talked himself through the audition by displaying a new-found virtuosity in making music with bells stuck on tennis rackets. For nearly a year he waggled his tennis racket the length and breadth of America. In Kansas City he nearly broke his neck swinging on a bar as the strenuous farce demanded. At Urbana, Ohio, a 'dry' town, he imprudently drank deep of the rotten liquor purveyed by illicit stills. After a disgraceful scene he spent the night in a police cell and, next morning, feeling very ill, was rescued by his disapproving company manager who paid a large fine. In Johnstown, Pennsylvania, he received the only notice of his acting days he ever kept. 'Charles Cochran played the part of Smart, the detective,' declared the town's newspaper. 'He certainly must have learned the art of acting in a stable with hungry horses; he did nothing but attempt to chew the paint from the scenery. A more ridiculous chump has never been seen on the local stage.'

A New York reviewer was more complimentary. 'Mr Cochran is a humorous vocalist of the funniest and most able order. He has a choice repertoire of racy comic songs, and his imitations of the London cabman, costermonger and other grotesque and outlandish types of English eccentric character, are true to nature and irresistibly laughable. His power of imitative facial expression is wonderful, he gives the English dialect "patter" to perfection, and altogether his characterisations are inimitable.' Such praise delighted Charlie who was beginning to lose confidence in his ability as a performer. Even so, the contemptuous note of the Johnstown review continued to depress him. While a good review naturally brings pleasure a bad one causes deeper emotion, and the victim tends to read it over and over again with the sort of masochistic fascination derived from sucking at the pain of a rotten tooth. Was he, Charlie repeatedly asked himself, really as bad as they thought in Johnstown?

He made one more attempt on the stage. In July, 1897, when he was twenty-five, he appeared in what was intended to be an open-air production of *A Midsummer Night's Dream*. Rain intervened and the performance was transferred from Central Park to Madison Square Garden. Among the cast of mortals in the fairy play appears the legend: 'Snug the joiner . . . Charles Cochran.' No more engagements came his way. In a Baltimore hotel that year he was an unimportant guest at a supper given by the American actor Richard Mansfield. There he met, for the first time, Herbert Beerbohm Tree who was touring America with a company that included the young actor Gerald du Maurier. Another guest was the beautiful daughter of a rich local citizen. Both du Maurier and Charlie competed for her favours. On this occasion it was Charlie who triumphed over his rival's debonair charm and engaged on a passionate though brief affair. A few months later, as Charlie commented wryly, 'some sordid local millions came between us' and the Baltimore belle married the scion of a wealthy family.

He adored women and could not keep his hands off them. In the easy-going atmosphere of provincial towns he found that chorus girls were attracted by his square, boyish features. They responded to his natural charm and were amused by his quaint English accent. He was good company and, although his comic acting may not have been all that brilliant on stage, in private life he knew how to make women laugh, an ability, he soon discovered, which eases the path to seduction. They were flattered by his appreciative interest and touched by his thoughtful manner in advising them on their little problems. He had an intuitive feeling for the right moment and sensed exactly when sympathy was needed, when laughter was called for, and when, inevitably, it was time for bed.

While his love-life prospered, though, his career had begun to falter. He remembered Mansfield and called at the box-office of the theatre where he was appearing. The office keeper told him that Mansfield was out, whereupon a deep voice resounded from the depths: 'Who is that asking for me? Why did you say I wasn't here?' The actor himself came in. After a short discussion he said: 'Young man, I'll give you an engagement. Come to me when my season opens.'

In the meantime Charlie had to earn a living. He found one as an employee of the Y.M.C.A. The work involved assisting the Church of England chaplain to the Port of New York and meeting new arrivals from liners. What churches did they attend in England? he had to ask them. If they belonged to the Church of England, he explained, he was there to guide and help them. At two dollars a week the duties were not congenial. He approached the first person he judged to have an Anglo-Saxon air. 'Are you English?' he enquired pleasantly. 'I did not come to this country to be insulted,' replied a furious Irishman. 'I'll throw you in the water!'

A week of this was enough and Charlie waited anxiously for news of Mansfield. He learned that the actor had been taken ill, then that he was recuperating. Still no word came through of preparations for the imminent season. A chance remark from an acquaintance that he was rehearsing in Mansfield's next play reduced Charlie to despair. He was mystified. Had he been forgotten? He wrote and had no reply. For days he sat alone in his miserable lodging and wondered what on earth he should do next. It was, he afterwards said, the bitterest moment of his life.

Suddenly a messenger arrived. 'Where,' Mansfield had demanded at rehearsal, 'is that young Englishman I engaged?' He had sent his stage manager to scour New York for Charlie on pain of losing his job. The young Englishman was found and entered Mansfield's company at a salary of forty dollars a week.

Richard Mansfield then enjoyed the same reputation in America as Irving did in England. He was a full-blooded romantic whose Richard III and Henry V were spectacular affairs presented with dazzling pageantry. One of his greatest successes was a dramatisation of *Dr. Jekyll and Mr. Hyde*. For years people argued about how he managed his transformation from the saintly Dr Jekyll to the villainous Hyde in a scene which invariably terrified the audience and even made some of them faint away. Many explanations were offered to account for this phenomenon but none of them was correct. Watching from the wings each night Charlie could see that Mansfield used no make-up or props. He depended entirely on changing the muscles of his face, on the tones of his voice and on the sudden switch from an upright to a crouching position. All his knowledge of theatrical effect was deployed in the wicked expression and the blood-curdling snarl which filled the dimly-lit stage with an atmosphere of horrid suspense.

Under such a master Charlie felt that he could be ambitious in the make-up he devised for the small rôles that came his way. He put on a large and impressive beard of which he was especially proud and marched off to take his place on stage. Mansfield darted an eagle glance at him.

'Who are you?' he said.

'I'm Cochran, Mr Mansfield.'

'Good God!'

Charlie never quite knew what he meant. He managed to play his minor part without reproof but soon found himself taking on duties as stage-manager. They interested him. As an actor, he decided, you were limited to a very narrow field. As a stage manager you worked on a much broader canvas, and since you were responsible for the look of the whole production your ingenuity was tested in a richer variety of ways. Stage-management, he increasingly thought, was greater fun than acting.

His impression was confirmed when, after the company had been on tour for some time, Mansfield summoned him to interview. They were at Pittsburgh where the actor's private railway carriage was halted in a siding. Since few hotels were luxurious enough for him he had fitted up this conveyance with expensive furniture and travelled everywhere accompanied by his own pictures and books.

'Sit down, Cochran,' barked Mansfield. 'Do you think, Cochran, you'll ever be a good actor?'

Charlie, fearing dismissal, replied that he was doing his best and thought he was improving.

'But,' Mansfield persisted, 'do you think you'll ever be as good an actor as – as I am?'

No, said Charlie, he would not dream of soaring as high as that, but, he added, he was not despondent. He began to think that his unusual conversation was yet another example of Mansfield's notorious eccentricity.

'Well,' Mansfield continued, 'I've been watching you. I don't think you'll ever be a great actor. How would you like to be my private secretary?'

Since Charlie's one concern was to keep himself in a regular job without having to worry about food or a roof over his head, he immediately accepted.

'Very well,' Mansfield concluded, 'you shall have ten dollars a week extra and be my private secretary.'

There and then Charlie set to work drafting letters for Mansfield to sign in reply to the heavy correspondence that arrived each day for America's most famous actor. Diplomacy was needed, and tact, not only in writing suitable replies but also in reading his employer's mind. On his first evening in the new post Charlie put before Mansfield the result of the day's work. Mansfield read and signed. 'Capital!' was his gruff comment.

Prickly, unpredictable, given to sudden moods of anger as quickly succeeded by moments of benevolence, Mansfield was not an easy man to work for. One of Charlie's duties was to find in each town they visited a quiet siding for the actor's private railway carriage. In one place he decided on what was a perfect spot looking out on a beautiful garden and elegant buildings. It was, he told Mansfield, who always demanded a quick answer to his questions, a young ladies' seminary. 'How very charming,' said his employer. 'It will be delightful to watch the charming girls at their play. Nothing more charming.' That evening in the theatre Mansfield smiled grimly at him. 'You damned fool. It's the State Lunatic Asylum.'

As time went on Charlie took over responsibility. He received Mansfield's friends at the theatre, transacted business for him and was deputed to handle the most delicate affairs. The actor had a violent temper and inclined to frenzies of impatience when things went wrong. At Cleveland, Ohio, the curtain failed to descend after Act I and the cast had to break their tableau and leave in sight of the audience. When at last the stage was set for the second act Mansfield had disappeared. He went home to sulk in private and was so angry that he smashed the furniture. No-one, not even Charlie, could persuade him to come back and finish the play. The result was an expensive court case in which Charlie gained a deal of incidental knowledge about the laws governing breach of contract.

The company travelled on to Washington and there Charlie met an old friend, Mabel Beardsley, whom he had not seen since his Brighton days. Aubrey was dead by then and his sister, who had discovered a talent for the stage, was touring in a company headed by the English actor Arthur Bourchier. Charlie was later to know Bourchier well. He had begun his career with Mrs Langtry and eventually established himself in comedies and farces, many 'adapted from the French' as the coy phrase had it, partnered by his first wife Violet Vanburgh. Mabel Beardsley could not be said to shine as an actress but she had presence and gave quiet charm to the flimsy rubbish in which she appeared. Off-stage she was a witty talker and an accomplished journalist who could turn out piquant newspaper articles. Charlie persuaded Mansfield to engage her for his own company. Although, as Mansfield often told her in his brusque way, she could not act very well, he liked her because her grace and conversation made his supper parties exceptionally pleasant.

One day, however, Charlie and Mansfield quarrelled. It was over some small difference, an affair so trifling that in later years Charlie could not even remember what it involved. Usually such matters were forgotten by the next day. This time the grievance endured. A confrontation took place in the private railway carriage and Charlie marched out. He went back on his own to New York and made a new friend in the actor Edward John Henley, brother of the poet W. E.. Charlie agreed with the general opinion that put Henley among the finest actors then playing in America. He had an excellent technique and, on occasion, flashes of genius, though he lacked stability and tended to drink too much.

Charlie now felt that he had learned enough with Mansfield to go into management on his own. With Henley as his partner he set up a school of acting in New York. They also launched a production of Ibsen's *John Gabriel Borkman* in which Henley took the leading role. The date was October, 1897, and Charlie, at the age of twenty-five, had taken his first step as a manager. Even though his financial backer suddenly died and brought the venture to an abrupt conclusion, he resolved that it would not be his last.

There had, furthermore, been an unpleasant incident at the Fifth Avenue Theatre. Although estranged from Mansfield Charlie still admired him professionally, and when the former put on the first American production of *The Devil's Disciple* Charlie was eager to be there – so eager, indeed, that anticipation made him drink rather more than he could take. He arrived at the theatre in a state of noisy belligerence. On being refused admission he started a fight which led him to spend a few uncomfortable hours in a police cell. Once again Mansfield did the unexpected. He materialised in Charlie's hour of need and, with sardonic amusement, bailed out his former employee.

Perhaps, Charlie concluded, it would be better to leave New York for the time being. On reflection he decided he should quit America entirely and return to England. He begged a loan of fifty pounds from his sister Minnie and, once more in the company of Scotson Clark whom he had persuaded to join him again, he started the voyage home in a murky tramp steamer which was all they could afford. After seventeen days of misery they disembarked at Leith in Scotland where Minnie's loan awaited him poste restante. Why, enquired his thrifty sister in her letter, was he in such dire straits after holding such an important job with Mansfield? His reply explained that, never having had money while out of an engagement, he had been unable to save any. He also showed that he had learned one of the most important conditions of being an impresario: 'It would never do to let my pals in N. Y. know my true financial position as I hope to return to America before long and, in that country, when a man is "broke" he is down – very much down.' When he came to Brighton for a few days, as he proposed, he would not let anyone there know that he was hard up. And since, he ended, he would be 'pretty well dressed,' he was sure they would not think so. He knew that the successful showman must, above all, radiate confidence, optimism and prosperity. No-one otherwise would do business with him.

iii
HOUDINI AND THE MUSIC-HALL

'One cannot withhold real admiration for the great race of music-hall performers. Their generosity is proverbial. Their sympathy was as wonderful as their comradery. Many of them had fought wonderful single combats against ravening audiences, and tamed a many-headed and hostile monster until it fawned and ate out of their hands'.

CHARLES B. COCHRAN

He came to London by way of Edinburgh where he paused long enough to admire the surprising number of pretty girls he saw in Princes Street. From his Bloomsbury hotel, shrouded in a thick and mysterious fog, he went on the rounds of managers and agents. In New York he had known all the theatre people whereas in London most of them were strangers and he did not enjoy having to start all over again. The few acquaintances he already had were kind to him. Mabel Beardsley welcomed him with an invitation to a tea party she gave for Max Beerbohm, Robert Ross and artists like Sickert. The chit-chat, of a fashionable Yellow Book flavour, made him uneasy and went over his head. Yet everyone was pleasant to him because he had known Aubrey Beardsley long before they had and they treated him with deference. When the tea cups were put away and the others had gone, Mabel gave him, in a friendly gesture, a number of Aubrey's pictures and personal belongings. The latter included a flannel shirt of a startling green hue.

A few days were spent in Brighton placating Minnie and assuring his parents, especially his anxious mother, that his future was brilliant and that, no, he was not in debt to all the money lenders in New York. He walked on the front and thought back to the time only a few years ago when, at Dover, his dream of fame as a comic singer had vanished into humiliation. In America he had known a plight even worse. Maybe there was more to come? The prospect did not worry him. Already he was a gambler who got his thrill from the fall of the dice, an optimist who looked beyond immediate failure to a vision of ultimate, golden success. On Brighton front he wore his one smart suit and flourished his cigar with an air. Then he packed his exiguous bags for another assault on London.

On the strength of their meeting in America, Beerbohm Tree gave him a box at the theatre and entertained him to supper. When, though, he asked him for a job, Tree advised him in his grandest manner to go back to America where a young fellow would find better opportunities. He secured an engagement to play another old man role in a provincial town. His part was that of an elderly solicitor and his big scene drew gratifying laughter. The star comedian was furious. 'The little bugger is funny,' he snarled. 'But they pay to see *me* being funny. We don't want another funny man.' That was Charlie's last appearance as an actor.

Very soon he was moneyless and could not afford to pay for lodgings. In a studio lent by a friend, shivering beside an empty grate, he wrote an article on Aubrey Beardsley's schooldays and sold it to an editor for the price of his breakfast. At the Café Royal he met an author called Ranger Gull who a few years later was to play a vital part in his life. Gull made a steady eight hundred pounds a year by manufacturing sensational stories for the Amalgamated Press. 'Now, let me see,' his editor would say to him, 'have you any plans for your Grand Serial? I think we will have a little Reincarnation story this time – ancient Egypt, you know. You might be in a quad at Oxford; Commemoration time.' And Gull would speed back to his country retreat where he industriously produced the correct number of words, no more, no less, in good time to keep the presses rolling.

Gull at that moment was almost as hard up as Charlie and had no serial on hand. Charlie had just written a controversial article attacking the undue influence said to be exercised on the London theatre by the American impresario Charles Frohman. The article was much talked about and Gull wrote a reply, prompted by Charlie, which stirred up the argument further. To keep the pot boiling the two disputants cast anxiously around for another topic. They found it in the 'No Popery' issue and made fifty pounds between them from a slashing polemic.

The money he earned with journalism enabled Charlie to visit Paris and to see, among other things, the new Rostand play, *Cyrano de Bergerac*, in which Coquelin was making a great impression as the braggart hero. Charlie's impresario instinct told him that here was a perfect rôle for Mansfield and he sent him an urgent cable. Mansfield bought the rights and, on a visit to London, asked Charlie to come back with him to America. Charlie was overjoyed. His attempt on London had failed, he had known starvation and, at times, walked the streets by night for lack of a bed. America, by contrast, glittered with promise.

He took charge of shipping over a batch of costumes Mansfield bought from Irving as a job lot to dress his production of *Cyrano*. The New York première took place in October, 1898, and gave Mansfield one of his greatest triumphs. After eight weeks of packed houses the company went on tour preceded by speculators who bought up tickets and sold them at huge profits. In Columbus touts queued throughout the days and nights of a weekend to make sure of seats when the box-office opened. On Monday morning there was a riot. A disappointed queuer fired a gun and shot a man. Another was stabbed.

The company of more than a hundred travelled America with vanloads of scenery and accessories. Mansfield, as usual, lived in his private railway carriage where he rested as much as possible to husband his strength for the arduous tirades and wearing physical demands of the role. He got up late, and over breakfast would read letters and discuss the day's routine with

Charlie. After a walk of several hours in Charlie's company he went back to the carriage for more rest, a light meal and the evening performance. Once that was over he relaxed at grand supper parties where he entertained the famous: Henry Irving, Sarah Bernhardt, Mrs Langtry. Though flattered and intrigued by mingling with the great, Charlie began to long for a free evening when he could see his own humbler friends. Moreover, now that Mansfield had reached the peak of his career he was surrounded by a retinue of business managers and Charlie no longer had the responsibility he enjoyed in earlier days.

He felt he was getting nowhere and told Mansfield of his aspiration to be a manager. The actor suggested that, if a suitable play could be found, he would provide the finance and let him take control. Charlie, it happened, had seen just the thing in London, a farce that starred the comedian Weedon Grossmith. Mansfield arranged for him to go back to London with another manager, A. M. Palmer, in the hope of negotiating the rights. Palmer was already well known in London to all the important managers and actors and, thanks to his connections, Charlie made useful acquaintances. They went down to Haslemere and took lunch with Bernard Shaw whose plays were becoming known in America. The vegetarian dramatist thoughtfully provided a leg of lamb for his guests. Palmer, however, was then restricted to a meatless diet and ate generously of the vegetarian dishes that were also on the menu. Only afterwards did he realize that he had done their host out of his proper share and left him hungry.

For the first time Charlie, whose experience of England had chiefly been limited to Brighton, explored his native country under the guidance of an American colleague. He had heard much of Dickensian good cheer and looked forward to honest English fare beside a roaring fire in comfortable hotels. The reality of tinned soups and pallid blanc-mange and meagre gas fires left him sighing for the hearty steaks of America. Another, sharper disappointment was a cable from Mansfield ordering him to give up the idea of negotiating the Grossmith play and return immediately to America. Charlie refused and stayed in London where he was now determined to try his luck.

In 1899, at the age of twenty-seven, he took an office in Chancery Lane and began his management career with the touring company of a comic opera called *Paul Jones*. The stage-manager was Gilbert Laye, father of Evelyn who much later became one of Charlie's pet stars. The venture proved, in his own words, 'moderately successful', and he began signing up performers as a theatre and music-hall agent. He was his own master now, free of Mansfield's caprices and answerable only to himself. Success or failure depended on his judgment, and his alone. He had established the principle on which he was to operate for the rest of his life.

One of his early clients was Ehrich Weiss, otherwise known as Houdini the Handcuff King, who astonished audiences by escaping from padlocked barrels and, under the expert eye of Scotland Yard officials, freeing himself from iron handcuffs in half a minute. He could 'walk' through brick walls and make an elephant 'disappear' from the centre of an open stage. Less sensational turns included the singer Odette Dulac whom Charlie brought over from Paris at the high salary of a hundred and five pounds a week. Now that he was an agent he often went to his old hunting ground in Paris looking out for talent at the theatres and music-halls he had known from youth. There he witnessed the rise of the young Maurice Chevalier and of Mistinguett. Often, in his badly accented French, he sought to persuade her to London. '*Mon vieux coq*,' she would reply in her gravelly voice, 'they wouldn't understand me.' Once he took A. B. Walkley, the stately drama critic of *The Times*, to see Mistinguett in her dressing room. A sculptor was modelling a bust of her while she gazed critically at his work. With both hands she lunged forward and tore out lumps from the clay bosom the sculptor had given her. 'My tits don't look like *that*!' she exclaimed, much to the discomfort of the erudite gentleman from *The Times* who knew more about Molière than Mistinguett.

Charlie soon wearied of booking music-hall turns, even though his flair often made money and built up his reputation. A frequent bugbear was the ancient Charles Morton, often referred to as 'the father of the halls,' who, almost despite himself, helped to create the institution known as music-hall and profited exceedingly. When Charlie knew him he was an obstinate octogenarian, white-whiskered, venerable, usually enthroned in a managerial stall at the Palace Theatre drinking cups of tea and beating time to the music by tinkling his spoon against the saucer. Charlie would argue the benefits of putting on a revue, then something of a novelty. Steadfastly Mr Morton refused to have anything to do with such a new-fangled idea. He preferred the old songs and the old performers. Once, however, Charlie got his own back. He arranged an audition for a mediocre singer on his books, hardly imagining that Morton would approve. But she happened to sing a number dating from the time when Morton was young.

'I love the old songs,' quavered he. The singer could, he added, open that evening. 'Perhaps you can get her to take twenty-five pounds a night?'

Charlie, who privately assessed her worth at no more than eight pounds, thought Morton was being sarcastic. Then he realized the veteran spoke seriously. He pressed his advantage. 'She might accept the money you offer, Mr Morton, if you give her a long engagement.' 'Certainly, she can have six months as a trial.' The young lady was allotted 'a nice spot about half-past nine or a quarter to ten' and stayed at the Palace for nearly two years, emptying the stalls whenever she appeared and increasing the bar takings enormously. Perhaps the old man was not so silly after all.

Charlie was still so determined to sell him a revue that he commissioned one on his own initiative. For the music he turned to Herman Finck, Bohemian and *bon vivant*, consummate musician and pillar of the Savage Club. Finck had begun his career as violinist in a theatre band at the age of fourteen. Conductor of the orchestra at the Palace for some twenty years and later at Drury Lane, he knew everything about the difficult art of accompanying acrobats, music-hall singers, dancers, prima donnas and performing bears. Orchestra players are a tough and cynical lot but he had no trouble in dragooning them: he could play all the instruments in the band himself and his technical prowess was unequalled. He was a genial and well-known figure in London clubs and had a reputation for wit.

This took the shape of puns which he issued in an irrepressible stream, although today they would be thought tediously elaborate. Of a theatrical colleague named Volnay who was noted for his extreme thinness Finck remarked: 'Volnay – his name should be Beaune.'

He wrote dozens of revues, ballets, musical comedies and operettas. None of them survives, and all that remains of his energetic output is the catchy music-hall song 'I'm Gilbert the Filbert, the Knut with a K' and a tenacious drawing-room piece called 'In The Shadows'. The latter sold over a million copies as sheet music, but since Finck only left three thousand pounds when he died in 1939 he had probably spent most of his royalties on the lavish club life he enjoyed. 'In The Shadows' is one of those insidious tunes which, once lodged in the mind, drives you mad with its pitiless refrain. On a cab journey once the composer was infuriated by his driver who whistled the melody ceaselessly. He asked the cabman where he had heard it. 'My old mother plays it all day long at home,' said the cabbie. 'Then you must be sick of it?' suggested Finck. '*Sick!*' spat the cabbie venomously. '*Sick*, guv'nor? Well, I tell you that if I only knew who wrote it, I'd . . .' Finck hurriedly pressed a large tip into his hand and got out.

The revue was completed and offered to Morton. It went as far as the board of the Palace but the directors feared that the licensing regulations, which then forbade stage plays in music-halls, might cause problems. Although the project was dropped Charlie regarded the setback as only a temporary one: he was determined, sooner or later, to produce a revue. He went on commissioning music from Finck to accompany the various little burlesques and sketches he put on with, it must be said, no great success. At night he spent much time in clubs with the composer whose droopy moustche, big teeth and embonpoint gave him a curious resemblance to Arnold Bennett. Finck remembered Charlie as a vivacious drinking companion in those early days. One evening, after a jolly session together, Finck and three others took a four-seater cab home. Charlie joined them and, since there was no seat available, climbed out through the window as the cab rumbled along the streets. They heard scrabbling on the roof overhead and Charlie suddenly appeared at the other window to haul himself in. Despite the torrents of rain that were pouring down outside he continually repeated the performance, through the window, over the roof and back through the other window again, until it was time to drop him at his flat in Victoria Street.

After only a few years in London, Charlie had made for himself a wide range of acquaintances. He belonged to many clubs, half a dozen at a time, and was even a member of several Parisian *cercles*. The one he most enjoyed was the Eccentric, then in Shaftesbury Avenue opposite the old London Pavilion. He usually went there late at night for tripe and onions after the restaurants closed to mingle with friends like his old hero Arthur Roberts and a dancer from the Gaiety Theatre called Storey. The latter's great parlour trick was to strip the cloth from a loaded supper table without upsetting any of the dishes and then to jump over it and land on the far side in a split. There were no printed menus at the Eccentric. Members would arrive and ask the waiter what was for supper. He would point at a famous music-hall impresario, a notoriously dirty eater, and reply: 'Look at his shirt-front!'

The long-vanished Punch Bowl was another of Charlie's favourite clubs. It was run by a sculptor who loathed the stage and refused to accept actors as members, so that when Charlie was proposed his connection with the theatre had to be discreetly suppressed. The club was in Regent Street and frequented by *Punch* artists, authors and men like Charlie's old friend Scotson Clark who had starved and struggled in America with him. The finances of the Punch Bowl were meagre and did not allow of employing regular waiters. Instead, members served in rotation and put on white jackets when their turn came to wait at table. Other members were sometimes puzzled by the unfamiliar faces of white-jacketed attendants who served them. They were bailiff's men whom the proprietor had mollified with generous drinks and persuaded to act as waiters in order to keep up appearances.

In these clubs, where Charlie would eat and drink until it was time to go home for breakfast in the morning, many schemes and ideas were floated and discussed. Some of them, by the light of dawn, had lost their glamour and were abandoned.

Others seemed better able to withstand the colder and more sober inspection of the day after. Among them was a production of *Les Deux Aveugles* by Offenbach which Cochran did in an English version at the Tivoli music-hall. It was a one-act piece which, on the first night, was badly received by an audience impatient for the popular comedians who came later in the bill. After that it was put on at the beginning of the evening when the auditorium held only a sparse handful of waiters and early arrivals. More profitable were the sporting events and variety turns Charlie sponsored at the Crystal Palace. Yet while these brought in the money he still had not forgotten his main ambition of theatre management. With an actor friend he took the Royalty Theatre on a short lease and presented a farce called *Sporting Simpson*. It failed to attract. This he followed with *Lyre and Lancet*, a new play by F. Anstey, the author of *Vice-Versa*. Despite good character drawing and amusing dialogue that evoked frequent laughter, Anstey's piece did not run either. Moreover the venture was pathetically under-capitalised and Charlie had to rely on money-lenders to help him out with his immediate needs. Sums were raised and notes of hand were given. The interest to be paid seemed small at first but gradually, like a devouring monster, it grew and threatened until there was nothing left to placate it. In 1903 Charlie went bankrupt.

iv
A TERRIBLE TURK AND PERFORMING FLEAS

'And what a funny animal is that public with which the showman has to deal! After a lifetime spent in catering for it, my knowledge of it, so far as being able to foretell its approval or disapproval, remains much what it was when I started my career.'

CHARLES B. COCHRAN

A first bankruptcy is like a first-born child: the preparations are long and anxious, the delivery is painful and the worry long. With the second the process is easier, and by the time of the third everything goes much more smoothly. Charlie was to experience not one but several bankruptcies.

Not for an instant did he betray anxiety to the outside world. He ate in the finest restaurants and drank at the most exclusive clubs. His oddly square features radiated prosperity and contentment. His hat was newly brushed, his suits were elegantly cut and his shoes sparkled. In his tie he wore a large diamond stock-pin. From Chancery Lane he moved his office nearer to the West End in the Adelphi, and finally from there to a small street off what Diaghilev used to call 'Less-ess-ter Square'.

Behind the scenes there were struggles to pay off what seem, years later, to have been small amounts of money but which then were substantial. Having, in a moment of expansiveness, offered a job to his brother Alec a few months previously, Charlie was reduced to asking him to act as his guarantor for repayment of a forty-five pounds debt at seven pounds fifty a month. In many ways Charlie was a Micawber who lived permanently in the expectation of something turning up. It usually did. At the time of his first bankruptcy his saviour was the wrestler Georges Hackenschmidt who agreed to pay fifteen pounds a month until all debts were liquidated. His creditors were satisfied and Charlie obtained his discharge in a remarkably short time.

On a visit to the Folies-Bergère he had admired the technique of the young Russian Hackenschmidt. Soon afterwards, while talking to an acquaintance on the steps of the Tivoli, he saw the wrestler come down the street with a friend. They were introduced and Charlie worked hard to persuade him to stay in London for a while. In a hotel room Hackenschmidt displayed his athletic form, iron-hard with smooth, easy-rippling muscles, and at lightning speed did a few hand-springs for his admiring onlooker who declared that he was the most superb physical specimen of humanity he had ever seen. The wrestler's first appearance in a London music-hall had been inauspicious. Charlie promised him better things.

As he left the hotel he met a journalist he knew and, full of enthusiasm, rushed her up to Hackenschmidt's room for the wrestler to exhibit himself again. The result was a full page article entitled 'Is Strength Genius?' in the *Daily Mail* next morning. Charlie showed it to the controller of a big music-hall syndicate and exacted a trial engagement at seventy pounds a week. A steady flow of articles and photographs began to appear in other newspapers thoughtfully cultivated by Charlie. Having secured the engagement there remained the task of presenting his new client. A master of ceremonies was needed, a man who knew foreign languages well enough to take instructions from Hack's Belgian manager and to handle his opponents, mostly foreigners with names, said Charlie, that 'sounded like sneezes.' While sitting in the Café Royal with the manager he saw a figure resplendent in glossy top hat and wearing a monocle. 'That's the kind of man we want,' said the manager. 'Very well,' said Charlie, 'I'll ask him.' His companion watched in astonishment as Charlie went up to the man, offered him the job and received his acceptance. Charlie did not reveal that he already knew him as a man-about-town in need of money. The art of the impresario lies in winning over businessmen as well as audiences.

Under Charlie's persuasive guidance Hack did record business at the Tivoli and the proprietor insisted on a further engagement which Charlie agreed at more than double his original fee. In time, though, receipts fell off. The wrestler had no showmanship and lacked the skills of presentation. There was little excitement or suspense as he dourly laid his opponents on their backs within a minute or two, and audiences were disappointed by the absence of drama. Something had to be done. Charlie did not know much about wrestling, but he was aware of its great popularity in Lancashire. To Liverpool he went and leased for three months the Prince of Wales Theatre which was then up for sale. The newspapers were fed with stories about the great wrestler and his challenge to all comers. Just as public interest was at a feverish height the owner of the theatre, Mr Cleaver, had second thoughts and repudiated the agreement although keeping the rent paid in advance. He feared for his licence and thought that the wrestling event might prejudice the sale of his property. Charlie refused to move out and engaged an array of men bearing sandwich boards, hundreds strong, parading the streets and announcing that Hack would positively appear. Mr Cleaver retaliated with a rival army claiming that he would not. There were frequent scuffles between warring sandwichmen. Charlie won and the publicity was enormous.

On the opening night, just as the doors were unlocked to admit the public, all the gas lights went out. They had been expertly cut off. Within half an hour Charlie found someone to mend the pipes and switch them on again. The performance was crowded and successful. Mr Cleaver, however, did not easily give up. In the morning Charlie found the theatre locked and, at the head of an advance party, took the place by storm. As he rounded the corner of a passage an enemy hit him on the head and he was grabbed and thrown out. He returned to the attack and eventually the theatre was captured. The triumph proved a hollow one: all the seats and light fittings had been removed. He was beaten.

Returned to London he schooled Hack in the craft of show-manship and persisted with his efforts to make him a star of the music-hall. They languished until one day another wrestler, Madrali 'The Terrible Turk', challenged Hack from the stalls or rather, his manager, a cross-eyed Italian by the name of Pierri did so. Pierri always opened business negotia-tions by saying, 'Antonio Pierri very straighta man; cannot tella lie,' which Charlie countered by murmuring 'Yes, as straight as a cork-screw.' The Italian did not mind insults so long as money was to be had. He paid Madrali five pounds a week which he counted out in coppers and threepenny bits to make it seem a lot. Always complaining about the vast amounts of food his simple-minded charge consumed, he would speak of him eating each day 'a whole legga mutton' while filling him up with huge sacks of rice which he bought wholesale.

On the night of 30 January, 1904, Hackenschmidt fought Madrali at Olympia. Traffic jams around the hall were enor-mous and every ticket was sold. Madrali arrived wearing his long fur overcoat and Turkish fez under the escort of Pierri who introduced him as 'The Sultan's favourite', a description he applied to all the wrestlers he managed. Hack slipped in and paced up and down his dressing room shivering with nerves. Time was called and Madrali moved his great bulk slowly across the ring. His opponent rushed forward with sudden speed, grasped his huge body with encircling arms, raised his shoulder high and threw him violently to the ground. There was a thud, as when a sack of potatoes falls, and Madrali sprawled on the floor groaning with the pain of a shattered arm. In those few seconds Hackenschmidt became a national hero.

The sport of wrestling had won national status too as a result of Charlie's astute promotion. Other wrestlers were to perform under his management, Turks, Russians, monosyllabic Poles given to hurling referees out of the ring, but none of them possessed the glamour and dignity of Hackenschmidt. He thriftily put on one side the large fees (minus commission) Charlie passed to him, and, as we have seen, helped him generously over his bankruptcy. At the end of his wrestling career he settled in a Hampstead flat to cultivate a taste for Greek philosophy and for intellectual chit-chat with Bernard Shaw. The physical appetites of his huge frame remained as strong as ever. At dinner in Charlie's home one evening he ate nine eggs, a porter-house steak and a whole Camembert cheese. In reply to a hospitable enquiry as to whether he would like any more the giant thoughtfully said: 'No thanks. I have to dine with some friends, so I will not spoil my appetite.'

Other opportunities attracted Charlie's restless eye. At a picture-house called the Gem in Great Yarmouth he exhibited films which he grandly billed as 'Electrical Vaudeville' and, when a performer sang on stage to a film accompaniment, as 'Electrical Vocalism'. This was in 1904. While still keeping up an abundant flow of hypnotists, acrobats and singers to the London music-halls, he also went into exhibitions at Olympia where he had organized the Hackenschmidt-Madrali fight. Until the managers secured the Military Tattoo and other shows and exhibitions, the place had been something of a white elephant, and they were eager for new attractions. Charlie gave them what he called 'The Mammoth Fun City'. Besides filling the cavernous spaces with coconut shies and roundabouts he also engaged a menagerie and a circus. From Paris he brought over a troupe of wrestlers who, with noisy rodomontade, challenged all comers from the platform. There was a 'mumming booth' where Fred Karno, Charlie Chaplin's early patron, staged performances of *The Murder of Maria Marten in*

The Red Barn and other ghastly melodramas of the sort Charlie had watched as a boy at Lindfield fairs. Not far away stood an 'Indian temple' draped in tapestries and housing the 'Sacred Bull of Benares', a placid hump-backed beast which ate from golden vessels and blinked a dull eye through clouds of incense at gaping punters. From time to time a Sinhalese attendant, chanting in his native tongue, would draw the curtains and a barker would solemnly announce that sacred rites were about to be performed which no Christian should witness.

Charlie had his failures, of course. One of these were a band of pygmies imported from exotic climes. 'They hardly drew their electric light bill,' he commented gloomily. The Sacred Bull did well, however, and so did a man who set out to break his own record for continuous club swinging. Throughout a session that lasted without a break for forty-nine hours he swung his clubs under the alert gaze of a specially appointed committee. The biggest money-maker was Sacco, the Fasting Man. For many days and nights he sat without food in a sealed glass-house and drank water only. An outraged doctor complained to *The Lancet* and attacked the show as degrading. Others insisted that it was unwholesome. Charlie saw an excellent chance of publicity. Since, he argued, he had rented the premises to Sacco he might find himself sued for illegal trespass should he try to end the side-show by evicting him. Having primed his Fleet Street friends Charlie staged a confrontation with Sacco's solicitor in front of a large crowd. The result was a torrent of publicity. He raised the admission fee from sixpence to a shilling and then to half a crown. On the fifty-second day when Sacco broke his fast and also his record admission went up to five shillings.

Charlie's right-hand publicist at the Mammoth Fun City was a beefy, heavily moustached character by name of Arthur Binstead who wrote under the pseudonym of 'Pitcher' (pitcher of tales) for *The Sporting Times*, better known as 'The Pink 'Un'*.

---

* Its first issue in 1876 was printed on pink paper which had been bought up as a cheap job lot. The owner, travelling on a train with a sporting parson, heard the latter call a paper boy and indicate his choice by pointing at *The Sporting Times* and saying: 'That one – the pink 'un'. From then on the paper carried as its masthead: THE SPORTING TIMES, otherwise known as THE PINK 'UN.

He was, like Herman Finck, a genial Bohemian who revolved around the bar at the Gaiety Theatre, Romano's restaurant and the dubious promenade at the Empire. His column was filled with piquant gossip culled from the race-track, the dressing-room and the gentlemen's clubs. As a press agent he had a genius for terse, pointed hand-outs that newspapers were keen to use. It became a tradition for Charlie to join The Pitcher on Saturday afternoons at the Tivoli when he held court among music-hall stars and their hangers-on. He was a crisp raconteur and told a tale Charlie liked of how he'd once been out driving with a friend and bumped into a phaeton containing a dowager-like female. A bill for damages was received and The Pitcher's friend invited the owner of the phaeton to tea. Tea was something never served in his home and he had to send out for it. When it was brewed it looked very weak, so he added a generous stiffener of old brown brandy. Next morning the dowager wrote that she would not dream of pressing her bill, the damage was not as bad as she'd thought, but would he kindly let her have the name and address of his tea merchant?

When the Mammoth Fun City closed down Charlie turned his attention to roller skating which seemed to contain the germ of a popular craze. He arranged for a rink to be installed at Olympia and very quickly London caught on to the habit. With the support of a roller-skate manufacturer other rinks were opened both in England and abroad. Charlie became managing director for a while of the rinks in Europe. He stimulated custom with prizes for the most beautiful girl skaters – and, when they ran off with handsome instructors, was not displeased by the 'scandalous' publicity that arose. With Berlin as his headquarters he toured Paris, Antwerp, Nice, Hanover and Hamburg, juggling adroitly with contracts and leases charmed out of reluctant municipal authorities. For a while a lot of money was being made. Then the fashion died and the rinks turned into shops and warehouses again. Thirty years later, driving through the Place Victor Hugo in Paris with an actor friend, Charlie heard him say: 'That used to be a rink called St Didier where my parents took me roller skating as a child.' Charlie glanced at the dreary garage that stood there and said, with an expression of distaste: 'Is that so? Well, I used to run it.'

While the main hall at Olympia was being used as a skating rink the management asked him to produce a show in the annexe on the lines of his Mammoth Fun City. The annexe was too small for such a large function, and so, he decided, the logical answer would be something quite the opposite. He found it in the idea of a Midget City peopled by dwarfs. A hundred of them were gathered together and housed in a miniature town which had its own little fire station, shops, theatre and circus. The project was advertised as 'Tiny Town', and on the night before it opened he booked a large circular table at the Savoy to entertain forty or so of the dwarfs. Since he had thoughtfully neglected to tell the restaurant manager who his guests were to be, the arrival of a chattering swarm of tiny people who scrambled up on chairs and sat with their heads just above the table caused astonishment which next day was reflected by a gratifying number of column inches in the newspapers.

The star of Tiny Town was a diminutive Countess, wife to a Papal nobleman and widow of the famous General Tom Thumb, Barnum's protégé. With her black cap and voluminous robes she looked not a little like Queen Victoria and, indeed, consciously modelled herself on the sovereign, an audience with whom had been a proud moment in her life. She was a Christian Scientist and cherished strict ideas of conduct. When obliged to greet a musical comedy actress introduced by a friend she was indignant. Why, she demanded, should she have to do with this heavily made-up mummer? Her fellow dwarfs were not so puritanical. One of them, a Hindu gymnast, suddenly vanished from Olympia and was sought for everywhere by the distracted impresario. Two days later he as mysteriously reappeared, weary but jubilant. A fashionable beauty out for a lark had smuggled him into her Mayfair home where forty-eight hours of champagne and orgies had exhausted his professional agility.

An American friend who had also organized a midget city on Coney Island cabled Charlie for new attractions. He remembered the Westminster Aquarium of his youth and replied: 'Performing fleas'. At the old Aquarium audiences had been promised such sights as 'twelve Fleas in the Orchestra playing

on different Instruments of proportionable size . . . Four Fleas
playing a game at Whist . . . A MAIL COACH drawn by four
Fleas completely harnessed, the Coachman and Guard, (also
Fleas) dressed in the Royal livery . . .' Performing fleas were
unknown in America, but once Charlie convinced his friend
that they could be found the deal was agreed. A Scotsman who
had shown fleas at the Aquarium was commissioned to train a
band and escort them to America. Charlie was in Coney Island
the day their season opened and saw with pleasure large crowds
gathered outside the booth. Alas, the show did not go on. The
Atlantic crossing had robbed the industrious fleas of their
energy. Three were dead and the rest had not a jump left in
them. Next morning they all gently passed away. Their trainer
ascribed the tragedy to insect powder used on the ship. Charlie
was not to be discouraged and took him on a visit to the slums in
pursuit of fleas. All they could find were bed bugs. There was
not a flea to be had in the whole of New York. California,
however, was said to be a Golconda of fleas and urgent
telegrams soon brought dozens of boxes crammed with tiny
livestock. By then the Scottish expert, disappointed and home-
sick, had slipped off home on a steamer. America was never to
see Charlie's performing fleas.

Charlie's existence, full as it was of performing fleas, midgets,
pygmies and fasting men, still left him time for women. He
already had a paternal side to his character that they found
sympathetic, and he knew how to listen to them. The gift of
diplomacy which enabled him to handle temperamental wrestlers, awkward music-hall performers and difficult prima
donnas also gave him a supreme advantage with ladies. He had
a quiet but formidable charm and round eyes which, when he
decided he wanted something, sparkled with irresistible sincerity. One evening in 1902 he had met his author friend
Ranger Gull coming out of a public house accompanied by a
young and pretty girl. Gull introduced her as Miss Evelyn
Dade. What had a sixteen-year-old female been doing in a pub?
There were attractive blushes as it was explained that, curious
to see what there was about a place that attracted so many men,
she had accepted Gull's facetious dare to go in. As they walked
home Gull promised to return later that evening and throw a

pebble at her window. Charlie looked at her reflectively. Miss Dade interested him.

Both he and Gull went out to dinner. At the end the author was so full of whisky that he collapsed on a sofa. Charlie remembered Gull's promise to Miss Dade. He duly threw a pebble at her window, a romantic gesture which led to further acquaintance, much against the will of her widowed mother who reprehended her only daughter's infatuation with a man of the music-hall and circuses, a man-about-London and, worse, a man-about-Paris. A passing resemblance between Charlie and the comedian Arthur Roberts inspired Evelyn to paste on the walls of her bedroom photographs of the latter cut from newspapers. Her mother, in a rage, tore them down.

After much unpleasantness at home two uncles were summoned to a family council. One of them, recently appointed to a new job in Dublin, suggested he take her with him secretly. A letter from Evelyn told Charlie that she was destined for an Irish convent and implored him to rescue her. They had a clandestine meeting in a Dublin sweetshop and he learned that her uncle was to see her off at the railway station next day. Charlie arrived in due time and observed her anxious relative bidding her farewell at the window of her carriage. Since Uncle did not know Charlie, the hopeful suitor boldly stepped into the compartment next door and took a seat. Uncle departed after a final goodbye. Once they were sure he had really gone Evelyn and Charlie skipped out of the train, collected their bags and took the next boat to England.

In 1905, four years after she had first met him, Miss Evelyn Alice Dade married Charlie Cochran at a register office in Henrietta Street, Covent Garden. She was then twenty years old and he thirty-two. There was no time for a formal honeymoon. After a bottle of champagne and biscuits at the old Covent Garden Hotel Charlie hurried off to an important business appointment with the proprietor of the Middlesex Music Hall. In the evening, as was his habit, he visited three music-halls looking for new talent and sizing up the acts he had booked. Mrs Cochran stayed at home.

They did, however, enjoy a honeymoon of sorts. Soon after the marriage Charlie came across a boxing referee of his acquaintance at Romano's. The referee invited him and Mrs Cochran to his seaside home for the weekend. Just as they were getting out of the train he warned them that his wife might be a little unwelcoming since he had not been back for a week. Mr and Mrs Cochran went reluctantly with him to the house. As forecast, their involuntary hostess, who at first took Charlie for a boxer, would not speak to them. Gradually her icy manner thawed and soon they were on the best of terms. All was undone next day when her husband took Charlie out and did not return until late at night, so incapacitated that he had to be helped up the steps to his front door. As the two of them struggled and stumbled, the small son of the house danced around delightedly exclaiming at the top of his voice, to the great interest of the neighbours, 'Father's drunk again! Father's drunk again!'

Chapter Two
CHARLES B. COCHRAN

'I do not believe in alibis for theatrical
withdrawals. When I take my shows off
it is because they cease to attract.'

Charles B. Cochran

---

i
A MIRACLE

'I produce plays or entertainments because I like them, not
because I think they are what the public wants. Whenever I
have departed from this rule I have invariably failed.'

CHARLES B. COCHRAN

We must no longer call him 'Charlie'. In the days of his
maturity it was a nickname he allowed to be used only by his
wife, his very closest friends and his mistresses. Quite early on,
when he had established himself in London, he decided to be
known as 'Charles B. Cochran'. This was the style he used in
signing letters – though for intimates he unbent so far as to
subscribe himself 'C.B.C.' – in publicity material and in official
documents. He was a man of great dignity. From his manner
and dress, always immaculate, always in perfect taste, you
might have taken him to be a solicitor, a fashionable surgeon or
a confidential man of business, anything, indeed, but a showman. 'Showman' was a title he gloried in. A friend who once
described him as such to his face abruptly pulled himself up and
apologized. Cochran explained that, far from being offended,
he was charmed. A showman he was, and the happiest

moments of his life had been when the public agreed with him that his shows were worthwhile. On those occasions when they did not respond to his invitation 'Walk up, walk up, ladies and gentlemen,' he cheerfully admitted that the public had been right and the showman wrong.

His own experience on the boards had taught him to appreciate acting. In America he learned the arts of management and production. His eye for colour, which led him to collect pictures by Toulouse-Lautrec and others at a time when they were unknown to the general public, made him a sensitive judge of stage design and costume. His feeling for talent, however odd, and his insatiable curiosity about the freaks of human nature, gave him unlimited sympathy with a very wide range which extended from the clown Grock, whom he presented at the Palace, to the spectacular religious play *The Miracle*.

In the days when he was still involved with skating rinks he kept a permanent suite at the Hotel Bristol in Berlin. He used the bar as his office and paid for his drinks, or not, by shooting dice with the race-course owners and trainers who came there. It was the best place he knew of for picking up gossip and information about what was going on in the theatre. His main source was the head barman who could tell him all the latest developments and which were the most interesting and worthwhile. One evening in 1910 Cochran arrived and put his usual question: 'Hermann, what is new for me to see?' Hermann recommended Max Reinhardt's production of *Oedipus Rex* at the Schumann Circus. The show was heavily booked, but Hermann, who made a speciality of obtaining the unobtainable for his customers, had no trouble in getting seats for Cochran.

He went to *Oedipus Rex* and was enthralled. This was his first experience of arena drama and for days afterward the memory of crowds surging from all sides to kneel and pray before the King's palace haunted him with its moving effect. When he came out of the theatre he decided he must do something similar. Back in London he arranged an option to rent Olympia for the coming year and returned to Berlin on the track of the producer Max Reinhardt. Reinhardt had gone to Budapest with his company and Cochran pursued him there. On the train he had a sudden vision of Olympia as a cathedral: at one end he visualized a huge rose window looking down through massive columns on the performance of a mediaeval mystery play.

Max Reinhardt had begun his career as an actor and excelled at portraying old men when he was only in his twenties. Gradually he moved over to direction which interested him more than acting and gave him the opportunity of developing his novel ideas. These included replacing the old star system with crowd work, the use of lighting and stylised scenery to vary the appearance of actors, and, above all, the direct involvement of the audience by extending the stage into their very midst. What had most impressed Cochran was his handling of immense crowds and the skill with which he organized their movements.

Cochran joined him in the Hungarian Hotel, Budapest, at a large supper party which went on for hours. Afterwards, until six in the morning, the two of them discussed ideas in a café. At first bewildered by the grandiosity of Cochran's project, Reinhardt soon became enthusiastic. Why should he not stage the Delhi Durbar 'mit grossen Elephanten'? Cochran tactfully guided him away from this notion and towards his original concept of a mystery play.

'But the story,' Reinhardt insisted. 'Have you one?'

Cochran spoke eloquently of the gleaming rose window, of dim religious light, of crowds surging mysteriously through the great spaces of Olympia. He had little more than this to offer, but his vision convinced Reinhardt, who gave him an introduction to the writer Karl Volmöller of Berlin. Within twenty-four hours, spurred by the Englishman's exuberance and wheedling charm, Volmöller produced the scenario for a wordless spectacle based on a mediaeval Provençal legend featuring a nun to whom the Madonna makes an appearance. It was called *The Miracle*.

Reinhardt, aiming high, suggested Richard Strauss as composer of the incidental music. Cochran shrewdly objected: Strauss was too great a figure, he argued, and likely to demand impossible conditions which Olympia with its poor acoustics could not fulfil. For commercial success they needed a lesser man, a second-rater whose music would appeal to the general public. His choice, a perfect one, fell on Engelbert Humperdinck, prolific musician and fervent Wagnerian, who is remembered today only for his anodyne *Hansel and Gretel*.

The part of the Nun called for superlative qualities of dancing and miming. Few performers able to supply these were available, and, a little reluctantly, Cochran agreed to audition the Russian ballerina Natalia Truhanova who was so keen to work under Reinhardt that she offered to travel at her own expense from Paris to Munich for an audition. The audition took place in Humperdinck's cottage outside the city. Truhanova, wearing the latest Parisian fashion and moving in a cloud of expensive perfume, descended flamboyantly upon the simple dwelling of Herr Humperdinck, much to the disapproval of his wife who was more accustomed to the homespun jollities of *Hansel and Gretel* than to the cosmopolitan sophistication of her unwelcome guest. Frau Humperdinck peremptorily dismissed her son to another room so that he might not be contaminated by sinful relations. Despite the weariness of a long car journey from Paris to Munich and then an hour's drive to the cottage, Cochran and his colleagues watched the scene with amusement. Frau Humperdinck stood by in grim silence and offered them not one drop or crumb of refreshment.

Having changed into an outrageously transparent costume, Truhanova began dancing to a piano accompaniment by Engelbert Humperdinck, he having been ordered by his wife to sit with his back toward the siren. At her first high kick a picture tumbled from the wall. As her entrechats grew in exhilaration the whole cottage shook and ornaments trembled dangerously. From time to time Humperdinck's son peered into the room and was sharply ordered back by his mother. When it was all over Reinhardt murmured that Truhanova deserved the part because she had been such a sport. On the departure of her guests Frau Humperdinck opened every door and every window to purify her cottage of the alien presence and its sinful perfume. She aided the cold night air in its task by whisking back and forth waving a towel. The matrimonial bed, which had been profaned when Truhanova shed her street clothes upon them and changed into her daring costume, was taken up and its linen vigorously washed.

For the equally important part of the Madonna Reinhardt had wanted Ida Rubinstein, although she proved unavailable. One day Cochran happened to see Volmöller's wife, a beautiful Italian. 'There,' he said to Reinhardt, 'is the Madonna.' Although she had never acted she did well at audition and was engaged. How was she to be billed? She gave Cochran a list of Italian Christian names and a list of Italian towns. From them he chose 'Maria' and 'Carmi', little knowing that Maria Carmi was to be one of the greatest successes in the venture. The leading male rôle of the Spielmann, or minstrel, fell to the Viennese comedian Max Pallenberg, later a riotous Ko-Ko in the Berlin production of *The Mikado*.

The designer was Ernst Stern, Reinhardt's art director, who took Cologne Cathedral as the inspiration for his setting. Artist and practical workman to an equal degree, he had a gift for solving problems with the simplest of methods. 'When in doubt,' he would murmur, 'mask with a little black velvet.' Speedily, unerringly, he produced designs for some two thousand costumes, each with its individual motif and each with its individual belt, buckle, hat and shoe. Buckram was cleverly used to make garments hang the way he wanted, and everything was slightly exaggerated as it must be in the theatre to give, paradoxically, the effect of reality. Once the costumes had been made they were painted in order to show wear and travel stains. The army thus created for *The Miracle* looked like something out of a Dürer canvas. They were accompanied by dogs which Cochran had rounded up by scouring Hungerford Market and picking out the shaggiest specimens he could find. Stern even specified the colour and markings of the horses he required. Cochran took him to the winter headquarters of the Sanger circus and delighted him by selecting twenty-five horses, mostly piebald and patterned exactly as Stern had shown them in his sketches.

A numerous company of technicians took over the huge bare hall of Olympia on the 10 December with orders to have everything prepared for the opening performance less than three weeks later. Whereas in the theatre lighting effects are not difficult to achieve, at Olympia miles of cable had to be laid and hundreds of different lamps provided before work could begin.

With the pantomime season coming to its peak there were not enough specialist electricians available to operate lighting cues. While a cast of fifteen hundred people milled about down below, on gantries and flying gangways above a small band of men worked feverishly to complete elaborate lighting schemes. When the leading players rested, Cochran himself posed as the Nun so that Reinhardt and Stern could experiment with hues of green, yellow, blue, pink and red in their attempt to achieve the mystic aura they sought.

The miracle of *The Miracle* was that it opened on time. An orchestra of two hundred players and a chorus of five hundred voices combined with subtle lighting and rhythmic crowd movements to create a spectacle of a sort that London had never seen before. The great barn of Olympia was transformed into a vast cathedral-like setting dominated by the rose window of Cochran's original vision. On the opening night all the complicated machinery, hydraulic lifts and lighting bridges and platforms as big as the stage at Drury Lane, functioned with perfect smoothness. Cochran's first big production was a triumph and very much his own personal creation. His was the initial idea, and his the nurturing of it, which had brought success. From the very beginning and right up to the sensational première, he controlled and directed every aspect of the undertaking down to the smallest detail. The cut of a tunic worn by supernumerary, the texture of a dog's coat and the shape of a wimple were as important to him as the construction of the rose window and the placing of the giant pillars which soared up into the infinity of the roof at Olympia.

Yet although two performances a day were drawing audiences of about ten thousand the takings remained stubbornly less than expenses. To make a profit Cochran needed twenty thousand people to fill the seats daily. His old friend Ranger Gull wrote a piece attacking *The Miracle* as a Popish plot and sermons were preached in many London churches, but this welcome controversy did not stimulate ticket sales and the general public failed to respond. Then Lady Northcliffe, wife to the most powerful newspaper magnate of the day, saw a performance and was surprised at the small audience. She brought her husband to it and he, as a result, ordered one of his publications, *The Daily Mail*, to run an article deploring the scanty attendance at so fine a spectacle. This was not the sort of publicity Cochran wanted. Next morning, however, the *Daily Mail* asked him to let them have the figures for sales on the day before the article appeared and those on the following day. Northcliffe wanted to show the powerful effect of his newspaper's intervention. It was unfortunate that, far from increasing, business had dropped and less money had been taken on the day after the article. This, Cochran decided, he dare not reveal, and he blandly produced figures which showed a big leap. The story was taken up by other newspapers. The ruse worked. After ten days the box-office takings nearly trebled and people were being turned away. Much, much later Cochran told Northcliffe the truth of what he had done. 'You'd have been a damned fool if you hadn't,' grunted the press lord.

A rueful symmetry decreed that it should be Northcliffe who also, involuntarily, brought the successful run to an end. At a time when *The Miracle* had firmly established itself and was turning away thousands of would-be spectators, it was obliged to make way for the Ideal Home Exhibition which the *Daily Mail* had booked into Olympia. The date of the Exhibition had long since been reserved and *The Miracle* closed at a loss after a hundred and forty-three performances instead of with the profit it would have made had it survived a few months longer. Cochran was not dismayed. He had created a thing of beauty and, to do so, inspired some of the finest theatrical talent of the day. If *The Miracle* had made his name it had also given opportunities to many young actors and actresses. So large was the cast of hundreds that for years afterwards he was constantly meeting people, utter strangers, who would come up to him and speak gratefully of the chance he had offered them. Among them was a thirteen-year-old girl who played one of the children. Her name, she later told him, was Gertrude Lawrence.

How would he follow up *The Miracle*? He was asked to become general manager of 'Shakespeare's England', an exhibition organized at Earl's Court by Mrs Cornwallis West, alias Lady Randolph Churchill. That dominating female had set the project alight with her enthusiasm although she neglected much of the dull administration needed to make it run smoothly. Cochran moved in and readjusted various arrangements. She countermanded his orders. Her new colleague quietly restored them and took no notice of her. He put on a circus in the Empress Hall as a minor part of the attractions which drew far more paying customers than the Shakespearean element of the exhibition. Mrs Cornwallis West took due note and became his friend.

All this was small beer, however, and when Olympia became vacant he longed to fill it again with some big show. The circus he imported for 'Shakespeare's England' had put him in touch with the German zoo-owner Carl Hagenbeck. A learned and enterprising zoologist, Hagenbeck founded an animal park outside Hamburg where the beasts wandered in apparent freedom rather than being cabined in narrow cages. Foxes and chamois darted up and down artificial mountains. Lions and tigers loped through glens separated from the public only by deep wide trenches. Cochran decided he would bring them over to Olympia and feature them as the 'Wonder Zoo and Big Circus'. All he needed was many thousands of pounds.

From his own pocket he financed a deposit on Olympia and on Hagenbeck. A wealthy but aged animal lover offered him twenty thousand pounds at generous terms. (Cochran not only had the gift of charming money out of people: much more important, he always knew the right person to approach at the right time.) Conditions were agreed and contracts drawn up, at which point the old animal lover thoughtlessly died of a heart attack. It was too late to withdraw yet there was not enough money to continue. As Cochran walked miserably down Bond Street he passed the offices of Keith Prowse, the ticket agents. An idea struck him. He went in and asked to see the managing director. The latter, somewhat surprised, heard Cochran speak eloquently of lions roaming Olympia and monkeys swinging on the beams of the great hall. There would, his unexpected visitor continued, be two hundred and fifty horses caracoling expertly and five hundred Barbary apes performing remarkable evolutions. Lots of money was waiting to be made. By the time Cochran finished, Keith Prowse had agreed to advance ten thousand pounds in return for sole booking rights on the seats.

Still more cash was needed. In Regent Street Cochran met by chance a journalist he had known at *The Daily Mirror*. The journalist, as journalists often are, was out of a job and so keen to find one that he would, he said, produce five thousand pounds for whoever offered him one. Not taking him very seriously, Cochran proposed to engage him at Olympia. Promptly he was rewarded with the five thousand pounds for his coffers. Once the show opened at Christmas, 1913, the money was quickly repaid. Keith Prowse, too, had their funds back within two weeks of opening and made large profits.

The customers, sixty-three thousand of them on the first two days, entered Olympia and saw, to their right, numbers of lions rambling in freedom on a mountain. Close by there lolled twenty polar bears almost, but not quite, near enough to touch. Trapeze artists flew back and forth up in the dome missing each other by inches as they crossed. Barbary apes jeered and chattered at the gaping spectators while zebras trotted and an elephant circulated with nonchalant unconcern.

Cochran's favourite performers were the chimpanzees Max and Moritz. They rode bicycles and soon developed an artery of skills that outpaced the deftest trick cyclist. Like human comedians they loved laughter and could never get enough of it. Moritz, indeed, acquired a habit that his human counterparts often suffer from: having gained a laugh with a certain trick, he would repeat it over and over again until the effect ended up boring the audience. At this point the trainer would sit him up alone on a high shelf while regaling his partner Max with favourite delicacies. 'You call yourself a comedian,' said the trainer severely, 'you're a rotten actor! Just because you get a laugh you have to queer your act by repeating yourself over and over again! You're not worth a dollar a week!' As the bananas and oranges flowed generously in Max's direction a repentant Moritz sat on his own muttering and crying. The lesson was learned. It was something Cochran remembered when the comic actors he later engaged for his theatrical productions made the error of milking an effect dry. 'You remind me of Moritz,' he would begin gently . . .

ii
DELYSIA AND OLD BILL

'I am accustomed to temperamental storms. In the world of
theatre I have invariably found that the performer without a
temperament is not worth while.'

CHARLES B. COCHRAN

One of the busiest theatre managers in Paris early this century
was a dapper young man called André Charlot. Before he
reached the age of thirty he had been, at one time or another,
manager of the Folies-Bergère, of the vast Châtelet which
specialized in epic melodramas, and of the Palais Royal which
housed traditional French farce. Cochran met him in 1908 on
one of his Paris trips and found him a useful acquaintance. Like
General de Gaulle, who, although understanding English perfectly, always conducted business with Anglo-Saxons through
an interpreter, Cochran preferred to have a bi-lingual expert
available when negotiating contracts with the foreign stars he
imported. Charlot amiably helped out on such occasions, for
he knew Cochran's language well, his fluency having been
encouraged by his English wife Florence.

Charlot's reputation soon crossed the Channel and in 1912
he was invited to take over the Alhambra Theatre, then in a
state of bankruptcy. A few years later, having restored it to
prosperity, he became its managing director and launched on a
career in London which for sparkle and inventiveness often
rivalled Cochran's. In the early days, at a time when Cochran
desperately needed money, Charlot took him on as a partner at
the Alhambra. The arrangement did not last long, since a
smooth collaboration between the two individualistic characters was impossible. There were no violent quarrels, no stormy
scenes, but after a while they agreed to part on friendly terms.
Each personality was different from the other. Charlot was
obsessed by technical matters. He loved such minutiae as the
exact placing of a spotlight and the precise cueing of a thunder
machine. Cochran employed the best technicians he could find
and left them to get on with it: so long as the lighting expert

produced the effect he wanted and the designer created the illusion he sought, he did not bother himself with the mechanics of the thing. While exercising vigilant control over every aspect of a production he was content to delegate the technical side to others. Charlot nourished a strange distaste for publicity whereas Cochran, who revelled in it, had a genius for ensuring that his productions were widely talked and written about. Another difference was that Charlot enjoyed finding raw talent, cultivating and polishing like a cutter with a diamond until he could present it as his own creation. Although Cochran was just as alert to promise, his method was not to influence it directly but to provide the circumstances in which it could flourish. 'Charlot giveth and Cochran taketh away', remarked a wit. This was true, for example, in the case of Noël Coward. Charlot gave him an early opportunity with *London Calling* but it was Cochran who stepped in and enabled the promising young man to reach the heights.

In the nineteen-twenties and thirties Charlot and Cochran were to be rivals. Friendly in private life, in their professional work they often played tricks on one another, as when Cochran scheduled the first night of *Ever Green* to clash with an important opening arranged by Charlot. Reports of enmity between them were useful publicity, and Cochran, for one, slyly encouraged rumours in the interests of free advertisement. Their main field of conflict was in the sphere of revue. Cochran, as we have seen, had already tried to introduce in London the sort of thing that had impressed him in Paris. When a language does not possess a term to describe something, it borrows the word from another tongue, which is what has happened with *revue*, an old-established feature in France defined as an end-of-year entertainment in which brief scenes, often with music, comment on events over the past twelve months. Erudite historians trace the first *revue* as far back as a work by the thirteenth-century lyric poet Adam de la Halle. In England, during the nineteenth-century, the form emerged vaguely in burlesques by the prolific James Robertson Planché and, with more sobriety, as family entertainments provided by Mr and Mrs German Reed. The first London revue as we know it today is generally agreed to have been *Under The Clock* (1893), which, directed by Seymour

Hicks, was deliberately modelled on the Parisian genre and satirised theatrical topics. Inspiration for the title came from *The Times* rubric at the head of its list of entertainments, which showed a clock face and books. Irving, Tree and Lady Bancroft were among the targets, and also Augustine Daly, the American actor then playing Shakespeare in London.

Revues began to proliferate in London. *The 'Revue'* at the Coliseum was devised by an expert specially imported from the Folies-Bergère. *By George!* at the Empire celebrated the Coronation of 1911. A new style of American music called ragtime encouraged the trend and inspired revues with such titles as *Everybody's Doing It*. In 1912 Charlot himself launched his first revue which, obeying the mood of determined flippancy, he baptised *Kill That Fly!* A neater title he devised for a subsequent revue was *5064 Gerrard*, the incantation spoken by ladies at the telephone exchange when callers rang his box-office. At least he had made sure that people knew where to telephone for seat bookings.

In this rising tide Cochran, as usual, had ideas which distinguished him from the rest. All other revues at that time were of the sort known as spectacular and featured large orchestras, a big cast and elaborate scenery. Cochran aimed at the type of production he had admired in the Théâtre des Capucines and other small Parisian theatres where the style was intimate and the wit subtle. First he took a lease on the newly-built Ambassadors Theatre off Shaftsbury Avenue. Its Louis XVI style of decoration and colour schemes of pale violet and dull gold set a quiet, understated tone and, with its ambassadorial crests, hinted at distinction. Then he looked for a star. Paris, again, supplied what he wanted. Some years ago he had heard a young woman sing at a party given by the Anglo-French entertainer Harry Fragson. Born in Soho, Fragson was a *chanteur à accent* who shuttled between London and Paris singing in English for his compatriots and in Cockney-accented French for Parisians. 'Canoodling' became 'Les Jaloux' and 'Everybody's Doing It' was transmuted into 'C'est Pour Vous'. His baptismal name was Victor Philippe Pot which he changed for his debut into 'Frogson'. Realizing, however, that French audiences would translate this as 'son of a frog' he prudently altered it.

It is a fitting irony that the most celebrated tune he ever composed was 'Hello! Hello! Who's your lady friend?', since in private life he was consumed by jealousy and forced his mistress to telephone him regularly throughout the day so that he might check her movements when they were apart. His then wife, who so interested Cochran, often caused him agonies, for, husky-voiced and strangely attractive, she cuckolded him without remorse. He died at the age of forty-four, not long after Cochran met him, his father, the eccentric Monsieur Pot, having shot him dead in a quarrel over a discarded mistress.

'Why don't you go on the stage?' Cochran asked Madame Fragson when he heard her sing. Before she could answer, the jealous husband intervened: 'She would drive everybody out of the theatre.' His wife modestly agreed: she had tried it, she said, and had not gone beyond the chorus. A year later Cochran saw her playing a small part at the Olympia music-hall in Paris. Although she had only a few lines to say she delivered them with a tear in the voice, a trait which is inborn and cannot be acquired, and she had, Cochran sensed, a curious magnetism. 'Who is this girl?' he asked his companion. 'You must have met her as Madame Harry Fragson,' came the reply. 'They call her Alice Delysia.'

Having engaged Delysia for his new revue Cochran sought out another French performer called Léon Morton, a skeletal droll with a mouth like a rat-trap who had often amused him in Paris. The third principal he recruited was Max Dearly whose name may still be remembered by connoisseurs of nineteen-thirties French films. Max had elongated features that looked as if a flat-iron had been passed over them and a voice that crackled like a rusty hinge. He was small and might have been taken for a jockey – indeed, his life was divided between his dual passions for racing and the theatre. As a beginner he toured with an English mime troupe called 'Les Willi-Willi' and, when a member of it left, unexpectedly, took his name to avoid changing the printed programmes. His most famous number was the *valse chaloupée* in which, made up as an Apache, he danced with the beautiful Mistinguett. Women adored him, especially when he sang 'Tra-la-la-la-voilà les English' and other nonsense ditties. 'The most virtuous woman,' he used to say, 'can't resist a sympathetic little chap who knows how to make her laugh.'*

Cochran took possession of the Ambassadors Theatre on the 1 August, 1914. Three days later came the declaration of war against Germany and, with it, an end to theatrical activity for the time being. Too old for active service at the age of forty-two, he decided to continue laying his plans against the moment when London theatres were functioning again. The dancers he wanted were an English troupe called the Grecian Maids who had been playing Munich. Their journey home in the confusion of wartime led them back and forth across frontiers on a zig-zag route so bewildering that, said one of the Grecian Maids, it was only the sound of station porters speaking English which told them they had reached their destination. Another member of the cast was to be Arthur Playfair, an excellent comedian but much given to late-night parties that went on so long that he was occasionally unable to appear for the next day's performance. Cochran once heard that he had organized a bumper New Year's Eve celebration, and, fearing the worst, rushed to his home with the intention of keeping an eye on him. He was too late, the bird had flown and the performance was missed. On New Year's Day he received a doctor's certificate which read: 'This is to certify that Mr Arthur Playfair is suffering from "Excessive New Year's Eve".'

As with *The Miracle*, the basic idea for the new revue was Cochran's own. The plight of the Grecian Maids had suggested to him a situation where a foreign troupe of actors find themselves arriving, to their surprise, in an English theatre. What are they to do? Why, they will put on a show. Their leader, Max Dearly, was to get a laugh by saying: 'We have some English dancers, so why not give a French revue?' (Even then English dancers were established features of European revues). Cochran took his idea to several writers who none of them could

---

* One of his many stories established itself as a part of French film lore. His butler, he said, went every evening to the same cinema at the same hour to watch the same film. Why so? Max asked him. Because, said the butler, there was a scene where the heroine undressed beside a railway line. Unfortunately, at the very moment when the last crucial garment was about to drop, the train came in. Well? said Max. Well, said the butler, he was waiting for the train to be late one evening.

grasp what he wanted. Eventually he settled on Harry Grattan, a veteran who had begun his stage career at the age of four in *Uncle Tom's Cabin*. When he was twelve, a seasoned actor, he played Captain Corcoran in a children's production of *HMS Pinafore* directed by W. S. Gilbert. Having done everything there was to do on the stage, he had now started writing for it. Grattan quickly absorbed Cochran's notion and within a few days he produced the script. The title, deliberately nonchalant, was to be *Odds and Ends*.

The setting was uncluttered to the point of starkness. Mindful of Ernst Stern's advice – 'When in doubt, mask with a little black velvet' – Cochran made no attempt at scenery and draped the stage with black curtains. What he described as the essence of revue, 'lightness, colour, variety, speed', was provided by the script, the acting and the singing. The biggest problem was running order. Each brief item must contrast piquantly with what had gone before and must build up to the finale of the first half. The second number of the second half needed to be exceptionally good since its function was to persuade the audience that even greater treats lay in store. Again, the various numbers had to build up logically and smoothly to the number immediately preceding the finale. One method, as used by Charlot, was to write the name of each number on a card and then, by shifting and re-arranging the cards interminably, to juggle with them until he arrived at what seemed to be the perfect order. After which someone inevitably pointed out that, ideal though it might be, the running order was impracticable because of lengthy costume changes or the outraged protests of leading ladies who claimed that excessive demands were being made on them. Whereat the process began all over again and went on for many argumentative hours.

To help with the organization Cochran engaged a man called Frank Collins whom he had already known for some time. Once a clerk on the Stock Exchange, Frank did a lot of amateur acting in his leisure hours before turning professional. Cochran asked him to take over the show. He would, said Frank, but not as a stage manager and only if he were to be officially entitled 'director'. Then, he explained, since there were so many foreigners in the cast, he would be called 'Monsieur le

Directeur' and have prestige. Cochran agreed. 'How long do you want me for?' 'For life,' said Cochran. Frank pointed out that they might not get on together. 'I'll take the risk,' was the laconic reply. Their association was to last for twenty-eight years with Frank as his loyal associate and intermediary who relayed his orders to others and kept him in touch with everything that went on. He was an impeccable administrator and an ideal adjutant. Actors did not always like him since he was not much amused by their jokes and responded little to their banter. His dourness and his literal interpretation of his master's orders made him a forbidding and sometimes lugubrious character. He was a disciplinarian, tall and dominating, who ruled his fief with the stern authority of a headmaster. Cochran found him indispensable. Others, more used to the cheery informality of the theatre, could not bear him. His sombre suits gave him the look of an undertaker, a lay preacher, anything but a man of the theatre. He dressed, said a performer who knew him well, 'like a labourer in his Sunday best'.

By October the theatres were all open and Cochran launched *Odds and Ends* on the 17th. It was originally part of a triple bill and sandwiched between two one-act plays. As the run developed one of the plays was dropped and *Odds and Ends* accordingly expanded. At first, though, its reception was dubious. The audience found the stark setting unattractive and doubted even if it approved of this novel entertainment. Cochran persisted when he noticed that people had started coming back to see *Odds and Ends* again. He put in a new scene and invited the critics once more, taking care to distribute them among a public which had paid for its seats and consisted largely of enthusiasts for the show. This time, with the regulars laughing and applauding in advance, the evening went much better than the first night and *Odds and Ends* settled down to a handsome run of five hundred performances.

While Max Dearly in the course of time went back to Paris, Léon Morton and Alice Delysia stayed on in London. Morton's spindle shanks became a familiar Hampstead sight as he departed each evening for the theatre from his home in Fitzroy Road. He was a keen organist, and, when he bought an instrument too large for his flat, moved to Brighton into a home big enough to take it. Delysia was to marry again, twice, and to develop into a star whose accent, like Yvonne Arnaud's, was sedulously fostered as part of the charm which captivated West End audiences. One of her triumphs in *Odds and Ends* had been the recruiting song 'We don't want to lose you but we think you ought to go', which, thought the composer Paul Rubens, she sang more convincingly than anyone else. Her voice had not been trained and her middle register was a little vague, although her top notes, on the evidence of gramophone records, were strong and sweet. Any vocal failing was compensated by her sparkling personality which projected to the farthest reaches of the theatre and by her gurgling accent with its uvular r's. She was just as warm and effervescent behind the scenes where she delighted to cook up delicious meals, banging a steak with a rolling-pin to make it tender, lightly browning it and then pouring melted butter over it. '*Voilà!* You 'ave a wondairful meal,' she would say as she poured out her favourite drink, the mixture of champagne and stout known as Black Velvet. Much of her leisure time she spent on charitable ventures and entertaining wounded soldiers. When she received a decoration for her wartime work a dinner was given in her honour and a French colleague proposed the toast: 'Mesdames, Mesdemoiselles, Messieurs, there are two ways of making love . . .'. Delysia burst out: 'Don't be reedeeculous, I know two hundred and seventy-five.'

Having made a profit of five hundred pounds a week from *Odds and Ends* Cochran immediately put on a sequel in the following year called *More (Odds and Ends)* with the same players. This time the settings were not so austere. Delysia showed off a series of beautiful dresses and proved as well that her instinct for comedy was exquisite and sure. The chorus girls, wearing silvered top hats and striped bow ties as Victorian dandies, demonstrated a precision of attack and spruceness of costume that were rapidly becoming the hallmark of a Cochran evening. Mistinguett came over from Paris to see this Victorian number and reproduced it at the Folies-Bergère. It was copied by other Parisian theatres and even turned up in America. *More* triumphed as rapturously as its predecessor. Among its admirers was the esteemed but unpredictable actor-manager Sir Herbert Beerbohm Tree who saw it half a dozen times. He even asked Cochran to produce a revue at His Majesty's Theatre with himself as the star. It would, said the tactful Cochran, be 'vastly interesting.' But Tree went away on an American tour and the project languished, much to Cochran's relief.

More was succeeded in 1916 by *Pell Mell*, the third of Cochran's revues at the Ambassadors Theatre. The programme of *Odds and Ends* had contained the message: 'Pray be seated punctually at 8.30, as the plot finishes at 8.25.' That of *Pell Mell* announced that the entertainment could just as well be played backwards as forewards. No-one took up this apparent challenge to the bugbear of running order and the success of the earlier revues was repeated with, in particularly, an ingenious mime episode based on a Fragonard picture. The French flavour, as before, was pronounced, and Delysia and Morton clowned to the wild delight of their admirers. Delysia was, by now, earning a lot more money to feed an inborn extravagance which could not resist what was offered to her as something she called *une occasion*, or bargain. Queues of dealers formed regularly outside her dressing room to collect instalments on quite useless goods – fake pictures, rugs, shawls, furs – which she had bought through hire purchase. Her cupboards filled up speedily with unwanted objects. She also had a generous passion for adopting orphaned children. Callers at her dressing-room had to step carefully in order to avoid the numerous contented babies who crawled everywhere on the floor.

In between his work at the Ambassadors Cochran also produced a revue at the Empire. Having for so long been his own master he was at first reluctant to accept an invitation which meant his becoming a salaried employee as general manager. A percentage of the profits helped to persuade him and he revived the theatre's fortunes with *Watch Your Step*, an American import which included music by Irving Berlin. While rehearsals were going on he vastly increased business at the Empire by getting Horatio Bottomley to deliver a speech there every night. Bottomley in his day was a superb demagogue who could sway audiences in a manner that seems incredible now. To his talents as orator, journalist, business promoter and race-horse owner he added, later, that of confidence trickster, although at that time he was famous for patriotic addresses which sent young men dashing off to army recruitment offices and others scurrying to invest money in war bonds. Receipts quadrupled when Bottomley spoke at the Empire and his drawing power filled the theatre over and over again. He more than justified the big fees he needed to keep him in the kippers and champagne he devoured as his favourite breakfast.

Despite profits on his three revues Cochran soon found that the Ambassadors was not large enough to sustain his rising expenses. Having started Delysia at a salary of six pounds a week he was now paying her fifty, and fees and production costs were mounting steadily as he sought to keep up with more elaborate revues presented by André Charlot and other rival impresarios. He sold his lease and moved literally next door into the St Martin's Theatre which is separated from the Ambassadors by a narrow alley. His farewell to the Ambassadors consisted of a play called *Wonder Tales* in which the author's wife took the leading rôle as a fairy. She was, unfortunately, a woman of statuesque build, and at a children's matinée she popped up through a shaky trap in the Ambassador's small stage to be greeted by a shrill voice from the gallery which declared: 'Oh, Daddy! What a big fairy!'

The St Martin's Theatre was built at the same time as the Ambassador's, although through wartime delays it had only just been completed. The interior was Georgian in style and, with its gold leaf and neatly moulded plasterwork, suggested to one observer a private theatre created by some noble patron of the drama to entertain his guests. Cochran thus obtained the same effect of intimacy for his productions but with a seating capacity twenty-five per cent greater than that of its neighbour. He opened the theatre with *Houp-la*, a mixture of musical comedy and revue featuring Gertie Millar, the archetypal Gaiety Girl who, first wed to the composer Lionel Monckton, later set the fashion for all Gaiety Girls by marrying into the aristocracy and becoming the Countess of Dudley. A humbler member of the cast was the seventeen year-old Binnie Hale, engaged as understudy to one of the leading players. The latter had insisted on paying for and wearing her own clothes but would not allow her understudy to use them. One evening she fell ill and Binnie Hale had to go on in her place. What clothes was she to wear? The good-natured Delysia came to the rescue, and Binnie, rushing back and forth across the alley to the stage-door of the Ambassadors, was able, after plunging into Delysia's voluminous wardrobe, to wear a different outfit for each entrance.

One of the properties Cochran acquired when he took the St Martin's was a derelict scenery store over the road. He did not need it and sold it to a restaurateur who turned it into a café. During rehearsals of *Houp-la* Frank Collins and one of the musicians decided to have a meal there. 'We can only die once,' observed Collins with his usual pessimism. They did not die but, in fact, enjoyed an excellent steak. Collins told Cochran about it and he, in turn, recommended it to Delysia who was a passionate connoisseur of food. She liked the place so much that she became an habituée and, in fact, gave it a name. At dinner one evening she surveyed her retinue of admirers and hangers-on and remarked: 'Actors cling together like ivy, don't you think?' Since by then the restaurant was a favourite rendez-vous for actors working in nearby theatres, 'The Ivy' it was known as ever after.

Cochran took pride in the chorus he assembled for *Houp-la* and described it as 'perhaps the prettiest collection of girls ever seen on any stage in the world'. He was already setting a fashion in beautiful women, and soon other producers tried to tempt them away with offers of double their usual salary. Few things gave Cochran more pleasure than choosing a pretty face, grooming its owner, advising her on clothes and trying to find her a rich husband, preferably a nobleman into the bargain, on the pattern of Gertie Millar. During the First World War he drove about London in an electric brougham, and, after the night's performance, took the girls safely home while Zeppelins droned overhead and the occasional thump of a distant air raid was heard. Inevitably his interest in these young creatures often went beyond the paternal. The favoured one would find when she entered her dressing room each night a posy carefully placed beside the mirror. More elaborate bouquets would follow. She would be guarded at first with this beaming little man and his slightly red nose and his large cigar. He may have been old enough to be her father but his thoughtful attentiveness would gradually undermine her defences. Free tickets to his other productions were lavished upon her, and cosy little meals at the Savoy Grill. Sometimes, when Mrs Cochran was away, she would go back with him to his flat in Piccadilly. On other occasions the object of his adoration would find him tedious and a familiar speech would be heard: she liked and admired him as a person, she enjoyed his company, she thought he was the most interesting man she had ever met, but . . . 'You're cold,' he would murmur bitterly, 'cold, cold. Why are you so cold?' Next day he would have forgotten all about her in the excitement of chasing new prey.

If, in private, his life was punctuated by amorous adventures, in public he observed the conventions of the day with strictness. One of his revues at the time was called *At Half-Past Eight* and he had specifically designed it for the well brought-up young officer on leave and his sixteen year-old sister. The Lord Chamberlain, who inspected all theatrical productions for the slightest hint of immorality, gave the entertainment his approval. Business had started to fall off when a newspaper published some caricatures of the leading ladies. Cochran liked them and had them reproduced in an advertisement and hung them around the foyer. Next evening the 'house-full' boards went up and he was obliged to turn away queues of people. The Lord Chamberlain called him in and ordered the immediate removal of the pictures. Cochran, though he complied, was puzzled. He could see nothing objectionable about them. Ah, said the grave official, the artist 'seemed deliberately to have created the effect of feminine garments being blown up'.

Famous now as a purveyor of sophisticated revue, Cochran still wished to prove that he was just as discerning in the more serious reaches of the theatre. As he was fond of pointing out, had not his very first theatrical production been an Ibsen play, and obscure Ibsen at that? Moreover, his latest production, *The Hundred and Fifty Pounds Revue* in which he promoted Binnie Hale to an important rôle, had lost him considerably more than the sum mentioned in the title and he began to think that perhaps the vogue for such entertainment was dying out. He therefore put on *Damaged Goods*, an adaptation of *Les Avariés* by the French dramatist Eugène Brieux who specialized in *pièces à thèse*, or problem plays, well-wrought examples of dramatic carpentry which utilized contemporary moral topics adroitly enough to startle boulevard audiences without alienating them. *Damaged Goods* took as its subject venereal disease, a highly sensational matter then, and impressed the public by its sober treatment. The play continued for nine months and did so well that while it was still running Cochran produced *The Three Daughters of Monsieur Dupont*, another adaptation from Brieux, this time dwelling on the perils of that well-established bourgeois custom the arranged marriage and the unhappiness it caused when money took precedence over love. The role of the materialistic father was played by O. B. Clarence, (even in reference books he never divulged the secret of what those famous initials stood for), an Old Bensonian of wide experience, whose round innocent eyes and mellow voice often cast him as a smooth-tongued villain or a Trollopian cleric.* As Monsieur Dupont he said mellifluously to his daughter: 'All I ask is that you won't be obstinate, or refuse to let us present Antonin to you as a possible husband.' 'To marry nowadays, then, a girl has to buy her husband?' retorted the girl indignantly. Brieux's dramas were full of 'strong' scenes like this, and, while the social problems they examined have passed away and left his work irremediably dated, his technique was brilliantly effective at the time.

Nothing could have been more different from the moral tracts of Brieux than the next play Cochran sponsored. He spent the Easter of 1918 with his wife Evelyn at an hotel in Brighton and, as usual, had brought scripts to read. One of them was a romantic drama by the best-selling author Robert Hichens and the other a comic play based on a series of popular cartoons. The latter was badly written and badly put together, yet it made him choke with laughter. When he read it to Evelyn

---

* Perhaps the initials stood for 'Old Bensonian'. Clarence much respected Sir Frank Benson and was proud of his association with the cricketing knight under whose guidance he learned his trade through playing scores of parts.

she too laughed until the tears came. The piece which so amused them was called *The Better 'Ole* and had been turned down by all the other leading impresarios.

The author was a serving officer, Captain Bruce Bairns-father, a talented artist who created a character called 'Old Bill'. Under the title 'Fragments from France' he drew a series of cartoons depicting Old Bill, a phlegmatic and permanently disillusioned infantryman uprooted from his London haunts and plunged into the horrors of trench warfare. He is a scrounger and a beer-swilling cynic who refuses to be shaken by the terrible battles that go on around him. His two mates, young Alf and young Bert, act as comic feeds. 'When the war's over, I'm going to change my name to 'Enery.' 'Why?' ''Cause the blinking Kaiser 'asn't 'arf made a mess of the name of William.' As the din of heavy bombing is heard in the distance Alf says: 'What's that?' 'That's the gong for dinner,' grunts Old Bill. The noise of terrific shelling grows nearer. 'It's times like these that make Victoria Station seem a 'ell of a way off,' muses Bill. The most famous cartoon of all showed Old Bill, round-faced, big-eyed, huge walrus moustache bristling, stuck in a muddy shell-hole with his mates while buildings crash, rain drizzles and a hell of bombs and bullets thunders all around them in No Man's Land. 'If you know of a better 'ole,' says Bill in reply to some unprintable remark by Alf, 'go to it.'

This became the most famous catch-phrase of the 1914–18 war. Old Bill incarnated English stolidity and the English sense of humour in the front line. His dry Cockney wit and lavatory brush moustache represented patriotic doggedness in the way that Napoleon's *grognards* symbolised stubborn veterans of the Old Guard. Even today, when the circumstances that made Old Bill a much loved figure have disappeared, Bairnsfather's witty draughtsmanship still amuses and often moves.

The play he had concocted was clumsy and amateurish. During the Easter holiday Frank Collins, who lived in Brighton, came to tea and bore off the script together with that of the Hichens play and read them over the weekend. He returned them with the opinion that the Hichens piece would do, once various small changes had been made. And *The Better*

'Ole? It was piffle. 'A schoolboy of fourteen could write a better play than that.'

'That is the one I'm going to produce,' said Cochran.

Frank glared in surprise. His amazement was understandable. *The Better 'Ole* lacked a proper story, the narrative was childish and the technique crude. It contained nonetheless, as Cochran pointed out, three hundred of the best jokes made during the war. The Bairnsfather types, Old Bill himself and his stooges Alf and Bert, embodied the optimistic 'Tommy'. By 1917, Cochran judged, the time was ripe for a war play without false heroics. The virtue of *The Better 'Ole* lay in its complete simplicity, and throughout rehearsals he strongly resisted attempts by professionals to rewrite it.

The choice of theatre was crucial. He decided on the old Oxford music-hall with its ready-made atmosphere of Old Bill and beer, a venerable but run-down place now doing poor business. The auditorium was cleaned up and the foyer covered with imitation sandbags. Instead of a box-office a realistic dug-out handled tickets and bookings. Since a West End name was essential, Cochran engaged the comedian Arthur Bourchier to impersonate Old Bill. He was not quite right; his accent, as one critic put it, 'travelled from Devonshire to Yorkshire and back to Somerset by way of Maine', and his clowning tended to obscure the pathos of the rôle. His name, however, sold tickets, for which reason Cochran was ready to put up with his difficult behaviour. He bubbled over with self-love and once declared to Cochran: 'Charles, I am a great actor. Yes, I am a very great actor . . . In time to come, Irving will be recalled, followed by a gap, and then Arthur Bourchier.' 'What about Beerbohm Tree?' 'An ephemeral success which will not be remembered.' His grand opinion of himself was fuelled by a dislike of his fellow comedian Arthur Roberts that went far beyond professional rivalry. At four o'clock one morning he passed Roberts under the gas lamps of the Strand. 'Goodnight, Arthur,' he said. 'Time all good actors were in bed.' 'All *good* actors are,' riposted Arthur who usually won his rounds with Bourchier.

Two days before its first night in August, 1917, *The Better 'Ole* looked as much of a shambles as the blasted landscape of No

Man's Land where the action took place. Props had not been delivered, cues were missed and an air of doom hung over endless bungling rehearsals. Worse still, Arthur Bourchier, the star of the show, was not giving satisfaction. 'You have made a mistake in engaging Bourchier,' complained a sorrowful Bairnsfather. It was agreed that until the curtain went up he should spend all his time with the comedian explaining exactly how the rôle should be played.

At the opening performance on the 4 August it had been arranged to show magic lantern slides of the famous Bairnsfather cartoons while the overture was being played. Half-way into the early bars Cochran asked for the slides. They had been forgotten. Once discovered, a breathless electrician rushed them up to the cinema box and started projecting them. In his haste some of the cartoons, to Cochran's horror, were shown upside down. This only increased the audience's pleasure at seeing yet again well-known jokes which had become a part of the national legend. The spectators were with the play from the start, and before the last notes of 'It's A Long Way To Tipperary' had died away they were determined to enjoy themselves. 'I wouldn't take £10,000 for half my share,' said Cochran exuberantly, convinced that he had a hit.

Laughter began almost as soon as the curtain whisked up, and during moments of pathos there was an eloquent silence. The audience did not worry about the thin thread of narrative which held an unwieldy play together, a preposterous story in which Old Bill foiled a German plot to blow up a vital bridge and won the Légion d'Honneur from a grateful French ally. What mattered was the vivid presentation of a folklore anti-hero whose wry humour corresponded exactly with their own and said the sort of things they would have said had they possessed Old Bill's gift of the gab. At the end Bairnsfather was reluctantly obliged to take a curtain call from a house which rose to its feet and cheered him. *The Better 'Ole*, sub-titled 'The Romance of Old Bill, A Fragment From France in Two Explosions, Seven Splinters and a Gas Attack', was an ugly duckling whose potential only Cochran had been alert enough to perceive. It rewarded him with the greatest success he had known so far and ran for two years and over eight hundred performances. At one time there were no less than five companies touring *The Better 'Ole* in the provinces and the triumph was even repeated in America. Later in the run Cochran gilded the lily by incorporating a miniature French play into *The Better 'Ole*. It was based on the cartoons of Poulbot whose drawings of children playing at soldiers were a Gallic equivalent to Bairnsfather's more robust humour. Cochran recruited an actress from the Old Vic to take part in it, and so introduced Miss Sybil Thorndike to the West End stage. Given her later career, his judgment of her was curiously bleak. 'Her performance at the Oxford was a little too restless,' he wrote. 'She had at that time a number of mannerisms and lacked repose. Her voice also lacked flexibility. But she was a conscientious artist, and a charming woman to be associated with.'

No sooner had *A Better 'Ole* been launched, than he was up in Liverpool supervising the provincial try-out of *Carminetta*, a musical comedy starring Delysia whom he was now paying a hundred pounds a week. His new production, inevitably from the French, was vaguely inspired by the opera *Carmen*. An Offenbachian score, the work of Emile Lassailly who had collaborated with the old man himself at the Théâtre des Variétés, gave Delysia many chances to show off her impertinent glamour. Her compatriot Morton played the male lead, though with some misgiving, since, despite an English wife and three years' residence in this country, he still could not speak the language properly, a handicap which did not matter in the Ambassadors revues where his mimetic talent had been enough to see him through. To his surprise he was warmly hailed by try-out audiences. When, though, *Carminetta* arrived at the Prince of Wales Theatre he found that what had raised hilarity in Liverpool failed utterly to amuse London. Yet, thanks to Delysia, *Carminetta* had a respectable run.

With the Oxford, the Empire and the St Martin's already under his management, Cochran now added the London Pavilion to the growing number of theatres he controlled. A coaching inn originally occupied the site which, from the late eighteenth-century onwards, had always been a place of entertainment. Then it became a music-hall where the 'Great' Macdermott introduced his notorious 'Jingo' song. ('We don't want to fight, but by jingo if we do, / We've got the ships, we've got the men, and got the money too.') By the time Cochran took over it was, despite attractions like Marie Lloyd and Grock, in a state of penurious decline. He closed it for a month, ripped out the gaudy mirrors and tore down the gilt angels which had been the music-hall owner's idea of elegance. Within a month he transformed it into what he proudly described as 'a jewel of a theatre'. Jewel though it might have been for the audience, for the performers the theatre was hideously uncomfortable: built in an oddly triangular shape with the base looking out on Piccadilly circus, it housed the backstage quarters in a narrowing apex where harassed technicians and flustered actors cursed and stumbled over each other. To outward appearance, however, it was everything Cochran thought it, and when, across the façade in Piccadilly Circus, he strung electric lights spelling out 'London Pavilion – The Centre of The World', all patriotic Londoners agreed with him.

He opened in August, 1918, with a revue called *As you Were* adapted from the French *Plus Ça Change* by the veteran 'Rip', otherwise Georges Thénon, a bald and charmless misanthrope, later to die of alcoholism, who specialised in biting and sardonic dialogue. His cynical wit, duly toned down for Anglo-Saxon audiences, inspired a scene where a husband, weary of marital infidelities, is transported back through the ages in hope of finding a time when women are faithful and war does not exist, although of course he never does. Rip's venomous shafts were sweetened by Arthur Wimperis, a well-known revue writer who had started as a black-and-white artist and then floated into the theatre, for which he turned out lyrics, plays, libretti and revues. Later on he worked as a script-writer for Alexander Korda and wrote some of the latter's most famous films including *The Drum* and *The Scarlet Pimpernel*. He had an effortless wit and produced at least one epigram which has become a theatrical byword. Having sat through a music-hall programme in search of new talent he delivered his verdict: 'My dear fellow, a unique evening! I wouldn't have left a turn unstoned.'

Wimperis collaborated on *As You Were* with the composer Herman Darewski, who at one time was so prosperous that he ran his own music publishing company, though when he died in

1947 he left little more than his equally prolific colleague Finck. One of his early hits was 'Sister Susie's Sewing Shirts for Soldiers' which he followed with 'Mother's Sitting Knitting Little Mittens For The Navy' and 'Which Switch is the switch, Miss, for Ipswich?' Another that rings a bell today is 'The Villain Still Pursued her'. For *As You Were* he wrote 'If You Could Care For Me', a number which Delysia sang as Ninon de l'Enclos in the panorama of famous beauties through the ages. Her dresses, like all the others in the show, were designed by Paul Poiret, then the leading Paris couturier. One of them, a skin-tight black costume in which she appeared as Lucifer introduced by the punning lines:

'Down! Evil spirits! On your faces fall
'For here comes Lucifer – a match for all',

brought comment from newspapers and distress to the Lord Chamberlain who asked for it to be modified. Cochran, though grateful for the publicity, was a little irked that his lovely dresses, made by the finest designer in Paris, should be so criticized when other London productions were riddled with vulgarity. Was there, he thought, something peculiar about drama critics that made them unable to appreciate the beauty of women?

In his time Cochran was to be associated with most of the capital's theatres but the one he always felt the greatest affection for was the London Pavilion. Perhaps it was the very awkwardness of the place that endeared it to him. The stage was not much larger than a fair sized dining table and had only one entrance. This was so small that an actress in a period sketch would have to wait before making her entry so that her voluminous hooped dress could be lowered down on to her from the flies. Visiting producers whom Cochran showed round did not believe it possible for the show they had just seen to be played in such a tiny area.

His sentimental liking for the Pavilion was encouraged by the long run *As You Were* enjoyed. It was the first in a series of revues there which captivated the town and drew full houses at over four hundred performances. Between August when it began and the following December, *As You Were* earned good profits for both Cochran and his landlords. In the previous eight months of the year the Pavilion had registered a loss. Productions such as this were to give him his reputation as a master of revue, although he often protested that revues only formed a small number of the hundred and twenty or so spectacles he was to produce throughout his career. It irritated him, too, that his Pavilion shows earned him a nickname as 'The English Ziegfeld' – an irritation somewhat mollified on learning of his American rival's discomfiture when newspapers dubbed him 'The American Cochran.'

iii
PUGS

'Most boxers have extraordinarily little imagination – far less, in fact, than the smallest chorus girl . . . The boxer's brain in too many cases makes one complete revolution only every twenty-four hours, except where money is concerned.'

CHARLES B. COCHRAN

The thrill of boxing is sharp and concentrated. In team sports interest is diffused over a number of people; in boxing the focus is exclusively on two men. Armed with nothing but their gloves and their skill they stand in a lonely confrontation which must end with victory for the one and defeat for the other. Added excitement comes from the knowledge that big sums of money can be lost or won in the split second needed to fumble a left hook or deliver a lightning jab to the chin, besides, naturally, the spilling of enough blood to satisfy lady spectators at the ringside. Crude as neat gin and dramatic as any *coup de théâtre*, boxing is the ideal popular entertainment.

Cochran had been a fan of the sport ever since, as a small boy, he saw Jem Smith slug his way through bouts of murderous punishment. In 1914 he had already launched on his career as a boxing promoter by hiring Olympia and staging a match there between the popular Billy Wells, known as 'Bombardier', and the Australian heavyweight Colin Bell. Having recently been floored by the debonair French champion Georges Carpentier, the Bombardier was on his mettle. In the second round he smashed Bell's jaw with a tremendous right and won sixty per cent of the two thousand pound purse, a record amount of money for the time. As usual Cochran's publicity arrangements were unexpectedly original. They included the appointment of a parish priest, also a boxing enthusiast, to announce the rounds: when required, the venerable gentleman hustled into the ring wearing full canonicals and bawling through a megaphone.

Why did Cochran, so much a figure of the theatre, take up boxing presentations as well? To begin with, he enjoyed them himself, which was a good enough excuse to share that enjoyment with others. Then, as he always said, he was a showman, and it was the showman's function to sense public demand and, if possible, to anticipate it. During the 1914–18 War boxing had acquired a wider popularity. Commanding officers encouraged their men to take up the sport because it kept them fit. It also kept them out of ale-houses in garrison towns where large concentrations of idle military were prone to riots and other unpleasantness. In the Navy and the Royal Flying Corps boxing was seen as a valuable form of training and there were frequent tournaments. Boxing was no longer the preserve of the 'fancy', the public schools and the universities. A new and larger public came into existence. It brought with it the potential of bigger audiences, and wherever audiences existed Cochran was there to supply them with something watchable.

In 1919 he inaugurated his direction of the Holborn Stadium with a match between Bombardier Billy Wells, still an idol of the public, and Joe Beckett, the idea being to groom Wells for an eventual encounter with Georges Carpentier again. The Bombardier was not, however, in good form. His punches did not connect, his onslaught faltered, and twice Beckett's left hook sent him reeling to the floor. Beckett won, to the crowd's disappointment, and Cochran began to prepare him for a match against Carpentier.

He was, at the same time, promoting other matches, just as, in the theatre, he liked to be running half a dozen different projects simultaneously. He soon found that, difficult as it was to cast a play, matching up suitable boxers proved still harder.

Even when a boxer's record, weight, style and tactics had been taken into account, there was still the problem of whether his name would draw the crowds and whether the right opponent had been chosen to meet him. Sometimes a match would provide good boxing and a thrilling night but still fail to cover the costs. On one occasion Cochran added up the takings to find that his gate was one hundred and twenty-four pounds nineteen shillings less than the prize money he paid his two fighters. This may have been partly his own fault. As soon as it was known that Charles B. Cochran was in the market for boxers, managers and promoters followed his example and prices shot up accordingly. He became, reluctantly, notorious for what were then remarkably high amounts of purse money.

Intense competition forced him to offer more than five thousand pounds when he organized the next match for Joe Beckett. Cochran's protégé emerged triumphant in a rain of merciless blows that mangled his opponent and left him crushed on the floor. The way was now open for Beckett to meet Carpentier. Cochran flitted to and fro between London and Paris negotiating dates, money, quarters, venues. A programme was arranged and the big hall of Olympia booked. Publicity was set in motion and great expectations were aroused. At a late date Carpentier asked for a postponement. He was not perfectly fit, he explained, and he still had to complete his military service. More money changed hands, deposits were made and forfeits proposed. Was Carpentier afraid of meeting Beckett?

That, Cochran hoped, was what fans would think. Meanwhile he embarked on the most disagreeable task a showman has to bear, that of refunding their money to disappointed spectators who had been looking forward to the match of the year. He hastily cobbled up a bill of not one, not two, but three contests between various champions in an attempt to make up for Carpentier's absence. Had he gone mad? asked commentators astonished at such prodigality. On the contrary, his gambler's instinct was proved correct, for in the end very few refunds were needed and his triple bill sold out almost immediately.

At last, on the 4 December, 1919, the long-awaited European

heavyweight championship fight between Carpentier and Beckett was scheduled at the Holborn Stadium. Few contests, before or since, have aroused such interest. Profiting from the fact that he could have filled the place ten times over, Cochran priced his ringside seats at the enormous sum of twenty-five guineas and standing-room at five guineas. Carpentier arrived at Victoria to be met by a tumultuous crowd. He came to the evening performance at the London Pavilion where, from his box, he was invited on to the stage and addressed the audience in French, which his compatriot Delysia obligingly translated. Then he retreated to the training quarters at Stanmore which Cochran had organized for him, there to jog and spar and imbibe the cuisine specially prepared for him by his manager's mother-in-law, a cook who knew exactly what it was prudent for a heavyweight champion to eat and what not.

On the night tens of thousands of people anxious to hear the result thronged the streets outside the Holborn Stadium. Inside, the Prince of Wales and other notables took their seats. The Prince carried his cigar, observed Arnold Bennett who was there, in the same manner as his grandfather had. Film cameramen were precariously suspended over the balconies, their feet supported by loops of rope which Cochran, always attentive to the smallest detail, had thoughtfully provided for them. Everyone expected Beckett to win and the bookmakers confidently laid odds on him. The two men faced each other and silently took stock. Carpentier's left flickered out over Beckett's nose. Beckett responded by pushing him back to the ropes and going into a clinch. They broke. Beckett swung an upper cut and missed. Carpentier feinted and smashed a lightning right to Beckett's unguarded chin. The Englishman collapsed. In stunned silence he was counted out. The fight had lasted seventy-three seconds and achieved a gate of thirty thousand pounds.

Carpentier was borne shoulder-high out of the ring and women threw flowers at him. From Holborn a jubilant party sped to Delysia's flat in Knightsbridge. It was led by Cochran and Carpentier, no longer the tigerish fighting machine of hours before but once again the handsome young Frenchman who conquered London with charm as well as brawn. At

Delysia's home he was met by all the people involved in her current show and toasted, well into the night and early morning, with libations of Veuve Clicquot. Cochran rarely bet on his own promotions but this time, as a favour to a comedian friend, had accepted a wager on Beckett. The proceeds, together with his takings, made the seventy-three second fight a very profitable occasion for him. Even as the champagne fizzed he was laying plans for Carpentier to meet the world champion Jack Dempsey. Next morning the Frenchman signed a contract with him for twenty thousand pounds.

That, however, was only the beginning of the fight to get the fight. No sooner had Carpentier's manager left Cochran's office at the London Pavilion than a French group was offering a hundred and fifty thousand dollars for the promotion rights. A few days later, while Cochran was on the *Mauretania* in mid-Atlantic, another promoter offered nearly half a million dollars. The moment he arrived in New York he learned that William Fox, founder of the Twentieth Century Fox film company, had made a bid which topped even that. Many offers came tumbling in, some genuine, others cunningly devised to make Cochran increase his original stake. At his hotel the telephone burbled ceaselessly. Whenever he emerged he was besieged by speculators who, believing him to be worthy prey, invited him to finance hotels, oil fields and car factories.

The fact remained that his contract with Carpentier was unbreakable and that he had deposited two hundred thousand dollars in a New York bank as surety. All he needed was Dempsey's signature. The champion wanted the fight to take place in America, and his manager, hoping there was a time limit in the contract, delayed the matter as long as possible. Cochran retaliated by doubling the sum he had offered to Carpentier, who agreed as a result that he would not fight Dempsey anywhere but in Europe except with Cochran's consent. Of all Cochran's rivals only the American promoter Tex Rickard was the one who counted since he had an understanding with Dempsey. If Cochran had Carpentier under his wing, Rickard had Dempsey. Unless the two men came together there would be no fight. After close on two years of wary negotiation and of journeyings between London, Paris and New York, a deal was done. The contract was signed in a room at the New York Hotel Claridge which, said an observer, 'was lighted by a soft red glow given out by the roast-beef complexion of the English promoter, Charles Cochran.' Dempsey and Carpentier were also there and shook hands affectionately. 'I hope,' said Dempsey, 'nothing happens to the poor fellow until I get him in the ring.'

Despite his vast satisfaction at this triumphant ending Cochran began to feel ill on the voyage home. Violent headaches plagued him and he spoke of permanent weariness. The ship's doctor gave his opinion. It was, he said, a question of being over-tired. Back in London a specialist examined him, administered a spinal puncture and sent him to bed. He must, ordered the man of science, remain there and give up any thought of doing business. All correspondence and even newspapers were denied him and his affairs were carried on through a power of attorney. His wife Evelyn read his mail and asked advice of his closest friends. Since the news from America told of nothing but shattered promises and Byzantine intrigues against him, they advised her not to discuss it with her husband. His tenuous hold on life, they warned, might be broken. Important visitors called in alarm to report the latest developments. While he dozed fitfully, not truly sleeping or waking, she turned them away. The Carpentier Dempsey fight was slipping out of his hands, but at least she had saved his life.

For several months he lay in his bed. When he got up and was hale enough to read the mountain of cables which had amassed during his illness they told a tale of duplicity and manoeuvre which put an end to his dream of promoting the biggest fight ever. Partners had backed down, agreements had been altered and profit-sharing schemes annulled. The match eventually took place in New Jersey and Dempsey won. Cochran's original New York deposit was returned to him minus over a thousand pounds eaten away by fluctuating exchange rates. His reward for years of work and worry amounted to a grave illness and a total loss of more than five thousand pounds.

He went on promoting fights, though none of them had the lustre that would have been his had he brought off the great Carpentier/Dempsey event. Most of the day's well-known boxers fought under his aegis. One of them was Jimmy Wilde, the valiant little bantamweight. Another was Tommy Milligan whom he presented in the world middleweight championship fight with the American Micky Walker. It looked an assured money-maker although the initial investment was large. Cochran found a sponsor ready to back him in return for a half share in the profits from one of his successful revues. By guaranteeing Walker twenty-two thousand pounds, the highest purse ever offered, Cochran secured the American's agreement to appear. At first there were grandiose plans to stage the fight in an open-air setting at Blackpool. Legal objections squashed Cochran's bright idea and the venue was changed to Olympia. Then Walker's manager, a crafty manipulator who set Cochran many problems, demanded that the match be refereed by the Prince of Wales, no less. It is a suitable comment on the negotiations, which soon took on a surreal hue, that Walker's training quarters had been established in a houseboat owned by Fred Karno.

Cochran expected that the box-office would follow the usual pattern: early bookings for the expensive seats by enthusiasts, then a lull when the cheaper ones were taken up by the general public, and at last, on the day of the fight, a sudden upsurge encouraged by a flurry of comment and pictures in the newspapers. This time it did not happen. At the critical moment the notorious financier Jimmy White disobligingly committed suicide and triggered off a Stock Exchange panic which brought ruin to thousands. People who had booked seats by telephone did not claim them since they had more serious matters to think about, and references to the fight were pushed to the back pages. Cochran lost not only fifteen thousand pounds but also much of the profit on his next revue which he had to make over to his backer in addition to the half-share in his current production.

Perhaps lawn tennis offered him a more lucrative, even more dignified sport to promote? He engaged the famous player Suzanne Lenglen to tour the country giving demonstrations of her skill. As in boxing, he found that the big problem lay in matching the star with suitable opponents. His cynical view of the 'shamateurism' which pervaded this genteel recreation was confirmed in negotiations with female players who named outrageous sums for giving up their amateur status: when he offered them less they indignantly denied that they had ever thought of turning professional. On the other hand his experience of great women artistes in the theatre gave him an immediate sympathy with Suzanne Lenglen. He had always found the most gifted women the easiest to handle, and so it turned out in the case of Madame Lenglen. Her sensitiveness and her reaction to the public reminded him inescapably of Eleanora Duse. Their interesting acquaintanceship proved, however, expensive. His promotion of lawn tennis caused him another loss of five thousand pounds.

A moment came in the late nineteen-twenties when he decided it was time to withdraw from all sport and from boxing in particular. Despite his sometimes sensational losses on individual fights he had, in general, made money enough to satisfy reasonable ambition. What sickened him was the attitude of the boxers. They were greedy, stupid and unreliable. They would plead illness in order to get more money and wriggle out of contracts honourably arrived at. They forced him to break faith with the public by cancelling matches at which they had never had any true intention of appearing. The theatre business, ruthless though it was, could not compare with boxing for viciousness and rapacity. In future, he resolved, he would patronize boxing as a simple spectator. It was a decision he found easy to keep.

Chapter Three
REVUE MASTER

'I do not deliberately believe in setting out to
please other
people . . . If I say to myself that a play or revue
reaches my own
standard, I know I can do no more, and I need
not reproach myself
afterwards if others do not like it.'

Charles B. Cochran

---

i
PRINCE AT HIGH NOON

'To be a beggar at dawn, prince at high noon, and at dusk a
beggar again – such is the essence of every showman's existence
. . . C.B. is still a child who has never grown up; he plays with
fortunes as carelessly as an infant with its mother's diamond
necklace.'

JAMES AGATE

In the nineteen-twenties Cochran lived off Park Lane at a house
in Aldford Street. It was one of the many places in their married
life that Evelyn's gift for home-making turned into a haven for
him, a comfortable retreat from the worries and alarums of his
business career. The Renoirs and Lautrecs he bought in his
youth were cleverly 'offered' on the walls alongside framed
playbills. Furniture glowed discreetly, bowls of roses cast their
scent, signed photographs of his stars clustered on top of the
grand piano. At little dinner parties he gave for theatre folk

Evelyn was the perfect hostess. She never came into a theatre except at first nights when convention demanded that she appear at his side, usually wearing some fluffy new creation, her mouth twisted up at one corner in the typical mannerism that people noticed on meeting her for the first time. She and Cochran were, you would have thought, an ideal couple in the old-fashioned mould, he the older and protective husband going forth each day to win the battle of life, and she the quiet nest-builder running the home and devotedly tending his hours of ease. You would not have been wrong.

But truth has many aspects. It is true that once the early sexual excitement had faded Mr and Mrs Cochran fell contentedly into the humdrum but pleasant routine of slippers by the fire and meals served at regular times. It is also true that Cochran's appetite for pursuing women increased rather than diminished with the passage of time. The layman who sees the theatre only as a place of glamour tends to imagine that its inhabitants spend most of their time dallying with beautiful actresses. This naive attitude would not, however, have been entirely wrong so far as Cochran was concerned. His vast energies enabled him concurrently to manage half a dozen theatres, set up as many different productions and negotiate boxing championships while laying siege to young females with the pertinacity of a full-time seducer. Evelyn Cochran knew very well that he was consistently unfaithful to her. She could never reconcile herself to the knowledge and, as the years went by, the pain bit deeper. Outwardly she kept her pride and maintained a light and careless manner. Distress sharpened her tongue and she would, at carefully chosen moments, deliver acid witticisms in her characteristic lisp, mouth twisted up at the corner. At a dinner party one evening in the Aldford Street flat the company decided to play roulette. Cochran was involved at that time with a dancer, perhaps Tilly Losch. The green baize cloth was brought out and he remarked: 'It's awfully dirty.' 'Yes, Cockie darling,' replied Evelyn, 'just like your little friend's knickers.' Unaware that she had known his secret, he blushed deeply while his guests pretended not to have heard.

A guilty conscience urged him to ring her several times a day from his office and flatter her by asking her opinion on business matters. He plied her with frequent gifts of the chocolate cake for which he knew she had a specially sweet tooth. At first she enjoyed them but, as the smart little boxes went on arriving remorselessly, grew heartily sick of them. One evening, in a bad mood, she threw the latest offering out into the street where it landed on the head of a passer-by and ruined one of Mayfair's prettiest hats.

The betrayals were not so hurtful as the squalid shifts, the furtive secrets and the indirect revelations. A dressmaker once hinted maliciously at an affair with an actress. 'It's not that I mind the affair itself,' Evelyn complained. 'She's a very lovely and I can understand it. But to be told about it by *her*! That's what hurts so much.' She took her revenge in verbal attack. After an opening night in Manchester she welcomed the arrival of an actress at the Cochrans' breakfast table with: 'And how is our husband this morning, my dear?'

She became expert in judging what stage her husband's latest infatuation had reached. Years of experience taught her when to diagnose a preliminary skirmish, a successful offensive or a fully developed affair. On being presented to a new protégée she would murmur: 'I know you haven't slept with my husband because you don't call him "Cockie".'

Perhaps the wound might have been assuaged had they had children. For reasons never disclosed, probably medical, they did not, and that consolation was forbidden her. She took to drinking, contracted a dependence on alcohol and looked forward all day to the hour when, as she said, she could get 'comfy with nips of brandy'. In later years, as we shall see, frustration drove her into a form of sexuality which must have horrified Cochran who, however insatiable, remained with a few exceptions resolutely orthodox in his tastes. For the time being she contented herself with brandy. Her doctor, alarmed by this indulgence, advised her to substitute apples for her beloved 'nips'. 'But, doctor,' she retorted, 'I can't eat fifteen apples every night!'

The Cochran ménage was duplicated by that of his close friend and business colleague Seymour Hicks, later Sir Seymour. Actor, producer, author, dramatist and celebrated wit, Hicks was the incarnation of theatre, the essence of the stage. His partnership with the adorable Ellaline Terriss had the durability of a public monument and endeared itself to generations of audiences with a graceful display of mutual love, he dapper and gallant, she tender and affectionate. Off stage he was ferociously disloyal to her and rarely slept in the same bed twice. Yet the impeccable façade remained, and their skill at acting was such that, in the end, they really believed they were devoted to one another and lived out a serene old age as Darby and Joan. Nature imitated art with the most charming of consequences.

Hicks was Cochran's equal both for energy and an intricate private life. The lists of plays he wrote or produced or starred in occupy more than five closely printed columns in reference books. He actually built and managed two theatres, those known today as the Aldwych and the Globe, and had his darling Ellaline's initials carved in granite on the roof. Acting, writing a play or book and producing a musical comedy or two all the same time were not enough fully to occupy him, and so he began appearing at music-halls in addition to his more habitual West End visitations. With Cochran he devised in 1918 a pageant-cum-spectacle called *Jolly Jack Tar* as a patriotic celebration of the war's end. It had a cast of two hundred and featured the detonation of the Mole at Zeebrugge, a particularly daring wartime exploit, together with ingeniously filmed sequences depicting battle and victory. The mixture of revue, melodrama, musical comedy and film even included Cochran's favourite 'Pepper's Ghost' trick. A naval captain praying for guidance on the eve of battle was supposed to be visited by the ghost of Nelson. The illusion depended on a mirror being placed at a certain angle. One night it was slightly out of true, and beside the ghost of Nelson the amused audience was vouchsafed a glimpse of stage-hands swilling beer and guzzling bread and cheese in the wings. *Jolly Jack Tar* did not run very long. 'I lost,' said Cochran bleakly, 'several thousand pounds over the venture.'

Not much better was a play called *A Certain Liveliness* at the St Martin's where, as lessee, Cochran paid Hicks a large salary under the terms of their partnership. It is probably the only West End production this century in which a character makes a quotation from the Greek classics. 'A. B. Walkley is sure to notice it,' said the author at rehearsals. The learned critic of *The Times* did not disappoint and, alone of all the audience, drew attention next day to 'one of the most familiar sentences in the *Anabasis*.' More immediately rewarding was a transaction over the scenery, a splendid oak room built of panelling, bought from a Scottish castle, which Cochran sold after the short run to an American millionaire for thousands of dollars. And there was always Lady Tree to lighten the burden of rehearsals, horse-faced and wittily alert. With the greatest respect for her vast experience and reputation, Hicks deferentially explained how he wanted a scene played and suggested where he would like her to stand. 'Don't worry, Mr Hicks, it will be quite all right,' she smiled sweetly. 'You do your little bit of acting wherever you like. It won't worry me, and I shall be ready when you want me.'

The most engaging result of the Cochran/Hicks arrangement was *Sleeping Partners* which Hicks translated and adapted from *Faisons un rêve* by Sacha Guitry, prince of the boulevard theatre. Son of Lucien Guitry, France's greatest actor, and himself an actor-dramatist of glittering prowess, Sacha was to write, direct and star in a hundred and twenty plays and some thirty films. The leading lady was usually his wife (he had five in all) and the subject more often than not women, who gave him the material for cynical epigrams and insolent wit. Although the original play has the conventional boulevard cast of husband, wife and lover, it is much superior to the usual type of adulterous comedy. Despite the seventy years that have passed since the first production, many revivals have testified to the consistent vitality of a play which the author took only three days to write. The second act is a tour de force and consists of an extended soliloquy by the lover as he waits impatiently for the wife to arrive at their assignation. He pictures her leaving, calling a taxi and going through the various stages of her journey. He hears a car outside, rushes to the window and glimpses the flutter of a skirt . . . but: '*Merde!* it's a *curé*!' How, one wonders, did Hicks translate this for the benefit of respectable Anglo-Saxon audiences? He was, incidentally, apart from Gerald du Maurier, the only English actor able to rival Sacha for lightness of manner and brilliance of technique. The play ends with one of the best curtain lines ever written. The lover has persuaded the husband, who had been visiting his mistress, to go away for two days on a 'business trip'. 'He's gone?' says the wife. 'So we have the whole of life ahead of us?' 'We've something better than that,' replies the lover, 'better than the whole of life.' Better than the whole of life?' 'Yes. We've got two whole days!'

A year later Cochran brought over Sacha himself and his father to do a season at the Aldwych. They were accompanied by Yvonne Printemps, Sacha's second wife and the most talented of all his consorts. The 'Grande Saison Parisienne', as Cochran styled it, was inaugurated with a reception Lady Cunard gave in Carlton House Terrace. The audience included the French Ambassador, princesses and various dukes and duchesses. They quivered with surprise when Sacha, in paying tribute to the English theatre, declared that his favourite actor was Little Tich, the quintessence, for him, of genius. His father Lucien agreed with his preference and, when not appearing at the Aldwych, scoured the London music-halls to see over and over again Little Tich perform his famous dance with the big boots that were as long as he was high. There was an occasion when Lucien, majestic in black cloak and wide-brimmed hat, rose from his seat and commanded the audience: 'Get up, all of you, in homage to the world's greatest genius!' He hurried backstage and, kneeling down, kissed the tiny comedian on both cheeks.

Every seat at the Aldwych was filled and the season had to be extended for another week. The programme opened with *Nono*, a light comedy Sacha had written at the age of sixteen, and continued with other plays full of what *The Times* called 'gay, easy, witty cynicism' and 'smooth voluble patter'. The dramatic *Pasteur* revealed that Sacha was not just a virtuoso of the flippant. In the rôle of the pioneering scientist Lucien showed all his quality and was rewarded by forty curtain calls at the end. 'I have never known a greater night in a playhouse,' observed Forbes Robertson, an elder statesman of the profession. As Seymour Hicks left the theatre he remarked to his companion Gerald du Maurier: 'I shall be ashamed to act again.' He did, though, and without compunction.

The Guitry season gave Cochran an unqualified triumph, complete with the accolade of full houses, even on Derby Day, and the patronage of King George and Queen Mary in the royal box. Regular visits by what the English press called 'the incomparable family' became annual events in the London season. Cochran did not, however, make money on them and had to be content with breaking even in return for the honour of introducing them to English audiences, a situation which Peter Daubeny was to encounter when he mounted his own World Theatre programmes at the self-same Aldwych. Cochran bought the rights to a couple of Sacha plays, among them *Deburau*, a delicate re-telling of the celebrated mime's life which he presented successfully in New York and hoped to repeat in London with Seymour Hicks whom he thought ideal for the part. At first Hicks was enthusiastic and began learning his lines with gusto. Then he lost confidence. 'I am afraid,' he told Sacha. The latter was astonished. 'You only have to play it as you played *Sleeping Partners*,' he said kindly. Hicks was not to be persuaded and gave up the notion. Unable to find him a West End part for the time being, Cochran offered to compensate him with half the profit he made from renting the St Martin's to Moss Empires in return for fifty per cent of Hicks's profits. This handsome gesture earned him £199 from his partner to whom, under the terms of the agreement, he paid £6,500. Hicks had become, in real life, a sleeping partner.

Cochran's Francophilia encouraged him to embark on yet another expensive production with Edmond Rostand's *Cyrano de Bergerac*. He had an affection for this play dating from the time when he worked for Richard Mansfield. Its lush extravagance and flamboyant conceits had given the famous actor Coquelin one of his greatest roles as Cyrano, the voluble Gascon knight and embodiment of seventeenth-century *panache*. The play is very French and, of course, quite untranslatable. As James Agate remarked, it 'prates of the stars and breaks into the spangles of the sky-rocket. *Cyrano* is the Crystal Palace of poetry. In this play Rostand says nothing with unexampled virtuosity.' Not at all deterred, Cochran spent lavishly on scenery and costumes by the artist Edmond Dulac. For the tile rôle he engaged Robert Loraine, a larger-than-life

romantic actor, and denied him nothing in the way of accessories and refinements that in time began to exceed by far his
original budget.

The production of *Cyrano*, which he strove to make as
beautiful as possible, foundered on two of the commonest
shoals in the theatre. Despite more than twenty years' experience in the business Cochran allowed enthusiasm to outrun his
commercial instincts. The first problem arose when, after a
very successful first night at the Garrick and an encouraging
run of several weeks, he realized he had made the elementary
mistake of misjudging the seating capacity: however full the
house the Garrick was just not big enough to cover his costs and
show a profit, so that the longer *Cyrano* ran there the greater
would be his loss. The cast, with one exception, agreed a
reduction in salary, which he undertook to return before taking
any profit, on the assurance of his finding them a bigger theatre.
This became immediately available at Drury Lane where the
gorgeous scenery looked much better in its grandiose setting. It
was by now the summer of 1919 and the weather had turned
very hot, a warning of the second classic misfortune to strike the
production: a week after *Cyrano* moved into Drury Lane and
receipts had begun to flourish, a sudden heat-wave reduced
attendance and wiped out the profits Cochran might have
expected. He made a loss of some eight thousand pounds. This
was not the only experience that made him feel bitter when
people disdainfully referred to him as a 'commercial' manager.

He turned back to his old reliable cash-cow, the London
Pavilion, and put on a new operetta called *Afgar* with lilting
music by Charles Cuvillier, composer of *The Lilac Domino*. All
the new piece had in common with *Cyrano* was that it came from
France. Being set in a harem it needed careful adaptation for
English susceptibilities, even though Cochran interpolated a
scene inspired by the *Lysistrata* where the ladies go on strike.
(This was not because he rivalled A. B. Walkley in his knowledge of Aristophanes: he happened to have seen a comparable
episode in some French farce and stored it away in his mind for
later use.) Delysia was the star and he paid her five times what
she had earned in *Odds and Ends*. With costumes by Paul Poiret
and all the gloss which audiences had come to expect of a

Pavilion show, *Afgar* made up generously for the losses on *Cyrano*. So generously indeed that, after a dispute with the ticket libraries, Cochran made them buy seats as the public had to buy them, without a discount. This was the icing on the cake. Each performance sold out and standing room was full for three hundred performances. The cast included a youthful Lupino Lane, yet another emergent member of that omnipresent Lupino family which has peopled English theatrical history for what seems like untold generations. An actor who complained of insomnia was once advised by a friend: 'Have you ever tried counting Lupinos?'

Having made money with *Afgar* Cochran proceeded to lose some of it on a now forgotten musical comedy entitled *Maggie*. This was a truly Anglo-French production which, originally adapted from a Parisian show, ran for a time in London and was then turned back into a version for Paris where it had more success than Cochran achieved with it. *Maggie* illustrated one of the problems an impresario meets when he juggles with the very different elements of a show and tries to blend them into a pleasing whole. Cochran was already a master of the craft but on this occasion was defeated by one of his principal actors, a low comedian called George Graves who had gained a big following with his knockabout pantomime turns. The climax of *Maggie* flowered into a mannequin parade for which Poiret designed some of his most glamorous dresses. Cochran's producer Frank Collins spent an hour at rehearsals lighting the beautiful golden-haired blonde who was to appear in the finale, manipulating the limes to create subtle variations of gold and arranging hidden spotlights of green, red, blue and yellow to pick out the folds of her dress. The parade began with a little Quaker girl demure in white and grey. The next dress was more elaborate, and as the mannequins tripped forward their clothes became grander and grander to the accompaniment of increasing applause until the actor who played the part of the dress shop owner announced: 'Now I will show you my *pièce de résistance*, the dress I have planned in my head for years and years. Ladies and gentlemen – voilà! My Golden Girl!' Lights beamed, music throbbed, and on stepped the loveliest blonde in the world, her dress, stockings, shoes, cloak, hat and gloves radiant with gold. Suddenly George Graves made an un-scheduled entry. 'God bless my soul, Solly Joel's housekeeper!' he exclaimed in an ad lib reference to a then notorious million-aire from the South African gold-mines. The audience shrieked with laughter and the effect of Poiret's ingenuity and Collins's meticulous lighting was ruined. Though apparently spon-taneous, the intervention had been planned by a cunning trouper to milk an extra laugh for himself. Cochran realized, too late, the mistake he had made in engaging a comedian to play a part that belonged to an actor.

Another disaster in the Spring of 1920 seemed to confirm the bad luck which at the time waited on all his productions outside the sphere of revue. He brought over the American actress Laurette Taylor and featured her in a play by her husband called *One Night In Rome*. It was not very good, but he thought Miss Taylor's reputation would make up for the defects in the writing. Soon after the curtain rose at the Garrick on the first night there were hostile rumblings from the gallery. As the performance went on coins and stink bombs sailed through the air to land on the stage. The clamour of boos and whistles mounted until it drowned out the play. Cochran went on stage amid roars of disapproval and declared: 'I have brought this great artist 3,000 miles to appear in this play. I will ring down the curtain and give another first night at a later date.' Few evenings in the London theatre have been so turbulent. 'This is not like England!' shouted Seymour Hicks from his box. 'Who has done this foul thing?' enquired Robert Loraine with a fine flourish. 'We will none of us play tomorrow,' declared Gerald du Maurier. 'We will close the theatres as a protest.' In the auditorium all was confusion and behind the scenes hysteria flourished. Was it a Sinn Fein outrage? Were the ringleaders enemies whom Cochran had made in the boxing world? Much, much later it emerged that the outrage had been organized by an Australian who believed that his girl friend should have had Laurette Taylor's role.

Cochran made up some of his losses with a revival of *The Better 'Ole*, which had become something of an insurance policy when times were hard, and decided to mount another revue. As usual he peppered his authors with ideas and suggestions.

Chance remarks, items seen in newspapers, trivial incidents in everyday life, gave him the material for possible sketches and black-outs. This was discussed, sifted and much of it rejected. Time was needed for the refining process. His experience was that a revue seldom failed when it had been adequately prepared, and only if it had been put together in a hurry, without the leisure to substitute and rewrite, would it be doomed. His new revue was called *London, Paris and New York*, and for it he signed up the popular comedian Nelson Keys, usually known as 'Bunch'. Keys was the type who performed well so long as he had good material. Without the support of good writers he could not shine. Cochran gave him these and had his reward in an uproarious whirlwind of impersonations which started with a fat German bandsman and went by way of a romantic matinée idol, a passionate Frenchman, a Spanish brigand, a street singer, a Regency beau, a Cockney tipster, a drunken Admiral and a man-about-town to a Japanese juggler. In order to enhance his Oriental cheekbones as the juggler Keys had two of his side-teeth extracted. While Cochran was prepared to concede his talent he had no great love for him. He was obstinate and persisted in meddling with production matters that did not concern him. When the London Pavilion management received a large dentist's bill for the false teeth Keys ordered to replace those sacrificed on behalf of his art, Cochran's attitude became distinctly frigid.

A more congenial player in *London, Paris and New York* was Arthur Roberts, the idol of Cohran's youth. He was close on eighty years old and well past the days when his name commanded big audiences. Age had made it difficult for him to learn his lines, and he was disconcerted by Nelson Keys' habit of interpolating gags which often altered cues. 'Bunch' lost his temper and snapped: 'You seem to have lost your memory.' Arthur, who in the course of his extensive career had heard most of 'Bunch's' second-hand impromptus from the mouths of comedians long since dead, genially retorted: 'Well, it's obvious you haven't lost yours!'

London, Paris and New York was the first Pavilion revue without Delysia. Cochran atoned for her absence by engaging the magnificent Spanish dancer Laura Santelmo. She arrived late for rehearsal after a long journey direct from Spain. Señora Santelmo was tired, she was hungry, she could not speak English. The scene had been set, the chorus and band were waiting, and rehearsal fees were burning away. Still she would not co-operate. At last a Spaniard was found who knew English. He explained Cochran's wish that she should dress, walk through her dances and change costume so that the necessary timings could be made. She remained mute. Cochran pondered. 'Tell her,' he purred at last to the interpreter, 'that she has the most beautiful eyes in the world.' The message was transmitted. A smile lit up the dancer's sullen features. 'Tell her,' Cochran went on, 'that I think she is a most delightful person.' She beamed. Thereafter she did all that was required of her and with the best grace in the world.

Now that the Pavilion was fully occupied and kept busy for the next twelve months he was free to concentrate on another of his responsibilities, the Oxford, where in the past three years, starting with *The Better 'Ole*, he had run the place so well that his landlords were able to pay a dividend of thirty-one per cent. Thanks to him they had also cleared heavy mortgages and loans besides repairing and renovating the building. Encouraged by his success they agreed to let him keep the theatre at a fixed rental on the understanding that he would make extensive improvements there. The deal was done and he committed himself to spending twenty-five thousand pounds on reconstruction. The builders went in and work began. There were strikes. Contractors dithered and would not produce fixed estimates. One day the proscenium arch cracked and ominous showers of stone and dust slithered down the walls. It looked, at one moment, as if the arch were to collapse and bring down the whole building with it. Impassive, unperturbed, Cochran gave orders and coolly raised more money from his backers. He ended up by paying over three times the amount originally estimated. What did it matter, since he had created one of the handsomest theatres in the West End? The shabby old bar was replaced with an exquisite drawing-room in Louis XVI style. On the walls hung, not copies, but originals of eighteenth-century pictures by François Boucher and his contemporaries, the sort of treasures which today can only be seen in the

Wallace Collection. Above the fine china and expensive furniture hung pear-shaped crystal chandeliers. Cochran's greatest pride was the ceiling. As he wandered around the silent auditorium and looked admiringly upwards he swore it was the loveliest ceiling he had ever beheld in any theatre.

He called his theatre the New Oxford, for new it certainly was, having been rebuilt from bottom to top, and he opened with the revue *League of Notions* in January, 1920. The show was dressed with splendour. From America he bought rare silks that could not be obtained elsewhere. In New York he commissioned a team of embroiderers to create designs using the Batik process. Paris was searched for rare materials which had to be specially made up in Lyon, headquarters of the silk industry. He also imported from over the Atlantic stage lighting equipment which then was unavailable in England. His show girls came from America and his clowns were Italian. His stars were the energetic Dolly Sisters, Rosie and Jenny, who electrified the audience with their looks and their dash. The American duo conquered English society as well and were besieged with rich admirers like the businessmen Thomas Lipton and Gordon Selfridge. So close to each other were the girls, so nearly attuned, that as soon as one began a sentence the other would complete it. Although Cochran took a long time to discover which was which, the confusion did not really matter since each of them, it transpired, was as proficient in bed as the other.

Every penny of the thousands he spent on *The League of Notions* was his own, and he made it the most elaborate production he had ever staged. The curtain, a gleaming creation of silver tissue, rose to show Pierrot and Columbine and Harlequin dispersing the London fogs and preparing a revue. Visions of loveliness that had taken months to create flashed by in a second and were followed by others yet more beautiful. The Dolly Sisters in pearly costumes were joined in the course of the evening by Dresden shepherdesses all in white, by Elizabethans in vast panniered dresses, by Russian princesses wearing headpieces a yard high, and by eighteenth-century brides crowned with pure white wigs. A girl moved around in the 'Dance of the Silver Bubble' shadowed by a glittering balloon that seemed to obey her every gesture. A melodramatic impression of a Hell's Kitchen dissolved into a witty pastiche of old-time music-hall, the Dolly Sisters here in black top hats and coachmen's silken cloaks, which in turn gave way to a garden of dreams where the girls wore headdresses of astonishing complexity. To encourage audience participation the management distributed free tambourines to be rattled and banged in time with songs and dances. At the first night the future King George VI and his brother were glimpsed in the stalls vigorously wielding these unattractive instruments. The French politician Philippe Berthelot looked in with Lloyd George one evening. He was then engaged on wearying transactions at the League of Nations. The Oxford show, he observed, was much funnier than the real thing. Cochran replied without immodesty, that at least it had been more efficiently produced.

Having set up the New Oxford for what he reckoned would be at least another year's profitable business, he turned to the other theatres under his control. Like a juggler balancing with dextrous skill a bewildering variety of disparate objects, he deployed musical comedy, farce, drama and operetta in a quick-changing series of permutations and combinations. The Garrick was clamouring for a new attraction. The Apollo needed to be filled. The Aldwych was ripe for another première. More boxing matches were called for at the Holborn Stadium. As a sideline he had also taken on ballroom dancing displays at the Piccadilly Hotel. He had become, in addition, chairman of a new company organized to float the Palace Theatre and was committed to finding twelve thousand pounds for shares. And what about the Princes' Theatre? That was easy. His Pavlova season there was just concluded and he put in Sarah Bernhardt for a few weeks. The *grande dame* of the French theatre was now in her mid-seventies but remained indomitable. Despite a bad Channel crossing and several driving mishaps on the road, she was rehearsing at the Princess within two hours of her arrival. Her part in the new boulevard play was that, incredibly, of a young man, and she convinced the audience that she was indeed a youthful hero. The occasion was all the more moving in that she had recently had a leg amputated and was obliged to play sitting down. Parisian theatregoers were less respectful than Londoners. The news that she would have to wear a wooden leg inspired one of the crueller wits to remark, when he heard the traditional fusillade of knocks that signals curtain-rise in the Paris theatre: 'Look out! Here she comes!'

All Cochran's theatres were now fully booked up and playing to good houses, although the effort involved drove him to bed with nervous exhaustion. His doctors forbade him to attend the first night of *League of Notions* and he was grudgingly allowed to follow its progress every five minutes or so by telephoned reports from the theatre. At last they wrenched the telephone away and insisted he forget about the stage. Next morning, as a special concession, they permitted him to ring the box-office. The news was good and he sank back under the sheets. There he lay for the next two months fretting over the destiny of his theatres and trying to ignore the pain of arthritis in his leg. A Danish masseur treated him and was able to sooth the ache with his probing fingers. Evelyn hovered as a constant presence, affectionate, attentive, for it was only on occasions like this that she had him to herself, and she thought nostalgically of the early days, now long gone, when they had been alone together. A few years later, at the height of his negotiations for the Dempsey/Carpentier fight, he was to become even more severely ill. For Evelyn the disastrous effect on his business affairs did not matter when balanced against the pleasure, however fleeting, of his brief but total dependence on her.

In the Spring of 1921 they set off on a recuperative holiday. Paris always did him good, especially on this visit since he won twenty thousand francs at the races. Their destination was Spain which they reached by way of San Sebastian. Here, once more, his gambler's luck held out, and after an hour at the casino he returned to the hotel and astonished Evelyn by casually strewing twenty thousand pesetas over their bed. On the way back to London after their holiday he could not resist travelling via San Sebastian. This time he lost everything. Roulette, as if he did not know already, was no different from the theatre in its unpredictability.

They spent five weeks in Madrid. Cochran appreciated with a showman's expertise the glamour of the Holy Week processions and the spectacle of the Feria. The rich costumes and elaborate ceremony of bull fighting blinded him to the vileness of that ignoble pursuit. In Seville he came to love Spanish dancing, the throb of the flamenco, the intricate glide of the bolero and the languid charm of the malagueña. His companions and guides around Seville were his Russian counterpart Serge Diaghilev and the composer Igor Stravinsky. Diaghilev took him to watch the famous dancer Ramires perform in a tavern. No guitarist could be found and a harp player was enlisted. He, despite rhythmic clapping and strumming by Ramires, could not play what was required. At last he was asked to play what he knew. He obliged with a rendering of the only tune he had by heart. It was the old English music-hall number 'Champagne Charlie is my name'.

Diaghilev, said Cochran, was 'one of the most delightful companions I have known – he could charm a dead man to life.' So, too, could the Englishman, and the meeting of these two super-charmers vying with each other to please must have been an impressive sight. Smiling but wary, beaming yet alert, they circled and feinted with velvet skill. Diaghilev had set his heart on a London season and was determined to woo Cochran. The latter had come to Spain for a rest, although he was not the man to reject a deal when it stared him in the face. They talked and manoeuvred at lunch parties in the hot white sunshine at the Venta Antequera over menus that offered fifty kinds of *hors d'oeuvres*, oxtails, red mullet, twelve different types of fish and partridges. After one glorious meal preceded by a bottle of Manzanilla and followed by a cigar and the best coffee he had ever tasted, Cochran allowed Diaghilev to persuade him that what London needed most was a season of Russian ballet at the Princes. The Venta Antequera was Diaghilev's favourite restaurant. It soon became Cochran's.

A few months later Diaghilev and his cohorts installed themselves in the Princes at the peak of a sweltering heat-wave. They brought with them a ten-week programme of ballets new and old, favourites such as *Les Sylphides* and *Le Carnaval*, novelties like *Petroushka*, *Firebird* and a revival of *The Rite of Spring*. At Cochran's insistence a big event of the season was flamenco dancing by performers Diaghilev recruited during their stay in

Seville. Some audiences adored it, others hated it, but what could not be denied was that on flamenco evenings the box-office sold out. Was this due to the women's charming habit of acknowledging applause by wiggling their bosoms in sympathy?

Before the curtain rose and also throughout intervals Diaghilev arranged performances of new music – Prokoviev's Classical Symphony, Stravinsky's Symphony for Wind Instruments and pieces by modern British composers. Fourteen of the twenty-five works given, he announced with pride, were being heard for the first time in England. Patrons in the stalls anxious for a quiet drink or an intimate gossip were not so enchanted by Diaghilev's largesse. He bestowed it as much for his own pleasure as for anyone else's. 'Mine is the finest life in the world,' he told Cochran. 'I have seldom at any one time had £5,000 in the bank, but I live in the best rooms in the best hotels in all the European capitals in their best seasons, and I can see the Russian ballet every night.'

Large though the Princes was, it still could not accommodate all the grandeur of the Russian Ballet. Some of the orchestral players spilled over into stage boxes. Extras were obliged to dress and make up in quarters over the road. Manuel de Falla visited London to superintend his ballet *The Three Cornered Hat* and wrote a polite little message in Evelyn Cochran's autograph book. Prokoviev conducted his new ballet *Chout* and Picasso designed a setting for the flamenco dancers. *The Rite of Spring*, which only a few years previously had caused uproar in Paris, was heard with enthusiasm and earned a cool verdict from Bernard Shaw that 'if it had been by Rossini people would have said there was too much rum-tum in it.' Perhaps it is typical of Anglo-Saxon audiences that they were much more scandalized by Monsieur Prokoviev's action in taking off his coat because of the heat while conducting the dress rehearsal of *Chout*. Several ladies, it was reported, left in horrified embarrassment.

Cochran believed that the Russian ballet season was artistically one of his most satisfying promotions. His love for things Spanish found its ideal in flamenco dancing. Why, he was often asked, did he always include a Spanish dancer in his revues?

Because, he said, having to see his revues more often than anyone else, he felt he was entitled to five minutes in every show when he could slip out of his office at the back of the circle and be sure of a few moments' complete enjoyment. He did not, of course, make money on the Russian Ballet. 'To have done the Cuadro Flamenco in London,' he remarked gallantly, 'was worth the £5,007 which I lost on the ten-weeks season.' From which it is obvious that he and Diaghilev had not only their charm in common.

ii

THE LAST CHIP

'I am a few years older than when I started; but I have a good deal more knowledge, certainly more imagination, and I have not lost courage. There is a thrill about starting life all over again with retrieving one's own fortunes as the goal.'

CHARLES B. COCHRAN

Among the guests at luxurious receptions in the Aldford Street house was a shy young actress nicknamed 'Boo'. The daughter of Gilbert Laye, versatile actor and producer and composer who had been associated with Cochran in his early management days, she spent the whole of her childhood back-stage and in theatrical lodgings. At night the infant slept soundly in dressing-rooms until the final curtain signalled that it was time for her to be carried home in her cot. 'Boo' was the first word she spoke to her father when he asked her name, and 'Boo' was what friends called Evelyn Laye hereafter.

It was inevitable that she should go on the stage, although her parents did not wish her to follow their example, and as a young woman she made her first success in *The Shop Girl* at the old Gaiety Theatre. Her father obtained an audition for her with Cochran and she was accepted. Cochran frightened her at first. This immaculate man was what she had always imagined a great impresario to be: by day a spruce figure in dark suit and trilby hat with silver-topped cane and ever-present torpedo cigar, by night in white tie and tails with top hat and shrouded, always, in the rich aroma of cigar smoke. The people around him awed her too, musicians, composers, producers, and girls of dazzling sophistication like the Dolly Sisters and their statuesque Borzoi dogs which accompanied them everywhere.

Cochran sought to emphasize her youthful good looks as a contrast to the chic of all his other girls. He put her into his new London Pavilion revue, *The Fun of The Fayre*, and at rehearsals prowled through the darkened auditorium watching and listening intently. Suddenly his voice would bellow down from the gallery: 'Very pretty, dear, but I couldn't hear one word. Do it again.' Sometimes a message arrived in her dressing-room: 'Please speak up. CBC.', or: 'Remember, the audience would like to hear you. CBC.' On other occasions he would call personally and beam: 'Very nice, dear, thank you very much.' Under his benevolent though exacting rule, everyone rehearsed happily until five in the morning when he sent them all home in taxis. After hours of work in an empty theatre rehearsing implacably, he told her: 'My old friend Seymour Hicks came to the show last night and asked me: "What have you done to that pretty Laye girl? I can hear everything she says!"'

She soon felt at home in the Aldford Street house. Evelyn Cochran took her under her wing and introduced her to everyone, Evelyn radiant in chiffon, sweet, graceful, redolent of delicate perfume and charmed to welcome with a kiss an unusually beautiful young woman. *Fun of The Fayre* ran well and was only blemished by the failure of the Fratellini Brothers, the celebrated Italian clowns whom Cochran and the rest of Europe much admired and whom he had eagerly imported from the Cirque Medrano in Paris. On the first night, when the show was running late and their equipment got jammed in the narrow back-stage quarters of the Pavilion, they were hissed by an impatient audience. The Dolly Sisters once more, however, saved the evening when they did a pony trot number with the dancer Clifton Webb, later to be a Hollywood actor renowned for his portrayal of acidulous dandies – type-casting indeed, for such he was in private life. Another future Hollywood star in the cast was Cochran's own cousin, Arthur Treacher, who, towering and disdainful, became the incarnation of the English

butler in many films, actually playing Jeeves on several occasions. In his last years he deserted butlering and built up a
prosperous chain of superior fish-and-chop shops throughout
America.

One of the most difficult decisions facing an impresario is
when to take off a show. If a production is ailing, should he
nurse it along or should he cut his losses? If it is doing only
moderate business, should he rely on instinct and try his luck
with a replacement? By the Christmas of 1921 Cochran sensed,
rightly or wrongly, that the vogue for *League of Notions* would
soon have run out so he closed it and ventured into pantomime
with *Babes In The Wood*. It drew good matinées but poor evening
receipts, and he concluded that once the school holidays were
over the takings would be uniformly poor. Here was an occasion to cut his losses, which amounted to over seven thousand
pounds, and to try something new. This he did with *Mayfair and
Montmartre* which brought Delysia back to London as the star of
an extravaganza in the Grand Babylonian manner which, said
the *Manchester Guardian*, 'revealed an astonishing mastery of
finished flamboyancy. Mr Cochran's command of showmanship is as assured as ever.' At the first night booking was so
enthusiastic that he had to turn away business. After this,
though, the box office languished. Press notices were not
helpful, chiefly because he had included a light-hearted skit
on drama critics which the latter, for once themselves the object
of appraisal, did not take kindly. He knew them all personally
and was startled that they should object to what he regarded as
a friendly joke. Convinced that he was in the right, he argued
back at them and wrote letters to newspapers defending *Mayfair
and Montmartre*. Gradually receipts picked up and after six
weeks or so he began to recoup his production costs. Then
Delysia fell ill with a throat ailment and was warned not to
continue on pain of losing her voice for ever. A hurried replacement failed to save a show which had been built around her and
within a month it closed leaving Cochran with bills for over
twenty thousand pounds.

He was forty-nine now, the age at which a man could
reasonably expect to have mastered his chosen profession and
to build on established success. In the theatre, he knew, this

could never be so. You were only as successful as your latest production. *Mayfair and Montmartre* was a failure, and he, despite his long experience, must at the moment be accounted a failure too. The atmosphere in Aldford Street grew sombre. The increasing pain of arthritis in his legs made him short-tempered, and the silver-topped cane, once a dandy's accessory, became a genuine prop as he limped from room to room cursing all drama critics and swearing at his valet. When he was in a mood like this Evelyn crept fearfully about and spoke in whispers to the servants. Nothing must be said or done that was likely to aggravate him or worsen his temper. He raised his voice and carried on long, loud, angry conversations at the telephone. She looked forward to the evening when he would be away at the theatre and she could cuddle up with her brandy bottle and those blessed nips, alone, in a kindly haze that softened the harshness of existence and blurred unforgiving reality. Better still, she would have some woman friend with her, preferably younger than herself, who would give her the emotional comfort which she no longer expected to receive from her husband.

The New Oxford Theatre stood empty and he filled it quickly with a show called *Chuckles of 1922* which he imported wholesale from America to save labour and expense. At the London Pavilion he staged a version of the French musical *Phi-Phi* composed by Henri Christiné, author of popular songs for Josephine Baker, Maurice Chevalier and Harry Fragson. In Paris *Phi-Phi* had run for several years and made fortunes for all concerned. The plot is set in ancient Greece and the hero is Phidias, the sculptor nicknamed 'Phi-Phi', who has trouble with his wife over the beautiful girls he engages as models. The dialogue was, in its day, considered rather *schockingue*, though now it has an amusing coyness. There are many neat jokes – the characters are always meeting each other in the rue du Panthéon, the Odéon, the rue d'Athènes and other well-known Paris thoroughfares – and the rhymes are adroit. The music is pert and breezy with a ballet performed as a soft-shoe shuffle and a 'Greek dance' which turns out to be a 'Java' in disguise. One number sung by Mrs Phidias is a pastiche of Massenet and delicately laments a certain physical effect which his glamorous models produce on her all-too susceptible husband.

Such pleasantries would have been impossible in English for prim theatregoers in the nineteen-twenties. They were dropped and replaced with jokes of the feeblest quality. The adaptors, of whom there were several, committed murder on the misfortunate *Phi-Phi*. They mangled the libretto, they mutilated songs and they added lyrics of a coy awfulness like the following:

> 'Ding Dong Dell,
> Who'll get me who can tell?
> But one fine day
> Someone may
> Hold me like a spell
> If I fell
> You'd hear the wedding bell.'

Extra numbers by Cole Porter and Herman Darewski were stuffed into the score and Christiné's original music was overlaid by an unlovely patchwork of banal melodies. It is astonishing that Cochran should have allowed such a vulgarisation. The only explanation may be that at the time he was ill, harassed by the demands his numerous enterprises was making on him and losing money over-all at the rate of two thousand pounds a week. The sole advantage *Phi-Phi* could offer was an excellent cast. Evelyn Laye, in her first principal role, played Mrs Phi-Phi, and her husband was the fleet-footed Clifton Webb. Stanley Lupino darted around energetically as an impudent Mercury while the moon-faced Jay Laurier, a new recruit from the music-hall, displayed a talent which was later to make him the finest Shakespearean clown of his day. For old times' sake, Cochran had also included Arthur Roberts in the small but telling part of a charioteer. He wore a top hat wreathed with laurel and, safety-pinned on his capacious toga, a cabman's badge large as a soupdish.

It is only fair to say that Cochran himself had doubts about the production. He liked Christiné's music but knew only too well the difficulty of fitting English words to French songs. The book of *Phi-Phi*, he rightly feared, would be impossible to adapt, and he sought to camouflage the weakness of the English version with costumes and sets by Edmond Dulac. 'I felt all the time that *Phi-Phi* was a vulgar show,' he later wrote. 'I hated to have it on the Pavilion stage where I had done things of which I was proud.' But he had been desperate to find a new attraction and *Phi-Phi* was all that he could lay his hands on at that particular moment. As soon as it concluded its short run, he rented the London Pavilion to Douglas Fairbanks for the showing of his latest film *Robin Hood*.

In the late autumn he sailed for New York, hoping to find ready-made productions which he could ship over to London. His finances now were so bad that he could not afford to originate new shows and he eagerly snapped up, among others, Irving Berlin's *Music Box Revue* which he put on next year. It lost him eight thousand pounds. *Dover Street to Dixie* was another revue of which he had high hopes. He showed, too, courage in presenting it at that time, for the public attitude towards black performers was ambiguous. The revue was divided into two halves, the first all-white and the second all-black. On the opening night the first half went badly and Stanley Lupino fought without success to win over a glacial audience. Not long after the second half began, the frenetic black chorus and dancers galvanized the house with their delirious high spirits. When Florence Mills appeared, a throb in her bird-like voice, her arms and legs flittering vibrantly, she conquered at once. Every night she received an ovation before she started her number, so magnetic was her appeal, and she controlled her audience in the way that only a great artist can. There was pathos in her frail little figure and a lingering nostalgia in her famous 'Bye-bye, Blackbird' number that brought a lump to the throat. Cochran fell more than a little in love with her.

Dover Street to Dixie was the only occasion when he lost his temper in public. Up to then his outbursts of anger had been restricted to the Aldford Street house with Evelyn and the domestics as sole witness. He was still on very bad terms with drama critics over *Mayfair to Montmartre* and had, ever since, refused them admission to his first nights. One of them, Hannen Swaffer, was especially outraged by his mingling of black and white in the new revue. Swaffer is forgotten now but in his day he was a flamboyant self-publicist who made himself as notorious as the personalities he interviewed. Apart from actually printing newspapers, he had done everything in the journalistic world as editor, columnist, special correspondent, leader writer, reporter and interviewer. Gaunt, episcopal of mien, his neck swathed in a black stock and his lapels shrouded in a layer of ash from the cigarette that jiggled permanently between his lips, he made it his business to annoy and provoke with the maximum of clamour. When someone described him to his long-suffering editor as 'witty and irrepressible', the latter replied: 'I don't know about witty, but he's bloody irrepressible.' Noël Coward was one of the few people ever to silence him. 'I have always said,' observed Swaffer grandly, 'that you act much better than you write.' 'How odd,' riposted Coward, 'I'm always saying the same about you.'

Swaffer claimed to be shocked by the 'impropriety' of exhibiting white performers in the company of black ones. Sixty years ago the topic was something that would have made headlines in fish-and-chip newspapers and he chose it for his sensation of the day. Despite Cochran's embargo he contrived to smuggle himself in at *Dover Street to Dixie* as escort to a well-known first-nighter. Cochran soon detected the familiar face in the stalls, the cadaverous cheeks, the harsh voice grating. His face reddened, then purpled. He squashed his cigar beneath his foot and limped down the centre aisle. Face to face with Swaffer he seized him and pulled him out of his seat. Then, one hand at his neck, the other on the seat of his trousers, he shook the critic furiously and threw him out. 'Get out of my theatre!' he bellowed. 'Get out of my theatre!'

Anger made him forget his arthritis for a moment. It even, probably, did him some good as a means of releasing the frustration he was going through at the moment. None of his productions were doing well and his debts were mounting vertiginously. Another import, George M. Cohan's *Little Nellie Kelly*, failed to save him. He could no longer rely on his lighter shows to subsidise the more intellectual fare he enjoyed presenting. Within the space of a few months he mounted yet another Guitry season, a visit by the Comédie Française, a programme of Ibsen plays with Eleanora Duse and a season by the Russian troupe known as the Chauve-Souris. The art of the last-named, which blended mime with folklore and balladry, was described by James Agate as 'pure theatre'. Their effects, simple and understated, were obtained with an ingenuity that recalled Diaghilev's Russian Ballet. Having expected them to storm London, Cochran was disappointed when they barely paid their way. He inclined to agree with their leader, the squat, simian-featured Nikita Balieff, who sighed wittily: 'Bacon – particularly with eggs – will always be more popular in England than Shakespeare.'

Also caviar to the general was Eleanora Duse. In 1923, the year before her death, Cochran arranged her last London appearance and travelled to Paris whence he escorted her over here. Very frail, very delicate, the Italian actress shrank trembling from the crowds around her. As the train whisked her up through the Kentish fields, she preferred to sit on her case in the corridor so as to escape the tobacco smoke that filled her compartment. Was she old? No, ageless, for the Ellida Wangel she played in Ibsen's *The Lady From the Sea* had eternal youth. 'The voice seemed to me to be just as exquisite as ever,' wrote James Agate, 'the arms, with their grave dance, eked out the old insufficiency of words; the face, in moments of emotion, lit up from within as though a lime had been thrown upon it. There was the old ineffable grace, the childish importunacy, the raising of human dignity to a power undreamt of . . . Her features have the placidity of long grief; so many storms have broken over them that nothing can disturb again this sea of calm distress. If there be in acting such a thing as pure passion divorced from the body yet expressed in terms of the body, it is here.' Her performance in *Ghosts* suggested to Agate a comparison between the two greatest actresses he had ever known: 'She is always herself, her fastidious, beautiful self. So, you say, was Bernhardt. But Bernhardt had a hundred different ways of being the same person. She could shake Heaven and Hell; Duse breathes only a sigh. Sarah, in the mind, still flames and glows; Duse lingers like some exquisite, faint regret.'

Cochran's other big presentation of 1923 was Eugène O'Neill's masterpiece *Anna Christie*. He had seen it on his recent New York trip and was determined to give the London première, however much it cost him. The leading player was the

American Pauline Lord who won as great a success in London
as she had in New York. Her performance, Agate said, was
exquisite: 'Only a highly accomplished artist could have given
that suggestion of childlikeness and canaillerie, of maiden
virtue rudely strumpeted, of a loving heart, and the stare of the
street. Plain, if you like, slightly, undistinguished, the actress
gave you at her first entrance that indefinable sense of trouble
which marks the great players; and she has the gift of melancholy . . . And the gesture of humility with which, at the end,
she abased her head before her lover was one of the most beautiful I have ever seen.' It was as well that Cochran had, by now,
made peace with the critics and allowed them to attend his
first nights.

That of *Anna Christie* was a triumph. An excellent press and
enthusiastic word-of-mouth reports brought good houses for
the next few evenings. Unfortunately, having heard that *Anna
Christie* was 'the best show in town', fashionable audiences
arrived not knowing what to expect – the latest American farce?
gangster melodrama? burlesque? After the first act they were
bored and went out to dinner or night clubs. Takings plum-
meted. As Cochran remarked, *Anna Christie* proved conclusively
that there is only a limited public for a high calibre play in
London. And people called him a 'commercial manager' . . .

He was proud of *Anna Christie*, proud of Duse, proud of
having brought so many fine artists to the West End. Pride,
though, did not fill his pocket which was now dangerously
empty. His theatrical empire was much diminished and all that
remained to him were the Palace, the New Oxford and the
London Pavilion. Creditors were pressing him, associates to
whom he was deeply committed were becoming restive. One
of his biggest creditors, a large advertising agency, was sympathetic and called a meeting. Cochran appeared, spruce,
courteous, grave. His eyes sparkled with sincerity and determination. He was a man of business like them, he said. No-
one realized more clearly than he did the situation in which
he found himself. He spoke frankly, explained how recent disappointments had blighted his plans, and outlined wonderful
ideas he had for the future. What a shame if these projects, so
close to fruition, were to be destroyed when, with only a little

breathing space, he could bring them to a happy conclusion! More important still, he added, extra time would give him a much better opportunity to repay all the gentlemen assembled here. In his quiet voice he thanked them for their courtesy and for hearing him with attention. He mentioned figures, took out documents from well-kept files, knew immediately where to find the paper he needed to illustrate the point he was making. When he sensed that most of those present were on his side, he allowed himself a touch of geniality, a hint of unbuttoned charm. They agreed, almost unanimously, to grant him a year of grace. Bankruptcy was averted, at least for the next twelve months. What a pleasant fellow, they thought, basically a sound man who happened to be going through a bad patch. He talked their language and could see their point of view. He wasn't one of those slippery fly-by-night showmen nor a bucket-shop artist whose word you could never rely on. And yet, around this figure who looked and spoke like a prosperous banker, there hung an enticing aura of theatrical glamour which could not but impress and intrigue them despite their hard-headed preoccupation with balance-sheets and letters of credit.

He limped out in a fog of cigar smoke and good wishes. Perhaps his judgment had been poor. Certainly he had known a run of bad luck. When he pondered the debts he had run up, they did not seem an impossible load for him to carry. After all, he had made vast sums before and he could do so again. Small measures were of no use. He must think big, he must get away from the theatre and launch out in a wider area of showmanship, one that would attract a public far greater than that of Shaftesbury Avenue. A rodeo was the thing, and he would present it at Wembley during the British Empire Exhibition.

To America he went, and to Canada, returning with four hundred head of cattle and four hundred horses. At Tilbury Docks twenty coaches waited to bear off an army of whooping cowboys to Wembley. In the streets outside they cracked lariats to whip off the hats of passers-by and lashed policemen to lamp-posts. The foyer of the Piccadilly Hotel resounded with yodeling and bronco calls. Gordon Selfridge threw a party for the cowboys and prudently gave them white wine cup to drink.

They did not like it, thirsted for something stronger, and having found the way to his cellar, dug out bottles of champagne and played skittles with them up and down the grand staircases of Lansdowne House where he then lived.*

On most days two hundred thousand people crowded into Wembley for a non-stop spectacle of bull dogging, steer riding and bronco busting. In ten-gallon Stetsons decorated with gold and rubies, marksmen flourished six-shooters and shot the pips out of a nine of spades at fifteen paces away. They were among the few allowed to address Cochran as 'Charlie'.

Bulls thundered through corrals, horses reared, steers fell in the dust, hog-tied by expert lassos thrown with micro-second timing. An ambulance stood permanently by to attend cowboys with fractured legs and splintered arms. But what of the animals? Although Cochran invited RSPCA officials to inspect the pens, the corrals and everything else connected with the show, animal lovers were uneasy. One Saturday a steer fell badly during a roping competition and got up, to the distress of the audience, with a broken leg. The RSPCA brought a prosecution for cruelty and Cochran found himself in the dock at Wealdstone police court along with a gang of bemused cowboys. Although a persuasive QC extracted a verdict of not guilty from the magistrates, the bad publicity depressed attendance at Wembley. After the rodeo closed, Cochran added up the two sides of the balance sheet. He had reckoned that he could have made, or just as easily lost, fifty thousand pounds. The figures showed that he had done neither. After six months' hard work he was left with nothing at all. 'It was a gambler's last coup,' he remarked. 'I was all out to win, but I lost.'

He remembered his old colleague Charles Frohman saying that so long as you did not lose your last chip you were always in the game. Now he had lost his last chip and was out of the great game of show business he loved. In January, 1925, he filed his petition in bankruptcy. Liabilities were put at over a hundred thousand pounds, assets at two thousand. For the second time in his life he heard an icy Registrar detail a long series of 'rash

---

* The Savage Club now occupies, as its lounge, the vast bedroom he allocated to the Dolly Sisters with whom he was currently besotted.

and hazardous speculations'. Where were the ninety-eight thousand pounds he had lost on the New Oxford Theatre? What about the five thousand that vanished with the Dempsy/Carpentier fight? How did he continue to squander seven thousand on *The Music Box Revue*? And the thousand on the Guitry season? And the two thousand on exhibition dancing at the Piccadilly Hotel? He had not kept proper accounts; he had contracted debts without reasonable expectation of paying them; he had, in short, courted bankruptcy. The culprit shut his eyes and thought of Lucien Guitry as Pasteur, of Diaghilev and all his splendour, of Eleanora Duse and Sarah Bernhardt, of *The Miracle*, of the Chauve-Souris. The Registrar droned on.

Two months later, cherubic, courteous, he applied for his discharge from bankruptcy. The Registrar spoke severely. He had, nonetheless, to admit that nearly all the debtors were in favour. One of the biggest, the scene designer Joseph Harker, father of Gordon, had even offered to drop his claim. It was an exceptional case, observed the Registrar, but he was prepared to grant the petitioner's request. The chill air of the musty little room warmed perceptibly as creditors bustled up to the impresario and shook his hand in delight. One of them started singing 'For he's a jolly good fellow.' Others joined in. While the Registrar put away his papers with a disbelieving manner, people to whom Cochran still owed thousands asked him eagerly for news of his latest ventures and promised to finance him again. No, his last chip was not yet gone.

iii
ON WITH THE DANCE

'There was a festive party at the Midland afterwards, where all raucous and harsh thoughts were submerged in champagne . . . Not only was all anger forgotten, but I may add, the possibility of my getting a larger percentage of the gross was also forgotten.'

NOËL COWARD

'The public have paid a million pounds to see my shows in the course of my career,' said Cochran to reporters who surrounded him when he came out of the court-room. Carefully he disposed of ash from his cigar. 'In one year I made a hundred thousand pounds,' he went on. 'Today neither my wife nor I have a five pound note in the world. I am not a brilliant bankrupt.' His Rolls-Royce drew up and took him, Evelyn at his side, back to Aldford Street.

Rates have to be paid, and heating and lighting, and income tax and food. How, wonders the lesser mortal, did Cochran manage it? That was his secret. He was still a familiar face in the Savoy Grill. His chauffeur, his valet, his cook and his housemaids stayed with him. There was a clue in the fact that at some time or another he had made over the Aldford Street home and all his valuable pictures and furnishings to Evelyn, thus preserving them from creditors. One should not forget either that he had the gift of inspiring confidence, as the unusual scene of his bankruptcy meeting proved. Because he believed so implicitly in himself, everyone else did the same. All he undertook was done with such fiery enthusiasm, such energy, that his partners were lifted up and carried along solely by the force of his conviction. When he sought money for a new show he would produce a small piece of paper on which was written: 'I agree to pay Charles B. Cochran the sum of £x.' His partners would sign it without even knowing what the show was to be. Cochran's name and his reputation were enough for them.

As soon as he emerged from bankruptcy he spent days replying to the hundreds of letters that flooded in containing money, cheques, postal orders from sympathizers. Among his correspondents were many whom he had helped in past times of need. They did not forget him now. He hurried off to France and America in search of new spectacle. In between, as a quick way of raising money, he sat down and wrote his memoirs, over four hundred pages of them, which he called *Secrets of A Showman*. It is true that he reveals few secrets worth telling. Except where his failures are sensational and make a good story, he does not write of the disasters which hit him as liberally as the triumphs. Rivals like André Charlot hardly figure. His family is scarcely spoken of, and with Victorian reticence he had little to say about his mother, still less of his father. He even, falsely and maybe through mild snobbery, attributes his birthplace to Lindfield and not to Brighton. Yet his early experience of journalism helps to make *Secrets of A Showman* peculiarly readable. He tells a good anecdote and can sum up a character. What he says about the great players he has managed shows a discerning eye for creativeness and an inborn sympathy with the artistic temperament. He asked James Agate to write a preface. Agate, although a drama critic, was, save for a few periods of estrangement, a close friend. Himself permanently harassed by money-lenders and the Inland Revenue, he admired a book which revelled, without turning a hair, in debts on a mountainous scale and in ventures that could only harvest dazzling riches or the lowest form of poverty. 'I look to the future,' wrote Cochran in the last words of his book. 'It is full of promise.' Agate the perennial optimist would have agreed with him.

That promise was instantly fulfilled when Major Gluckstein, head of the Lyons catering firm, asked him to produce a cabaret at the Trocadero grill room. Cabaret was an American import which soon naturalized itself in London at the start of the nineteen-twenties. The 'Midnight Follies' at Queen's Hall offered supper tables grouped around a dance floor and, in between sessions of the Black Bottom and the Charleston, singers who took over to chirrup 'Ramona', 'Little Man You've Had A Busy Day', 'All The King's Horses', and as time went on, the Lambeth Walk. At the 'Cave of Harmony' Elsa Lanchester immortalized the song 'I've danced with a man, who's danced with a girl, who's danced with the Prince of Wales.' Negro bands were very popular and speciality dancers like Mrs Vernon Castle earned high fees at the Embassy. Ambrose, the supreme band-leader of the day and known to his mates as 'Bert', was king of the Mayfair Hotel. At the Kit-Kat his rival Teddy Brown's band earned a thousand pounds a week. Night-clubs and hotels paid out large sums of money and were rewarded with takings which, including the profit on food and drink, were as good as those on a successful revue or musical comedy.

At the Trocadero Cochran began with a shortened version of the Delibes ballet *Coppélia*. It had a corps de ballet of fourteen and an orchestra of more than twenty. The licensing authorities turned restive and banned performance on what they called 'such occasions as Sundays and feast days usually given up to mirth and happiness'. There was not, in any case, a great deal of mirth to *Coppélia*, enchanting though it is, and Cochran soon evolved a formula which lasted fifteen years until the outbreak of war in 1939. He staged, in effect, miniature revues between half-past eleven and midnight. They had titles like 'Piccadilly Circus', 'Night Lights', 'Eve in the Park' and 'Going To Town'. The bill usually consisted of half a dozen musical numbers, solo and concerted, which followed each other non-stop. These were interspersed with acrobats and eccentric dancers. The quality of Cochran's product was shown in Doris Zinkeisen's costumes and settings, Oliver Messel's designs, and choreography plotted by Diaghilev's star Massine. The printed programmes were themselves minor works of art. Each had an elegant full-colour cover by a well-known artist. One of them, for a show called 'Round and Round', was in circular shape and held together by a central pin so that when you revolved it two chorus girls appeared to swing each other round.

Cochran never had a written contract with Lyons. Everything depended on a verbal agreement and a handshake. Once he had settled his formula, production costs stabilized and varied little from year to year. Often he would draw on his other current shows for a number or two, and at curtain-fall the chosen performer would rush off to the Trocadero ready for action at half-past eleven. A given cabaret could run for a year, and its first night would be almost as glamorous as a similar occasion in the theatre. His first-night table, ever decorated with pretty women, had to be enlarged over the years to accommodate all the celebrities who showed interest. The glitter, the flowers, the champagne were, however, but the window-dressing for all the hard and often tumultuous preparations. Rehearsals began at midnight on Sunday when the last diner had left and the place was empty for the cast, dress-makers, stage-hands, orchestra and wig-makers to sit down at an early breakfast after the first run-through from start to finish. Then it all began again with, if lucky, fewer halts for discussion. A third run-through might possibly go smoothly. If not, a fourth was needed while Cochran, bowler-hatted, warmly overcoated against draughts, lolled in a gilt chair and relayed instructions through his assistants. There were, in addition, regular rehearsals each Wednesday to check for signs of wear and to preserve the original sparkle. The Trocadero was well equipped with a proper stage and an orchestra pit, although the apron stage which ran out and around and on which the girls made their entrance was uncomfortably narrow. Tables under and next to the apron stage were, naturally, much sought after since they gave the most interesting viewpoint of the girls' charms as they flashed by. They were also the most hazardous. It sometimes happened that a footing was missed, a shoe came off, and a gawping patron found a girl in his soup.

As soon as the Trocadero shows had got under way Cochran began planning a new revue. Raising money was easy. Some of the creditors at his bankruptcy proceedings were only too keen to lend him more, so confident were they in his skill. He also knew many rich businessmen who, realistic and down-to-earth though they may have been in the circles where they made their fortunes, could not resist the lure of the theatre. They were entertained at parties with champagne buffets and, after midnight, by a hand-picked troupe of chorus girls who performed numbers from Cochran shows. Lecherous and full of drink, they squatted on the carpet the better to appreciate the talent displayed for their benefit, especially in the high kicks. Afterwards Cochran would introduce them to individual girls. Interesting developments sometimes followed. Either then, at a carefully chosen moment, or next day, when the memory still tingled, they would sign the famous piece of paper guaranteeing sums of money for Cochran's next production, whatever it might be.

He had been impressed by the performance of a twenty-four year-old actor called Noël Coward in his own play *The Young Idea*. That same year Coward showed further versatility by contributing songs and sketches to André Charlot's revue *London Calling*. Cochran invited him to his office and proposed that he write the book for his new revue, the music to be provided by Philip Braham, an experienced composer whose 'Limehouse Blues' was a popular hit. Coward disagreed.

Cochran twitched in his chair. When, in his grandest manner, he offered a promising author the unique opportunity of writing the whole of a Cochran revue, he did not expect to be greeted with objections. The skinny young man, obdurate, driven by an implacable, all-conquering urge for success and a supreme confidence in his own ability, wanted to write all the music himself as well as the sketches. Smiling his usual bland smile to mask irritation within, Cochran pointed out that Braham was the man he had personally selected for the job. Moreover, he said frankly, he did not think Coward's music would be good enough. The bumptious young man insisted, and for two hours, in the weird voice which he had invented for himself and which was to become his trademark, a strangulated blend of vowels from his Teddington birthplace and consonants from the Mayfair he aspired to, he disputed the issue fervently. In this first clash between two iron-clad egos it was the impresario who won – but only temporarily, because Coward arranged his sketches in such a way that they led naturally into a song. Braham ended up by contributing only three numbers and Coward by writing the greater part of the book, score and lyrics.

Once again Cochran gathered around himself the faithful team of experts who had helped him in his early successes. Frank Collins, incisive, laconic, directed rehearsals in his icy martinet style. Cissie Sewell, the red-headed wardrobe mistress, had already been with Cochran for years. At auditions she would signify her likes and dislikes by means of coded gestures to her old friend Elsie April, Cochran's music director. Elsie was a Margaret Rutherford figure who travelled everywhere upon an elderly bicycle. Only five feet two inches tall, dressed in baggy woollen outfits of indescribable cut, she invariably wore, indoors and out, an appalling hat. 'Elsie, darling,' Evelyn Laye once enquired, 'do you ever take your hat off when you go to bed?' This enigma, like the song the sirens sang, remains unsolved. Elsie had worked for André Charlot until Cochran poached her. She belonged to the type, not uncommon among musicians, of technical genius with no corresponding gift of invention. A comedian would hum a tune to her amid the noise and bustle of rehearsals and, having simultaneously notated and harmonized it, she would play it over to him at the piano in an immaculate transcription. She had perfect pitch, a characteristic not always possessed by even the greatest composers, and after a show would berate a trombonist for having played a momentary E flat instead of an E natural. Singers feared her unforgiving accuracy. 'STOP! dear,' she would roar, giving her hat an exasperated shove, 'you didn't quite make that high G.' Composers respected and adored her since she always had the ideal solution to a difficult passage and bubbled over with suggestions that immeasurably improved their original efforts. 'Soling and heeling' was what she called it. Noël Coward could neither read nor write music, but had the much rarer gift of melody, and he was one of the dozens who owed her a great deal. Why, he asked her, did she lavish her talent on the work of others and yet never composed anything herself? She looked at him through her bent granny-glasses and replied evasively: 'Well, dear, I don't seem to have any time.' Once, however, she sat doodling at her piano and hit on a pleasing motif that went from F to B flat, down to F again and on to E flat ending up after a few bars on A flat. Coward over-heard, was immediately captivated, said it was very nice, and used it as the theme of 'I'll See You Again'. Or so the story goes.*

Among the rare pieces of music Coward had not written for the revue, to be called *On With The Dance*, was that of a ballet composed around Hogarth's *Rake's Progress* by Roger Quilter. It was staged by Leonide Massine, a refugee from Diaghilev's camp. The Russian impresario was outraged, for Massine had not only deserted him but abducted two of his star ballerinas including Nemtchinova. Cochran, Diaghilev protested, was not acting as 'a friend and a gentleman' by signing contracts behind his back. Nemtchinova was his pupil, his creation. 'As an old friend I can't help telling you that you should create your own works with your own artists,' Diaghilev continued, 'in-stead of using those created by others for purposes alien to the kind of show you put on – sometimes very well.' His majestic reproof did not crush the Englishman who knew, any way, that Diaghilev's reign was nearing its end.

---

* Coward himself always said that the tune came to him while he was stuck in a New York traffic jam.

One of the girls Cochran signed up for *On With The Dance* was a nineteen-year-old Hermione Baddeley. She joined him reluctantly for she would have preferred to work with André Charlot, whose intimate revues, less glittering than Cochran's, were a much admired cult in London and featured names such as Gertrude Lawrence, Jack Buchanan and Beatrice Lillie. But he could afford to give her only half what Cochran was offering and her practical-minded mother urged her to accept. Cochran, always in a hurry, paused to size her up again at rehearsal in her practice clothes. He took the cigar from his mouth and said: 'You've got very good legs, Hermione. Turn round.' She did so. 'They're good,' he went on, 'Very good, and do you know what? They're good all the way up. There are lots of beautiful legs around, but not many all the way up from the ankle to the top of the thigh.'

Her big number was 'Poor Little Rich Girl' which she performed with Alice Delysia, the leading lady. Delysia, the only member of the cast to have a private dressing-room in the cramped quarters of the London Pavilion, did not as a result put on airs. Small favours from the chorus girls, the loan of a vital hairpin at a time of crisis, were rewarded next evening with a large pear or a peach. Delysia would appear, fruit in hand, and beam: 'For the little girl who gave me the hairpin last night.' In 'Poor Little Rich Girl' she acted a French lady's-maid warning her mistress, Hermione Baddeley 'looking drained and far from healthy' as Coward put it, about the perils of her debauched life. It was, Delysia thought, the best item in the show, and Coward agreed with her since it became his first authentic song hit and sold more copies than anything else he had written. When, later on, he suggested that Gertrude Lawrence might also sing it in New York, the usually benign Delysia lost her temper. 'Noël,' she screamed with excellent command of English idiom if not of accent, 'is a sheet and a boogairr.'

For his chorus line Cochran recruited Florence Desmond, at eighteen even younger than Hermione Baddeley. He had seen this attractive little blonde during auditions and asked her to dance. After a few simple steps he said to his stage-manager: 'Tell her I don't want to see any more. That girl's got style.' She, fearing dismissal, quailed. He disillusioned her with a contract at ten pounds a week and an option of fifteen for his next show. She joined a troupe of girls whom he had decided to call 'Mr Cochran's Young Ladies.' While checking a proof of the programme for *On With The Dance*, or so he said, the idea of giving them such a title had come into his mind. Its publicity value was immense and it quickly became a catch-phrase to be used with humour, facetiousness and, often, envy. 'Mr Cochran's Young Ladies' in years to come provided a finishing school for young talent and famous performers were to graduate from it. Beauty was not the only thing he looked for at those long and tedious auditions in dark theatres shrouded with dust sheets. Did a girl walk gracefully? How did she stand in repose and what did she do with her hands? Was her hair naturally beautiful? Did she have expressive eyes? (He always quoted Yvonne Printemps, who, with decidedly irregular features, yet had the loveliest eyes in the world). Was her figure in proportion? Imbalance of feature did not matter all that much, since lighting and make-up could work miracles. Once she became one of his Young Ladies a girl was chaperoned, taxi'd here and there, even fed with the care devoted to raising prize cattle. Slimming is always a newsworthy topic, and one of Cochran's best publicity tricks was to put his Girls on a diet planned by a well-known medical specialist and intended, he gravely explained, to help them survive the exhausting rigours of dance routines. They put on weight healthily and stopped fainting at rehearsals. Newspapers everywhere took up the story and sales of wholemeal bread spiralled heavenwards. What a kind, thoughtful man was Mr Cochran, and how devotedly he tended the welfare of his Young Ladies! He was baffled when, despite all his avuncular attention and kindly presents, quite a few of them rejected the honour of sleeping with him.

The leading comedian in *On With The Dance* was Douglas Byng. Long before Danny La Rue was even born Douglas Byng had established himself as the wittiest drag artist of all. Over a period of seven years he was permanent fixture in Cochran's revues and played more than a hundred character parts at the London Pavilion. He regarded that theatre as an undergraduate might look on Oxbridge. 'We were a sort of large family of

Above left Charles Blake Cochran at the age of
seven;
Above right Cochran the young impresario sets up
a deal on the telephone;
Left Mrs Cochran, née Evelyn Dade, at the time
of her marriage;
Below right Cochran as the promoter of
Hagenbeck's Zoo;
Below left Mr and Mrs Cochran at a garden party.

CHARLES B. COCHRAN

MADRALI
The Terrible Turk.

GEORGES HACKENSCHMIDT
The Russian Lion.

Above Cochran the wrestling match impresario. The sensational match between Madrali and Hackenschmidt lasted only a few seconds during which Hackenschmidt threw Madrali to the ground and broke his arms

Below Cochran behind the scenes at Olympia where he presented *The Miracle* and other spectacular shows

A scene from Sacha Guitry's *Mozart*: Sacha on far right,
Yvonne Printemps as Mozart second from right

Augustus John's design for the second act of O'Casey's *The Silver Tassie*

Cochran with Noël Coward and some of the 'Young Ladies' on board ship at Southampton. Cochran travelled often to New York, a city he loved: its hectic atmosphere suited his own restless personality

Poster for *Bless The Bride*

Cochran sizes up a dress for *Bless The Bride*

Cochran with Jessie Matthews, one of his early protégées

Tilly Losch in one of her 'speciality dances'

Cochran seen by 'Autori' at the height of his London Pavilion successes

Valerie Frazer, his last protégée – her legs, he told her, were 'cute legs – legs with personality'

The seaside tableau in *Cavalcade*

Cochran and Yvonne Printemps in Paris

Cochran discusses a point with Wendy Toye

Cochran at rehearsal with (l to r) his stage manager Frank Collins, wardrobe mistress
Cissie Sewell, Mrs Cochran, musical director Elsie April, choreographer Buddy Bradley

Noël Coward at the time of *Cavalcade*   The new Sir Charles and Lady Cochran

The last bow

children and Cocky, as some were privileged to call him, the biggest child of all,' he remembered. 'Every show he put on became a great new adventure because of his tremendous enthusiasm.' In private life Byng had a *tic nerveux* apt to alarm those unaware of it. Suddenly, and with an agonizing jerk, his head would twist round, his mouth gape in a painful rictus, his eyes goggle in alarm. For over ninety years this neurological disability plagued him, although on stage he used it to enrich the grotesques he played and to lend them a crazy distinction. In the gallery of baroque females he created, one recalls with affection Flora MacDonald, Minnie the Messy old Mermaid, Boadicea, Naughty Nellie Gwynn, Black-out Bella, Nanna of The Manor, and, vulgarity attaining the sublime, Doris the Goddess of Wind. He belongs to the great pantomime dames of this century. Among his music-hall acts was a one-man pantomime in which he played not only the Fairy Queen and Demon King but also Principal Boy, Heroine and Dame. Fond memory will always cherish his rendering of:

'Who'll come and roll mother's pudding?

'Who'll come and flatten the dough?

'Who'll fold the ends, and straighten the bends –

'You know where good puddings go.'

As James Agate remarked, 'Mr Byng is not near the knuckle, he is the knuckle itself.'

One of the sketches Noël Coward wrote for him in *On With The Dance* was called 'Oranges and Lemons'. He and his fellow actor impersonated two middle-aged ladies, one a spinster and the other a widow, preparing for bed in a Bloomsbury boarding house. After much pointed bickering, stays and corsets are eventually removed and billowing night-dresses put on. The lights go out. Two drunken guests, both men, blunder in. They each pile into a bed and are met with screams from the widow but, from the spinster, the helpful remark: 'Well, young man, and what can I do for you?' Byng's partner as a middle-aged lady was Ernest Thesiger, that unique and much mourned eccentric player. His cavernous features, his emaciated cheeks, his wide mouth, staring eyes and long pendulous nose served him equally well as a mincing cleric or as a gibbering Frankenstein. A *mariage de convenance* with an understanding wife enabled him to pursue his lifelong hobby of embroidery, a passion shared by his royal friend 'dear Queen Mary' who probably gained him his CBE. He once published a stimulating volume entitled *Adventures In Embroidery*. Until the age of eighty he went on acting, although he had never seemed anything but very old. One day in the Tube someone looked hard at him and said: 'Excuse me, but weren't you Ernest Thesiger?' According to Donald Sinden he replied: 'Madam, I *was*.'*

Rehearsals of *On With The Dance* were spread over a month and followed a timetable which Frank Collins had laid down with meticulous care. At ten o'clock sketches were rehearsed in the London Pavilion. At eleven Massine was supervising ballet at rooms in Poland Street. An hour later Elsie April ran through musical numbers in the stalls bar of the London Pavilion. At one there was an hour's break for lunch, after which the same routine was taken up in the afternoon. Another rehearsal room Cochran used was the Helvetia Club, and here he had a second confrontation with Noël Coward. Originally Coward's percentage had been based on the book and lyrics he wrote. As he pointed out, however, after the contract was signed he had contributed nearly all the music as well, and surely that entitled him to a bigger share? In the drab Helvetia, lit with bare electric bulbs, redolent of stale cooking and half-eaten oranges, where a jangling piano beat out harsh rhythms to which chorus girls danced for the fifteenth time that day, the two men argued at length. Coward, snappy and on edge, pressed the justice of his claim. Cochran, tranquil and impervious, explained that he could not possibly ask his backers for any more money. With charming openness he described his financial arrangements. He was the essence of reason and exuded commonsense. Perhaps, if the show succeeded, Noël might leave it to him to decide upon a further reward? With reluctance, outmanoeuvred by this approach, Coward agreed.

One Sunday the whole company went by train, luncheon provided with the compliments of the management, to Manchester where the try-out was scheduled for the Palace Theatre.

---

* Thesiger once asked Somerset Maugham: 'Why do you never write parts for me?' 'Oh, but I do,' replied Maughan, 'only Gladys Cooper always plays them.' (Sheridan Morley *dixit*.)

Rehearsals continued throughout Monday and the dress rehearsal proper began at eight o'clock in the evening. Again, and
yet again, the players sang the refrain of 'Fête Galante', a
vicarage garden party treated in the spirit of musical comedy:
    'We're six dirty little choir boys
    'With really frightful minds,
    'We scream and shout and rush about
    'And pinch our friends' behinds . . .'
It did not seem at all funny on the fifth repetition while
stagehands toiled to get the lighting right and Frank Collins
glowered in the stalls, intervening from time to time with yet
another suggestion from Mr Cochran who sat beside him
wrapped in a thick overcoat, hat tipped back on head. They
worked on through the night. By three o'clock on Tuesday
afternoon they had not yet completed even the first half of the
show. People read newspapers while awaiting their call, first
the evening editions, then the morning editions, and finally the
evening editions once more. The auditorium was dotted with
sleeping figures overcome by exhaustion. Douglas Byng did his
boarding-house sketch four times. On the fourth occasion he
could not deliver his black-out line. He had fallen asleep.

Cochran decided to end the misery. Hot coffee and ham and
eggs were brought in while he told the manager of the Palace
that they could not possibly open that evening. The manager
demurred. Postponement was out of the question, he went on,
the house was sold out for the rest of the season. His stage staff
would pull them through. Rehearsals started again and concluded with just enough time for everyone to have a bath and a
quick rest before the opening at seven that evening. Cochran
limped on stage before the curtain went up and, fearing the
worst, explained to the audience what difficulties had beset his
company. Then he sat in his stall, smiling, waving at friends,
benevolent and cheerful, with not a hint of the agonies that were
gnawing at him. Despite their rankling disagreements, Coward
had to admire his tremendous courage. Spontaneous applause
broke out frequently during the evening, the many scene
changes went with smoothness, no-one lost his or her voice, and
at the end there were happy speeches to a rapturous audience
and baskets of flowers trundled on stage. Afterwards Cochran

presided over his vast first-night table with champagne and more flowers at the Midland Hotel. He could hold out no longer and fell asleep. Friends carried him, still sleeping, to his bedroom.

More trials awaited him. While taking a bath in his hotel suite, he was assailed yet again by an irate Noël Coward so transported with fury that he irrupted into the bathroom even before the water had gurgled down the hole. The uninvited guest had noticed that *On With The Dance* was billed as 'Charles B. Cochran's Revue,' whereas had not he, Noël Coward, written nearly all the score, all the book and directed into the bargain all the sketches and several of the numbers? His voice shook. He raged. He stormed at the naked showman who sought to preserve dignity with a towel. Cochran heard him in polite silence. When he judged that the typhoon had partly blown itself out, he offered a gentle explanation. Posters and programmes, he stated, have to be printed a long while in advance, and they had naturally been prepared before Coward took over such a large part of the show. With Chesterfieldian diplomacy, *suaviter in modo sed fortiter in re*, he praised Noël's genius and complimented him on his wonderful contribution to the show. Everyone, by now, knew the true state of affairs and in any case would realize what a large amount of the credit was Noël's. Personally, Cochran went on, he was immensely proud to have had the opportunity of introducing such an original talent to the public. He foresaw a starry career and even finer achievements ahead. Together they could do great things. Once more hitching up the towel which had began to sag around his prominent middle, he invited dear Noël to take sherry with him in his sitting-room. They sat and, like old friends, discussed the triumph of *On With The Dance*. What a night it had been! What a splendid debut for the English theatre's most gifted composer, lyricist, actor, director and playwright! The flattery poured out in a smooth and emollient stream.

But Coward never received the extra percentage Cochran had promised him. He never forgot and he did not forgive.

Chapter Four

COWARD, O'CASEY AND BARRIE

'Mr Cochran has a way of crossing his hands –
when he is talking to you – which is entirely
cat-like . . . His eyes wander from the ceiling to
the carpet as though in search of flies or mice. He
can purr – and does – after a good dinner; and I
have heard him at times, when the Censor was
being tiresome, emit sounds that were very like a
miaou. His most cat-like quality, however, is his
mind. *One has never any idea of what he is thinking.*'

Beverley Nichols

---

i
ONE DAM' THING AFTER ANOTHER

'Sentimental reasons, however, are *not* the thing in business, as I
have learned to my bitter cost over the years. Cochran, Charlot,
John C. Wilson. I have been taken advantage of by all of them
and downright cheated by some of them.'

NOEL COWARD, 17 MARCH, 1961

You are as young, the saying goes, as you feel. To other people,
however, you are as young as you look. No-one, except those
who have a preference for the elderly, is excited by wrinkles and
grey hair. It is futile attempting to palliate the ravages of time
by claiming that you are young at heart, or by argument that
the dwelling has aged but not the tenant within. The cruel fact
is that although the passing years may ruin the flesh they do not
lessen the sex urge. In his mid-fifties Cochran's fair hair was

thinning and whitening, his girth was fattening and his face becoming more rubicund, yet his desire for women remained insatiable. He followed the principle enunciated by Alexandre Dumas that a man should attempt to seduce every presentable female he met. Naturally there would be repulses, but, said Dumas, the law of averages would ensure a satisfactory number of conquests.

Cochran was better placed than most in that, ageing though he looked, girls slept with him for the sake of his patronage and influence. Some, impressed by his strong personality and Napoleonic aura, felt affection for him. He had now, as many men do, reached a point of satiety with conventional debauch. True, he still enjoyed the unspoiled charms of fresh young girls who came his way, but he often found he needed a sharper stimulus than their innocent arts could provide. This was furnished by professional females who specialized in what the trade knows as water sports and the golden shower. They would straddle him and urinate on his body with gratifying accuracy. Better still, he would lie at ease in a hot steaming bath while the dew sprinkled over him from above.

Evelyn, too, had developed individual tastes. A strong Lesbian flavour permeated the ardent relations she sustained with young and pretty girls who came into her circle. She entertained them at cosy little tea parties and took them with her on the social round. Her frustrated maternity found an outlet in cossetting her chosen favourites, advising them on what clothes to wear and helping them with their careers. She became intensely fond of them and cocooned them in loving affection. They repaid her with a devotion that brightened her life and helped, with the aid of brandy, to make it worthwhile. Meanwhile she kept up a witty façade against the unhappiness her husband's philandering caused her. When he published his memoirs, *Secrets of A Showman*, she threatened to write her own under the title *Twenty-Five Years of Leading Ladies*. She was pleased at the witticism and repeated it a number of times to a number of different people. Cochran made sure that it never reached print.

His empire had at last found permanent headquarters where it was to remain until the end of his career. This was at 49, Old

Bond Street, in the West End, telephone numbers Regent 1241, 1242, 1243, telegrams to be addressed to 'Cochranus, Piccy, London'. For a time his letter-heading was 'The Cochran Corporation Ltd.', a proud title inscribed over his initials CB followed by the image of a crowing cock, the symbol he used as a book-plate in the exquisitely bound volumes in his private library and as a mark of ownership for his art collection. It was, in more ways than one, very suitable. The Cochran Corporation, with a cumbersome list of directors and formal obligations, did not last long and must have been a temporary expedient to overcome a passing financial difficulty. Cochran was too independent a spirit to be bound by company rules and the need for directorial assent to his ideas. Such an arrangement fettered his imagination, and, although it might have saved him from his bankruptcies, limited his creative freedom. Soon his letter heading became no more than the simple legend 'Charles B. Cochran'.

The office in Old Bond Street was famous in theatrical circles. You approached it by way of an asthmatic lift, not quite so decrepit as the equally celebrated conveyance which led up to Ivor Novello's eyrie at the Strand Theatre, nor so overwhelming as the one you took to reach Binkie Beaumont at the Globe. It moved slowly and deliberately, like its owner, before decanting you upstairs into modest and surprisingly unpretentious quarters. A corridor lined with valuable paintings formed the introduction to a set of rooms where a small staff administered royalties, theatre rents, leases, contracts, wages, box-office figures, catering receipts and bulging files of actors and actresses and directors. They communicated with the outside world by means of candlestick telephones through which they asked invisible operators to connect them with exchanges known as Welbeck or Paddington or Popesgrove. A lady typewriter, as the more old-fashioned still referred to her, handled his correspondence and took down the dictation he recited in a low, even voice. The walls of his own office, a small but comfortable den, were decorated with framed photographs and playbills. Most cherished of the latter was a bill for *Sindbad The Sailor*, the Brighton pantomime which nearly fifty years ago had inspired his love of the theatre.

Among those who knew this office well was Noël Coward. His disagreement with Cochran over *On With The Dance* had still not been resolved. At the dress-rehearsal Evelyn had helped to smooth matters. After a particularly violent quarrel she went up to Coward's room and paused at the open door. 'Noël,' she cooed, 'I've come to say how lovely it all was, not that I wanted to, but Cocky said it would be diplomatic.' Coward forgot his anger, burst into laughter, and peace was restored.

Such wifely diplomacy did not help in the longer term and no reconciliation seemed possible. After *On With The Dance* had been running some four months, rumours circulated among the cast that it was to be taken off. No-one could understand this, for it was doing excellent business and bookings extended well into the future. One day Cochran suddenly ripped out nearly everything Coward had written and put in its place new material by Ronald Jeans, an ex-stockbroker, founder of the Liverpool Repertory Theatre and now a well-known revue writer, though by no means as distinguished as Coward. The result was called *Still Dancing* and Cochran described it as a second edition of the original show. The reason was that yet another dispute between impresario and writer had created an impasse. Neither man ever referred in public to this final battle, though it was bitter enough for Cochran to gut, ruthlessly, everything associated with Coward that could be suppressed under existing contracts. His antagonist cannot have been displeased that this 'second edition' ran for only half the length of time that *On With The Dance* held the stage at the London Pavilion.

The gifted but pushy young man from Teddington was only one of the many challenges Cochran had to deal with at that moment. He had lately been appointed general manager of the Royal Albert Hall and discovered that it was by no means a good business proposition, since the type of entertainment allowed there was strictly limited by Victorian regulations. A parliamentary bill was introduced to amend these restrictions and met with strong opposition in the House of Lords. Opponents of the bill described Cochran as a 'British Barnum' who would desecrate the venerable edifice with boxing matches and performing fleas. He would, they claimed, turn it into a home for circuses and like vulgarities. The regulations were eventually changed but still left untouched the rights of people who owned some thirteen hundred seats, originally bought by their ancestors for the life of the building and permanently available to them except for ten days in the year. On big fight evenings, when tickets were at a premium, a band of seat-holders would parade the steps offering places to the highest bidder. When Cochran organized a New Year's Eve Ball and needed to cover the well with a dance floor two of them insisted nonetheless on occupying their seats. He accordingly had a piece cut out of the floor so that they were given access. On the night two little old ladies arrived and took possession of their seats, where, as in a mousehole, they sat through the evening with the shuffle of dancing feet overhead and the blare of the Charleston floating down to them.

Although Cochran was a salaried employee, a clause in his agreement allowed him to rent the hall to himself. Thus Cochran, as promoter, rented the Albert Hall from Cochran, the manager, and introduced one of his 'discoveries', the Russian scientist Lev Theremin, inventor of a radiophonic device which, if you advanced your hand toward or away from it, produced musical sounds. A fascinated audience watched Theremin as he stood before his machine and, by waving his hands in the air, conjured up the thin trembling tones of *The Song of The Volga Boatmen*. The ingenious Theremin could also bring colour out of space. In a darkened hall, he evoked with his pliant hands rays of red and green and violet which changed into the hues of the setting sun. Bernard Shaw was invited to a performance and sat dumbfounded. Gerald du Maurier, also in the audience, commented with glee: 'It is a wonderful invention – it has silenced Bernard Shaw!'

Another of Cochran's presentations at the Albert Hall was the opera *Boris Godounov* with Chaliapin as Friar Varlaam. Despite the notorious echo, long a bugbear of the place, Chaliapin thrilled a huge audience and Cochran made a profit. After the performance he took the Russian to dinner at the Savoy with Evelyn Laye and the actress Ivy St Helier. During the first half of the meal Chaliapin concentrated on Ivy St

Helier. Then, for the rest of the evening, he occuped himself with Miss Laye. 'Do you know,' he crooned at her in his ravishing deep voice, black eyes a-glitter, 'thair is von theeng that I would weesh so much to 'ave before I die?' She shook her head in flattered bewilderment. ''Ow I weesh,' he went on tenderly, 'oh, 'ow I weesh I could 'ave von leetle babee by you.' She blushed and twirled her wine-glass. Later, when she and Ivy went home together, the latter asked her what she had thought of the great man. 'Most impressive', she replied, not wishing to hurt Ivy by revealing the compliment paid her. 'I think he's damned odd. Do you know what he said to me?' asked Ivy. 'He leaned across and started all this deep-toned, deep purple stuff you know, and then he said he had one wish, and that was "to 'ave von leetle babee" by me. I nearly hit him over the head with the bread-plate.'

When invited to renew his agreement with the Albert Hall for another five years, Cochran preferred to leave: he had done what he wanted to and shown that, in spite of legalistic restrictions, the Hall could be a commercial success when properly run. In any case his attention span was brief and once he had accomplished something he was anxious for more novelty. This he found in the plays of Luigi Pirandello, then a little-known Italian playwright familiar only to scholars of the foreign drama. There was no money in Pirandello, just as there was none in the Old Vic season Cochran put on at the time, but he regarded his three week presentation at the New Oxford Theatre as a gift to intelligent English playgoers. During a reception for Pirandello, one of the guests asked Cochran to point him out to her. 'There he is,' said Cochran as Pirandello came down the stairs talking volubly. 'But surely,' enquired the astonished lady, 'he's going to shave off that nasty beard before he *sings* tomorrow?'

Another season full of prestige was devoted to the Guitrys who brought with them Sacha's new play *Mozart*. Yvonne Printemps as the twenty-year old composer dazzled the town with her elusive charm and crystalline voice, while Sacha added a witty footnote as the chaperon Baron Grimm. At the same time Cochran did not neglect lighter, more lucrative productions, such as *Blackbirds* in which Florence Mills, recorded Agate, was 'a superb artist, whether she is imitating the epileptic frenzy of a witch-dance or indulging in her native melancholy. The notes she warbles are real wood notes, and you would say that her voice is untrained. Untrained because of her astonishing facility. This singer has taken her high C and come down again while more ponderous prima-donnas are still debating the ascent.'

The London Pavilion was taken up with *Cochran's Revue of 1926*, another olla-podrida by Ronald Jeans which starred that most Parisian of entertainers, the lady known as Spinelly, and the dancer Massine whose evolutions impressed Agate as 'snatching from the air a pose which a sculptor would have frozen for all time'. The Manchester try-out was trying in a particular way for Spinelly who wilted in those dour surroundings and yearned after her native boulevards. Other veterans of Cochran revues, Douglas Byng and Ernest Thesiger, were hardier. They put up at a famous Manchester theatrical digs run by the macabre Miss Wood. Byng's father had died on the previous Friday and Miss Wood complacently declared: 'I knew it. I smelt hyacinths when I came into this room – always a sign. When are they going to bury him?' 'Next Thursday.' 'He'll never keep,' she sniffed.

Duggie Byng was now a permanent fixture at the London Pavilion. He appeared in Cochran's next production called *One Dam' Thing After Another*, a characteristic Twentyish phrase which the Poet Laureate John Masefield abbreviated to *ODTAA* as a title for one of his books. With Byng was Sonnie Hale, at first sight an unimpressive figure, slim of physique and short of stature, who wore heavy horn-rimmed glasses and looked like some dim young man just started on an obscure career in the City. Yet he was among the best revue artists of the time, a thoughtful performer who worked ceaselessly to perfect his technique as singer, dancer and actor. He was partnered by Jessie Matthews, one of Cochran's new protégées. She had been born over a butcher's shop in Berwick Market, Soho, where her father kept a stall. After a childhood of what the little Cockney girl called 'three or four in a bed, bread and scrape for supper some nights, and a swipe from Dad if we got in his way,' she took up dancing. Cochran had auditioned her for the children's troupe in *The Music Box Revue* and, interested by her big round eyes and bee-stung lips, had given her a part as a fluffy chicken popping out of a casserole to sing Irving Berlin's 'Down on the farm'. Charlot then snapped her up and despatched her to America in one of his revues. Cochran sent a cable ordering her to report at 49 Old Bond Street as soon as she returned. This she did and found him wreathed in the usual cloud of cigar smoke.

'What a hell of a flop you've been!' he greeted her.

She stared, not comprehending him. 'From what I hear,' he went on, 'you weren't worth the £18 they paid you.'

'They paid me £30.'

'That's not what I was told.'

'Are you calling me a liar?'

She threw him a furious goodbye and stamped out. An aide rushed after her. 'Miss Matthews! Come back. C.B. was only pulling your leg.'

Cochran's red face beamed at her. He offered her £60 a week rising to £100, then £150 and finally £200.

'Would I offer a contract to a flop?'

The music for *One Dam' Thing After Another* came from Richard Rodgers and Lorenz Hart. One of the big numbers was 'My Heart Stood Still', a phrase inspired by a near escape from a car accident in Paris when the two songwriters had imprudently entrusted themselves to a volatile French taxi-driver. 'My heart stood still,' said Rodgers as he recalled the unnerving experience. 'That's a song title!' exclaimed Hart, and they wrote one of their most successful hits around it. At rehearsals Cochran gave the song to Jessie Matthews and she sang the refrain, 'I took one look at you.' Cochran said: 'I like it, but we've got to have a verse.' Hart was in the stalls, hat on the back of his head, ever-present cigar jutting from his mouth. 'You wanna verse? he asked, scampering up to the stage. He leaned against the proscenium and scribbled on a bit of paper. 'How do you like this, babe?' The babe liked it, so did Cochran, and in the '7th Dam Thing' she sang it to her partner Sonnie Hale with whom, off-stage, she was already in love.

Another fresh new talent was the youthful Max Wall who

pranced his way eccentrically through a bit of nonsense entitled 'Make Hey! Hey! While the Moon Shines.' Among the chorus of Mr Cochran's Young Ladies who danced with him was Anna Neagle. She had already performed in Cochran's shows at the Trocadero, things like *Merry-Go-Round* and *Champagne Time*, and after three years in the chorus longed for bigger rôles. Cochran, however, saw her only as a chorus girl, one of his best girls in fact, but wondered if she was really suited for the stage. Would she not be happier, he once asked her gently, if she gave it all up, married and raised a family? The richness of talent in *One Dam' Thing After Another* extended even to the orchestra, where the pianist was the amiable Leslie A. Hutchinson. He had come from his native Grenada with the aim of reading law, but changed his mind and, as 'Hutch', sang in a deep chocolate-brown voice to his own accompaniment. On the piano lid there reposed, inevitably, a large silk handkerchief with which he mopped his brow at emotional moments. Among the many charms of his act was the amused affectation he put into this flamboyant gesture. In Paris, where he had studied to become a concert pianist, he made the acquaintance of Cole Porter who doted on men of colour and took an attentive interest in this very handsome young man. The result was that Hutch won the song-writer's approval of his interpretations, especially 'Let's Do It', and sang with unique authority. He was an expansive personality who loved life, especially riotous parties. In Manchester, after a very late dress-rehearsal of *One Dam' Thing After Another*, he threw a splendid affair at the Midland Hotel which continued until the very late hours of the morning. One of the Young Ladies went to give Cochran a goodnight kiss and returned with a note from him which read: 'Ladies and gentlemen, please remember we open this evening.'

Cochran's mistress of the month was dancing among the Young Ladies, a dark-eyed smouldering beauty, and next to her was a young girl called Lily Shiel. *One Dam' Thing After Another* had been running for several weeks when Lily received from Cochran a letter praising her work and enclosing a cheque for ten pounds. Eager for the stardom which he predicted would be hers, she went to see him in his office. He promised her a bigger part in his next revue and came out from behind his desk.

Putting both hands on her shoulders, he kissed her cheek lightly.

'Perhaps we can discuss this tomorrow at lunch?' he suggested. Then, standing back, he looked her up and down. 'You're a very pretty girl, I think you'll go far.'

There was lunch at the Berkeley and cosy suppers. Lily played her captive adroitly, allowing him to go no further than kisses and working hard to keep his interest, while at the same time emphasizing that she was a pure young girl who lived chastely with her family. Unknown to him she already had a husband, a man considerably older than herself. She and this husband took a holiday after the revue came off and went to Torquay. A telegram arrived from Cochran announcing that he needed a rest too and would join her for a few days. She answered to say that office hours were from nine to six. No reply came. Back in London she asked Cochran why he had not joined her. 'I didn't like those office hours,' he said austerely. There were no more intimacies, no more tête-à-tête meals together, no more stolen kisses in taxis. Later on Miss Shiel changed her name to Sheila Graham, left the stage, became the consort of Scott Fitzgerald and launched out on her final metamorphosis as a Hollywood gossip-writer.

One Dam' Thing After Another made big profits. None of them went to Cochran. At the time he was heavily involved in boxing, and to raise finance for a big championship match he had been obliged to mortgage his interest in the revue. His backer took all the money and he was left with nothing. He did, however, make something out of it eventually, in an episode which illustrates both the unpredictability of the theatre and the complicated business arrangements which hid behind the legend 'Charles B. Cochran presents'. A few years later the producer of a New York show wanted to use 'My Heart Stood Still'. By reason of certain contractual rights in the song, Cochran received a windfall of two thousand pounds for giving his permission.

He hoped to do better with his next revue, which he had commissioned from Noël Coward. Despite their quarrels, nothing had altered his belief in Coward's talent. Both men needed each other. They were like the partners in an uneasy marriage who are constantly warring but who do not take the final step of separation because they know it is in their best interests to keep together. Nearly three years after *On With The Dance*, time for Coward's resentment to die down, Cochran lured him with the unambiguous offer to write single-handedly a new show for him. This time there would be no misunderstanding about credits or royalties, Cochran assured him. Before work began, Coward had suffered two humiliating flops with *Home Chat* and *Sirocco*, the latter so sensational that it became a byword in the theatre for the worst type of failure. After a run of golden success, Coward's luck seemed to have given out and he even thought of leaving the country. In a first hysterical reaction he begged Cochran to release him from the contract: whatever he did, he pleaded, was bound to fail, the public no longer wanted him and it wouldn't be fair to Cochran. The impresario soothed him with kindly words. In a few weeks, he said, the hubbub over *Sirocco* would be forgotten. In any case, he had engaged Coward to write the revue because he was the best possible man to do it. Overcome with gratitude for Cochran's benevolence and his unimpaired faith in him, Coward began work again. Cochran was genuinely confident but also realized that, with his recent disasters in mind, Coward would be more malleable, at least for the time being, and that this gave him a valuable negotiating lever. It was a unique opportunity to act both shrewdly and humanely.

As Coward left 49, Old Bond Street, the words and music of 'Dance, little lady' were already humming through his brain, so thoroughly had Cochran restored his self-esteem. What were they to call the revue? All the best revue titles had been used, and hours of brainstorming produced nothing worthwhile. Then someone proposed *This Year of Grace*. It was, thought Coward, one of the best titles he had ever heard. Cochran was anxious to feature a new discovery he had made while in Germany to see Max Reinhardt's production of *A Midsummer Night's Dream*. In this, Ottilie Ethel Losch, known as Tilly, danced the part of the First Fairy, and an audition afterwards convinced him that she had rare talent. She made her first appearance when aged seven at the Vienna Opera House, where she evolved into première danseuse. To London she came, now twenty-one years old and in the prime of her beauty with small piquant features, exotic eyes and a perfectly shaped mouth. She danced well enough, but her special gift was for arm and hand movements, and she executed her *ports de bras* with a supple grace that hypnotized her audience. When she auditioned for Cochran, she gave him the outline of a speciality dance which he put into *This Year of Grace*. She and her partner were posed in a Gothic arch subtly lit to give them the appearance of a stained-glass window. As Bach's Air on a G String floated up from the orchestra Tilly danced slowly around moving her arms and hands in exquisite gestures. 'Gothic', as the number was called, inspired an early disagreement and Coward begged for it to be dropped, since he thought it would slow up the pace. Cochran refused and it became one of the most popular items in the revue. How versatile Mr Coward must be, said an innocent admirer, to have written not only all the other music for the show but also the lovely piece that accompanied Tilly's dance.

Of the music Coward did write for *This Year of Grace*, 'Dance, Little Lady' and 'A Room With A View' were the two most popular items. The frenetic rhythms of 'Dance Little Lady' were performed by Sonnie Hale and Lauri Devine wearing masks which reproduced the vacuous expressions to be seen in night-clubs and restaurants where, as Cochran wrote, sounding a high moral tone, 'empty-looking youths danced with empty-looking girls in an empty shuffle.' One evening at Ernest Thesiger's home he saw a number of decorative masks his host had bought at a recent exhibition by a twenty-two year old artist called Oliver Messel. He was intrigued by their exoticism and beauty and had commissioned others for *Cochran's Revue of 1926*. Messel was a product of Eton and the son of a family connected with banking and stockbroking for generations, although an artistic leaven was supplied by his maternal grandfather Edward Linley Sambourne, *Punch* artist and illustrator. Handsome, vivacious, Oliver Messel combined the manner of what used to be called high society with an outstanding talent for design. Although in later years he became the uncle of Lord Snowdon and so a fringe Royal figure of interest to the tabloid newspapers, he will best be remembered as one of the outstanding theatrical designers in his day. The sinister masks he devised for 'Dance, Little Lady' were a cunning synthesis of the exotic styles he absorbed and made his own, among them negro art: he had, like Cole Porter, a weakness for black men.

Jessie Matthews sang 'A Room With A View' to Sonnie Hale as they gazed romantically through a window. The title, brazenly stolen from E. M. Forster's novel, had formed in Coward's mind while convalescing from a nervous breakdown on a Honolulu beach. Romance turns into Barrie-like whimsy at the last couplet:

'Maybe a stork will bring, this that and t'other thing to
'Our room with a view.'

In the New York production of *This Year of Grace* Coward himself sang it, much to the disgust of his friend the critic Alexander Woollcott, who opened a newspaper, in the company of Harpo Marx, and ostentatiously read it when the disgusting lines were reached. Coward giggled, then rallied and cooed the rest of it in baby-talk which sent an exasperated Woolcott storming out of his box. More characteristic of the wit audiences expected from him was the trio of sketches entitled 'Rules of Three'. Each of them parodied a well-known dramatist on the theme of the eternal triangle. The Barrie sketch opened with Jeannie darning socks and musing: 'Ah me – I often wonder if all the little pink toes of all the little pink babies in the world were counted, how many there would be.' Another was a French farce in which Jeanne pairs up with her lover Jacques while Jean her husband goes to bed with the maid. The deadliest of the sketches was the Lonsdale number in its mixture of snobbery and insulting wit. 'Kiss me like you did last Wednesday in the Royal Enclosure at Ascot,' murmurs the wife to her lover. 'Dear James,' she says, 'you're drunk – you must have been lunching with your mother.' The lover asks the butler if he likes his job. 'Very much, your Grace,' he replies. 'We are the only class left with any manners.' And when the husband makes his entrance, to be told by his wife that 'I love Jimmie, you know,' he answers: 'Of course I know – everybody knows. It makes a damned good story. I've been dining out on it for weeks.' Which leads one to think that, as some suspect Bacon of writing Shakespeare's plays, it may have been Coward all along who was writing Lonsdale's.

This Year of Grace opened in the Spring of 1928 and ran for over three hundred performances, bringing Coward his just reward of a thousand pounds a week in royalties. Tilly Losch emerged as Cochran's brightest star of the moment. Back-stage and in private life she was fiery and impulsive. Jessie Matthews shared one of the London Pavilion's tiny dressing-rooms with her and walked in sporting a new tweed suit of which she was very proud. There sat Tilly wearing an exact replica of it. 'Snap!' trilled Jessie, flattered to think that her taste was as good as that of the continental celebrity. Tilly stiffened. 'How dare you wear my suit!' she screamed and slapped Jessie's face.

Tilly's exuberant personality fascinated Cochran and he soon fell very deeply in love with her. Everyone knew of the affair and much speculation was devoted to the absorbing topic of whether they actually went to bed with each other. What is clear beyond a doubt is that Tilly owed her success entirely to her professional gifts and not to her skills in seduction. Evelyn Cochran watched resignedly as the affair went through its usual stages, the favours, the presents, the intimate suppers. Her husband and Tilly even had a party piece which they danced on social occasions, a polka where Tilly led Cochran, despite his arthritic hip, through a series of comical gyrations. Once, invited to perform at a reception, they were reluctant despite strong pleas from the guests. Evelyn walked over to him, smiled and said: 'Charles, dear, would you do your little dance if I went into a nursing home for the night?'

Tilly appeared in several other Cochran productions before slipping out of his orbit and leaving him with a regret he found hard to overcome. She married, first, Edward James, million-aire and would-be poet who was often thought, wrongly, to be an illegitimate son of King Edward VII, a frequent visitor at his mother's home.* He bought up Surrealist pictures when they

---

* He was, in fact, the grandson of Edward VII who had once tumbled Mrs James's mother in the hay. When James playfully added a beard to a photograph of his mother she looked 'the image of George V.'

were cheap and spent lavishly on founding a ballet company for Tilly. With Adolf Hitler he shared a passion for architectural follies and devoted his last years to building a fantastic city in the heart of the Mexican jungle, though this was long after his brief marriage to Tilly. Her second husband, by contrast to James who did not really like women and who, indeed, one memorable night had had carnal knowledge of Salvador Dali, was that rabid heterosexual the then Earl of Caernarvon. This marriage, too, soon ended in a divorce which, among other things, was doubtless encouraged by his lordship's custom of hammering impatiently on the bedroom door with his erect penis.

When *This Year of Grace* departed from the London Pavilion for its inevitable run on Broadway, Cochran filled the vacancy with a new production called *Wake Up and Dream*. Oliver Messel designed for him again, most notably the outfit worn by Tilly Losch as the Manchu Marchioness which, though it had the sheen of porcelain and folds as of silk, was made of thin rubber painted with delicate motifs. For the ballet dancers, who included Anna Neagle, he created futuristic dresses in white and silver. Another promising young designer whom Cochran engaged was Rex Whistler, then, like Messel, a handsome twenty-two year old. His mural decoration at the Tate Gallery had just been completed and won him early fame. One of the backdrops he painted in *Wake Up and Dream* earned applause on its own merit and provided a witty setting for Sonnie Hale's irreverent impersonation of Sir Thomas Beecham.

The music was by Cole Porter who put up at the Savoy Hotel, small, dark-eyed, nervous. 'I don't know whether you'll like what I've written,' he apologized, rubbing his thin hands together with anxiety. He went to the piano and played 'What is This Thing Called Love?' In the show this was performed by Elsie Carlisle, then a well-known radio singer and now the object of a small but faithful cult inspired by reissues of her gramophone records. Hutch accompanied her, having been promoted from orchestra pit to stage. Very soon he was to enjoy a celebrity in the West End that lasted over forty years. 'Let's Do It' was given to Sonnie Hale and Jessie Matthews –

'The nightingales in the dark do it,

'Larks, crazy for a lark, do it,
'Let's do it, let's fall in love . . .'

and since, off-stage and on, they were both doing it, Sonnie Hale not long afterwards divorced his then wife Evelyn Laye and married Jessie. Evelyn Laye was not only a star of Cochran's but also his personal friend and there were difficult situations as a result. With its brilliant Cole Porter score, *Wake Up and Dream* was a great financial success, and when Cochran sent it to Broadway he prudently, for appearances' sake, cast Jack Buchanan as Jessie's partner instead of Sonnie Hale. At the first night in New York Cochran came into her dressing-room and found her racked by emotional stress as well as professional nerves. He murmured the usual encouraging endearments, told her how hard she'd worked, how pleased he was with her, what a great triumph was in store for her. In her confusion she made a late entry and spoilt the opening scene. She came off to see Cochran in a rare public display of anger. His face purple with rage, he shouted: 'I take back everything. You've ruined the show. I take back every bloody word I said to you.' Then, just as abruptly, he regained control of himself. Everybody made mistakes, he said, and he was sure the rest of the evening would be perfect. It was.

Returned to London he began preparations for a new Coward show which was quite different from all that had gone before. Hearing by chance a new gramophone record of *Die Fledermaus*, Coward had thought of an idea for the operetta he recently toyed with writing. Visions of uniforms and crinolines and chandeliers floated into his mind. A plot was soon evolved and a first act roughed out. He showed it to Cochran whose flair for visualizing a complete play on the strength of the merest outline helped him decide on the spot to accept it. The new piece was to be called *Bitter Sweet*, a title eventually suggested by the actor Alfred Lunt.

Coward had been brought up, like his friend and contemporary Ivor Novello, on Gilbert and Sullivan operettas where memorable tunes accompanied rhymes and metres which clicked into place with satisfying precision. The simple but haunting melodies of *The Arcadians*, *The Quaker Girl* and *The Maid of The Mountains* had been a part of his youth. To these home-grown products Edwardian musical comedy added such glamorous imports as *The Merry Widow* and its lovely waltz, Ruritanian romances and splendid finales in which every dilemma was resolved with luscious concerted numbers. The music was always craftsmanlike and the words delightfully literate. Then, in the nineteen-twenties, American musicals built up their domination of the stage and only Ivor Novello, in the thirties, was left to carry on the tradition. Was it not time, Coward reasoned, to bring back something of the fragrant charm which had evaporated during the 1914–18 war?

He began with an opening scene in modern times when an ageing marchioness sees two young people falling in love, is distressed by their shallow, unromantic behaviour, and tells her own story in order to show them that real life is a matter of deeper emotions. The play then goes back to nineteenth-century Vienna and the ageing lady is shown as a beautiful young singer loved by a daring Austrian whom she marries but loses when he is killed in a duel by a bullying captain. When Cochran told his stage director Frank Collins of the plot, the latter reacted with typical pessimism. He predicted failure, as he had with *The Better 'Ole*. Why? 'It has no comedy,' he complained, 'and the hero is killed at the end of the second act.'

The flashback was a device which gave Coward an excuse to air his nostalgia for the atmosphere of Edwardian musical comedy. The rousing number 'Tokay' paid homage to the robust marches that, as in *Chu Chin Chow*, have always been a feature of the genre. 'Zigeuner' was a sympathetic pastiche of all the 'gypsy' ballads ever heard on stage at Daly's. 'If Love Were All' had the power of genuine sentiment, pure and undefiled, in a descending motif that wheedled and caressed irresistibly. Other numbers gave a hint of Coward the revue writer, among them a 'green carnation' quartet satirising aestheticism as *Patience* had done, but generally the tone was one of romantic sincerity, a mood summed up in the most famous song of all, 'I'll See You Again'. Never having suffered the faintest hint of tuition in composing, Coward evolved his music at the piano, usually in the key of E flat, the one he found easiest to play, preferring it, oddly enough, to C major which one would think to be simpler because it has no black notes.

The elaborate score was dictated to Elsie April, who 'soled and heeled' it with professional expertise in a way that preserved its unique inspiration. Coward, in gratitude, dedicated *Bitter Sweet* to her. He sang it with her accompaniment for Cochran's benefit. 'If we can put this on the stage us I visualize it,' Cochran jubilated, 'it cannot fail.' Later that day his manager at the London Pavilion remarked that he seemed in very good spirits. 'I've got an old-age pension,' Cochran told him. 'Coward's operetta is a gem, with a great title.'

Before it reached the stage, however, they needed a cast. On a talent-hunting expedition in New York they allowed themselves a little off-duty treat by going to see Mae West in *Diamond Lil* which she had written herself. Afterwards, in her dressing room, Coward politely inquired if she had anything else on the stocks. 'Sure, I'm writing a new play,' she beamed. What, said he, was the plot about? 'Well, you see,' she went on, 'it's about this guy. He's a cock-sucker and . . .' Cochran, always an observer, at least in public, of the conventions, turned puce and ended the meeting with a violent fit of coughing. Coward was disappointed: he had never, he observed later, 'heard a plot begin with so much promise.'

On another trip, this time in Vienna where they hoped to find the leading man of *Bitter Sweet*, they were informed of a very suitable tenor, young and handsome. His name, alas, was Hans Unterfucker. Cochran again coloured up with embarrassment, though in the end he was reduced to laughter when Coward argued that, however the name might be pronounced in German, he longed to see it on every hoarding in London and on every bus.

When they came home they decided to engage George Metaxa, the Rumanian actor and singer who, if not sitting on their doorstep all along, was currently appearing in *Wake Up and Dream*. He was thirty years old then, having begun his career as an unlikely chef de cabinet to the Rumanian Ministry of Agriculture and then switched to the English theatre where he specialized in playing exotic Russian noblemen. With three marriages behind him already, it was obvious that experience qualified him as a romantic hero, to play opposite the American actress Peggy Wood who, in Coward's words, 'could sing beautifully, look lovely and act well.' Ivy St Helier played Manon, the cabaret singer, a small part but a very desirable one, since her three songs included the wistful 'If Love Were All'. The villainous Captain was Austin Trevor, an excellent actor always 'in work', as the profession has it, yet so good, so reliable at turning a dull rôle into something worthwhile, that everyone took him for granted and he never received the credit he deserved. Other, more unexpected names in the cast were Robert Newton and the Swiss Hugues Cuénod, better known today as an opera singer and exponent of the French *mélodie*.

Throughout the preparations for their latest venture Cochran had tactfully given Coward a free hand. Although Tilly Losch devised the choreography and Ernst Stern contributed scenic ideas, Coward and his retinue were allowed to do things in their own way. This time, Cochran resolved, there would be no disagreements, and the programmes announced 'The Entire Production by Noël Coward'. He only appeared at the last run-through before the dress rehearsal, when the cast played in their everyday clothes and Elsie April accompanied at the piano. That performance, thought Coward long afterwards, was the most exciting he ever saw of *Bitter Sweet*. At the end of it Cochran thanked them in tones husky and emotional and added that he would not part with his rights in the play for a million pounds.

The Manchester try-out was ecstatic, the London opening at His Majesty's less so. Cochran overheard disobliging remarks from other first-nighters. 'Nothing much in that,' said one. 'Girls aren't up to Cochran's standards,' said another. 'I wonder when Coward's going to give us some funny lines,' interposed a third. The audience had come expecting revue-type wit and satire. They were confronted, instead, with romance. At the end the reception was fair. Both impresario and author had agreed in advance that no matter how many calls were heard neither of them would go on stage to take a bow. This did not prevent them from encouraging the applause. While Coward and friends up in the dome of His Majesty's clapped and shouted 'Author!', Cochran at the back of the circle cheered and cried out 'Cochran!'

The first two weeks of *Bitter Sweet* were difficult and Cochran had to nurse the show with care. He did so because he had complete faith in the production, a faith which Coward acknowledged with gratitude for his enthusiasm, generosity and trust. Then *Bitter Sweet* picked up and ran for nearly seven hundred performances, a record Coward only surpassed later with *Blithe Spirit* and its tally of close on two thousand. Bearing in mind Frank Collins's pessimistic forecast, Cochran agreed that *Bitter Sweet* defied 'all the accepted conventions of the musical play. According to the rules of the theatre it should have failed – but I always contend there are no rules,' he said. Another contention it bore out was a favourite one of James Agate, who held that the difference between the professional and the amateur is that the professional can do his job when he doesn't feel like it and the amateur can't do it when he does feel like it. Had not Coward written the charming second act while convalescing from an operation for piles and while being obliged to explain every painful detail to Marie Tempest, an inquisitive visitor at his bedside?

ii
THE COWARD YEARS – AND O'CASEY

'I think there is a lot of the artist in C.B. – more than there is in some or most of those who prate Art, and dress up once or twice a year in Burkian costumes for a Fancy Ball.'

SEAN O'CASEY

The late nineteen-twenties and the early thirties were, famously, the Coward years. During that time Cochran promoted and displayed to glittering advantage every aspect of Coward's talent as actor, director, composer, lyricist and playwright. Despite the frequent squabbles and disagreements that inevitably arose between two such obstinate personalities, a mutual artistic rapport kept them together. Coward knew that Cochran was the only man to whom he could outline an idea and be sure that it would instantly be grasped and taken up, its potential exploited and its realization assured. Like a successful newspaper editor or publisher, Cochran had an intuitive gift for generating projects and being able instantly to appreciate those suggested by others. What is more, he knew how to put them into action. Before his association with Coward ended, it had produced revues, an operetta, a musical comedy, a play and a spectacle which became part of theatrical history.

Yet although more and more room had to be made at 49, Old Bond Street for the bulging files of contracts, agreements and correspondence relating to the Coward shows, Cochran's activity in other spheres remained irrepressibly buoyant. In 1929 alone, the year of *Bitter Sweet*, he initiated seven other major productions. Among them were the revue *Wake Up and Dream*, Du Bose and Dorothy Heyward's play *Porgy*, another lavish Guitry season, the New York Theatre Guild's *Caprice* with Alfred Lunt and Lynn Fontanne, and three straight plays. The latter included Sean O'Casey's *The Silver Tassie*, which represented one of Cochran's famous *succès d'estime*, or, in more brutal terms, a noble artistic venture which turned out to be a box-office flop.

The production came about through a curious chance. Eileen O'Casey, the dramatist's wife, an actress just returned from an American engagement, had an interview with Cochran about a possible job. At first he thought of putting her into one of his cabarets at the Trocadero. He decided against it because her husband was much older than her and, Cochran added thoughtfully, 'You'd be out very late each night, and your husband is too nice a man for you to leave all that time. You sing very well; why don't you audition for *Bitter Sweet?*' She did and was accepted in the part of Jane, one of the girlfriends. Later, pleased with her work, he gave her another small part in *Helen!* Meanwhile she told him about her husband's new play, *The Silver Tassie*.

This, it appeared, had been submitted to the Abbey Theatre, home of O'Casey's great triumphs, and met with humiliating rejection. The anti-war theme, the symbolism and the elaborate stage effects required so daunted W. B. Yeats that he turned down this offering by the Abbey's greatest playwright. Cochran restored O'Casey's shattered hopes by asking for a copy of the script. As soon as he read it he decided to produce the play. One reason for his enthusiasm was the recent success of *Journey's End* which had a war-time setting. Most of all, however, he relished the chance of staging the work of a writer whom he considered to be Ireland's finest dramatist. As director he engaged Raymond Massey, and as designer he had the inspiration of commissioning Augustus John. At first John modestly argued that he knew nothing of the theatre and was unsuitable. Cochran badgered him politely, used all his persuasive skill and in the end got from him a setting of the important middle act which he considered to be 'a masterpiece of theatrical design'. It was typical of Cochran that, in his delicate handling of the artist, he employed as an emissary the young Eileen O'Casey to whose charms John was not unresponsive.

He was tactful, too, in his negotiations with O'Casey, who, still wounded by the Abbey rejection, was impressed by Cochran's determination to risk five thousand pounds of his own on the production. 'I have been agreeably astonished in Cochran's knowledge of art and Drama,' wrote O'Casey, who, like many people, associated Cochran more easily with revues. 'He has produced himself a scene called "Dance, little lady, Dance" in his latest revue, which is a marvel of Expressionism. And he has some lovely pictures by Cézanne, Renoir, Van Gogh, Degas and John.' Writing to a friend, he mentioned the Coward revues and added, with good-natured envy, '. . . so you see my boy GENIUS and ART sometimes have a reward greater than a cup of cold water.' O'Casey even, at one point, concocted a revue sketch himself under the influence of what, for him, was a new and strange department of the theatre. Cochran tried hard to place it on his behalf but apparently did not succeed.

The cast included Barry Fitzgerald, that excellent Abbey actor who the following year played comic rôles in *Cochran's 1930 Revue* and then emigrated to Hollywood where he gained a comfortable living but small artistic prestige as a 'loveable' Irish card in saccharine musicals. One of the understudies was a youthful Emlyn Williams deputizing for small parts and walking on 'as required', one minute a stretcher bearer and the next a tango dancer. Hours were spent rehearsing Catholic chants to be intoned off-stage during the trench scene of the second act. All the while the star of the play, Charles Laughton, as a maimed soldier crouched in his wheelchair, gargled away at perfecting his Irish accent. 'Will oi ever get it roight, damn an' blast,' he moaned. Suddenly laughter overcame him when he remembered a Dublin production of some oriental play in which a hooded figure turned to his neighbour and said: 'Methinks the wind of Allah boiteth mighty cold in the bazaar tonoight.'

Intense, cloudy with mysticism, full of rage at the waste of war, *The Silver Tassie* opened to empty seats and a short run. 'Puzzling', observed the *Daily Telegraph* cautiously. A 'great stumbling failure' boomed *The Times*. In the controversy that followed there were those who described Cochran as a saint for producing the play and others who thought he should be burned at the stake. One of his strongest supporters was Bernard Shaw who thought it 'a magnificent play' and told Cochran 'it was a magnificent gesture of yours to produce it. The Highbrows *should* have produced it; you, the Unpretentious Showman, DID, as you have done so many other noble and rash things on your Sundays. This, I think, will rank as the best of them . . . Bravo!'

A bravo from Bernard Shaw gave more delight to Cochran than the profits he failed to make from *The Silver Tassie*. In fact, he lost all the money he put into the play and took his reward from the pleasure of artistic achievement. In any case *Bitter Sweet* was now launched on a very profitable Broadway run and helped to subsidize his more experimental productions. In addition Coward had given him another play called *Private Lives* which he wrote in a matter of four days or so while suffering a bout of influenza at a Shanghai hotel. Neither the playwright nor his friends ever invested their own money in his plays, but on this occasion, so convinced were they of success, Coward and his leading lady, Gertrude Lawrence, each provided a third of the finance. The remaining third was suppled by Cochran. With a cast of only four characters and minimal settings, *Private Lives* was one of Cochran's most economical productions and had retrieved all expenses and even made a profit during its brief pre-London tour. Coward was triply blessed, since as leading actor he drew a large salary, as dramatist a handsome royalty, and as backer a third share of the profits.

Private Lives was the opening production at the Phoenix, a theatre newly built by Sydney Bernstein, presumably as a diversion from his more usual habit of constructing monster cinemas, or 'picture houses' as *The Times* used to call them within living memory. The designers included famous names like Gilbert Scott and Bertie Crewe, and artistic matters were supervised by Komisarjevsky who presumably was responsible for the copies of Titian and Giorgione which decorated the walls and for the safety curtain which reproduced an allegorical fancy by Jacopo del Sellaio. Bernstein asked Shaw to perform the opening ceremony but the latter was engaged elsewhere. Gordon Craig was approached. He tartly replied that since no-one ever asked him to work in a London theatre he could see no reason why he should open one. In despair Bernstein turned to Cochran who good-naturedly stepped into the breach. On the 7 September, 1930, while drenching rain swept along the Charing Cross Road and passers-by in buses looked out and giggled at him, Cochran, feeling rather a fool, water cascading from his bowler brim, pulled a string to reveal the Italianate façade. Trumpets blared and cinema cameras recorded his inaugural speech. Mr Gordon Craig, said Cochran, had declared that nobody would allow him to produce in an English theatre. 'I am going to rob him of that excuse,' Cochran went on. Mr Craig was publicly invited to produce for him whatever play he liked and with whatever company he chose. The small crowd of water-sodden spectators raised a damp cheer.

For many years Cochran had been trying to snare Craig, ever since the eighteen-nineties when, as penniless young men, they used to meet their friend the artist James Pryde in a famous Strand bun shop, hoping that one or other of them might be in funds. Craig replied to the Phoenix challenge by emerging from his Italian reclusion. They met and Craig asserted that the stage of the Phoenix was too small for his grandiose ideas. Cochran offered him the Albert Hall, Olympia, any building at all, for Craig's name assured unlimited backing. Other meetings followed. The Cochrans now lived near Marble Arch in a Montagu Street house off the verdant gardens of Montagu

Square, and here they invited Craig to lunch with Max Beerbohm as another guest. The conversation was enchanting.
Craig spoke magniloquently of his beautiful visions and thrilled
them with his dream of cloud-capped spectacle. Cochran,
judging that the iron was hot, proposed *The Fairy Queen* with
Purcell's music. Craig looked doubtful. Then what about some
Shakespeare? Or *The Masque of Comus?* Craig did not respond.
Soon afterwards a letter arrived by hand containing an ex-
quisite Craig woodcut in homage to Evelyn. The bird had flown
back to Rapallo, perhaps because his bluff was called, and
Cochran never had the privilege of working with the elusive
Craig.

At least, however, he knew he could rely on *Private Lives*,
although he was disappointed at Coward's wish to play it for no
more than three months when it could have gone on well into
1932 or even 1933. Long runs bored Coward, as they do many
actors, and the privileged position he had won enabled him to
indulge his whims. The short West End run gave a fleeting
glimpse of perfection, with an ideal cast of the author, Laurence
Olivier, Adrienne Allen (Mrs Raymond Massey) and Gertrude
Lawrence. Coward had sent the script to Gertrude Lawrence,
then in New York, and received a telegram: 'Your play is
delightful and there's nothing that can't be fixed.' Annoyed by
what he took for haughtiness, he riposted: 'The only thing to be
fixed will be your performance.' He later realized she was
simply referring to contractual difficulties, and yet another
squall in their temperamental relationship blew over. He wrote
of her, very perceptively: 'On the stage she is potentially
capable of anything and everything. She can be gay, sad, witty,
tragic, funny and touching. She can play a scene one night with
perfect subtlety and restraint, and the next with such obvious-
ness and over-emphasis that your senses reel. She has, in
abundance, every theatrical essential but one: critical faculty.'
Everything he had in mind when he conceived the idea for her
rôle came to life on stage, the wit, the romance, the swift
changes of mood and the rapid delivery. Olivier, thought
Coward, gave his rather 'wooden' rôle a plausible reality. He
also learned to curb his tendency to giggle. Throughout the run
Coward, straight-faced, teased him with many surreptitious

jokes. By the end Olivier was giving as good as he got. One of his lines ran: 'A friend of mine has a house on the edge of Cap Ferrat.' In an unexpected ad lib Coward asked: 'On the *edge*?' 'Yes,' replied Olivier, 'on the *very* edge,' looking him in the eye without a glimmer of amusement. He earned a big laugh on this and the line, slightly adapted, was incorporated into the play.

Like other plays which are excellent theatre if well acted, *Private Lives* reads badly. The dialogue seems thin and the lines bare. Yet when spoken by competent actors the phrases glow into life. One is reminded of the comment by T. E. Lawrence, who at the time was an unlikely pen-friend of Coward, that he had read through the script in an attempt to strike out redundant words and could find none. The serious theme which underlies the plot and the exquisite symmetry of the construction invite agreement with Sheridan Morley's opinion that this is the best of Coward's plays. Cochran would not have dissented, and his only grievance about *Private Lives* was Coward's objection to long runs which cut short its triumph both in London and in New York. He badly needed success at the moment. As managing director of the Palace Theatre, he had booked the Marx Brothers in the hope that their film reputation would attract big audiences. It did not, for the rapid wisecracks that amused cinemagoers failed to work on an English stage. At the London Pavilion *Cochran's 1931 Revue* was foundering abysmally. Coward helped him out with two new songs, 'Any Little Fish' and 'Half Caste Woman', and there were also music by Irving Berlin and dances staged by Balanchine, not to mention the début as song-and-dance man of John Mills. The revue flopped and closed within a fortnight. Did Coward have anything up his sleeve that might restore Cochran's fortunes?

Coward did, and since their collaboration was to last until 1934 it would be convenient to trace its development over the next few years before the inevitable break came. The history of *Cavalcade* is too familiar for repetition here. Everyone knows how Coward, inspired by the revolving stage Cochran had installed at the Adelphi, envisaged a spectacular production about the fall of the Roman Empire, the French Revolution or the Second Empire; how he had browsed through bound volumes of *The Illustrated London News* and formed a picture of a troopship leaving for the Boer War; and how he hit on the idea of a pageant telling the story of an English family through the years from Mafeking up to 1930. He spoke of it to Cochran who, with his customary knack, visualized the whole thing in a flash. The Adelphi was too small and the Coliseum was not available. It would have to be Drury Lane, both for capacity and money taking.

There were twenty-three scenes and six hydraulic lifts to be operated together with mobile footlights that gave Frank Collins and his technicians many an anxious hour. Cochran spent over thirty thousand pounds on new equipment, scenery, costumes and the various structural alterations that were needed to accommodate the biggest production London had seen for many years. More than twelve hundred actors and actresses came to auditions for a cast which demanded forty-three speaking parts and two hundred silent rôles. As, day by day in the bleak auditorium, Coward interviewed the stream of hopeful out-of-work bit players desperate for their thirty shillings a week, he became more and more depressed by the wretchedness, the smell of failure and the humiliated pride of ageing lives. It annoyed him when Cochran sent along three well-dressed girls to whom he had airily promised rôles on the strength of their society background. No, Coward objected, they were not the sort he wanted. Cochran persisted. A long argument ensued. At last Coward agreed, adding the proviso that he should engage for each of them two more from along those who desperately needed the work.

During rehearsals Cochran fell ill and was kept away from the theatre for long periods. This was just as well because his absence limited opportunities for disagreement. Coward on his own soon developed a gift for marshalling the large crowds who appeared in tableaux representing the departure of the troopship, a ball, a seaside resort, Victoria station with a puffing railway engine, and Armistice Night. One scene in particular gave immense trouble, a sort of kaleidoscope where various groups were spotlit rising and falling on the hydraulic lifts so that a chaos of dancers, radio announcers, evangelists, wounded soldiers and others flashed briefly over the stage. On this occasion Cochran was present. Wearied by constant lighting failures and the difficulty of synchronizing the lifts, Coward decided to cut the scene. It was unnecessary, he claimed, and a small transposition was all he needed to justify dropping it. No, said Cochran, the scene was good when he originally planned it, and even if they had to rehearse it for one, two, three or even more days, the thing would come right. Coward finally gave way and the episode remained, an essential prelude, Cochran believed, to the patriotic finale. After which, exhausted as much by his argumentative collaborator as by his illness, he retreated to a nursing-home and underwent what he described as 'a slight operation'.

Before the curtain rose on the first night of *Cavalcade*, stage-hands picked their way over ramps and underneath platforms that reared up into the flies. Rostra littered the stage, red danger signs abounded and guide ropes dangled everywhere to help the cast find their way in black-outs. That first night, said Coward later, was 'the most agonizing three hours I have ever spent in the theatre.' At first all went well and Cochran sat beaming in his seat, without a hint of the anxiety that filled his mind, the fear that at any moment the elaborate machinery could go wrong. The troopship appeared, the tableau was applauded and nostalgic music hall tunes drifted through the auditorium. The next scene involved complicated manoeuvres by several hydraulic lifts while two huge side-wings rolled into place. The move was timed to last thirty seconds as brief interval music played. The orchestra finished a waltz and, no sign of readiness being given, started again. They played it right through, and over and over. The audience became restless. Cochran stared ahead and kept a poker face. A frantic message came from backstage: one of the lifts was stuck and would take two hours to repair. The orchestra bravely repeated the waltz and the gallery started to clap derisively. As Coward prepared to announce disaster, the lift shuddered into action and, after an eternity of four minutes or so, *Cavalcade* went on to its triumphant finale. From his box Cochran urged the reluctant author to take a bow. Coward stumbled into the light, spoke emotionally and ended with the remark 'It's pretty exciting to be English.' Already much moved by the patriotic finale, the audience cheered him wildly. Only a short time ago the public had regarded him as a decadent, a bounder who lolled around in a dressing gown smoking cigarettes through an outrageous holder and who dabbled in drugs. Suddenly he had become a jingoist as crusty as any Colonel Blimp. It was an image that discomfited him as much as his supposed decadence had.

Cavalcade was the most sensational of the Cochran-Coward projects and ran for over four hundred performances. The massive resources and huge cast it involved would make a commercial revival impossible today, although it was recently produced for the first time since 1931 and, with the aid of amateur crowds, made a strong theatrical effect. At the time *Cavalcade* impressed other showmen anxious to combat the rivalry of films and they launched on productions containing steamboats and live animals (*White Horse Inn*) and vast sets that quite obliterated the actors (*Grand Hotel*). But Cochran knew that the production was unique and could not be repeated. He travelled to America in search of new ideas and to Russia where he toyed with the idea of bringing to England Stanislavsky's production of *Boris Godounov*. On the way back he stopped in Vienna to see *A Night in Venice* and, charmed by the piece, took an option on all the Johann Strauss operettas with the hope of producing at least one of them at the Adelphi. He never did. Neither did he take up a novel suggestion put to him by a Soviet official. Why, said this dour functionary, did he not bring one of his revues to Moscow? The government would pay him with supplies of timber and oil.

Instead of mounting a Strauss operetta at the Adelphi, he put on a new revue by Noël Coward. The latter now had the upper hand in their partnership. Fortified by the success of *Cavalcade*, he was able to impose his own ideas and his own methods of working. While on a holiday which took him round the world, he announced to Cochran, he had written and composed a revue called *Words and Music*. Every item had been carefully planned, including the running order and the cast he wanted. Settings and costumes were already designed. There were to be no alterations and the show was to go exactly as he planned.

Cochran could not but accept, although he did so with misgivings. Having by that time produced nineteen revues, he could claim to know something about the process. No revue could be entirely the work of one man, he held, and his experience showed that several minds were needed to create variety of material, costumes and scenery. A single brain, however versatile, could not encompass the speed and rapid changes of mood that were essential. The phrase 'A Cochran revue' meant something definite to the public; it was a trademark that guaranteed diversity and glamour and colour. The Coward revue, with its acrid satire and most of the costumes in grey or black, did not.

Words and Music opened to initial praise. It featured two of Coward's best songs, 'Mad About The Boy' and 'Mad Dogs and Englishmen,' the second of them given with éclat by Romney Brent. Born Rómulo Larralde in Mexico City, he had travelled by way of Paris and New York to London where he embarked on a varied career as singer, actor, director and playwright. Wearing a magnificent solar topee made apparently from leopard skin and with a clerical collar wrapped around his neck, he introduced, as 'The Reverend Inigo Banks', the song which haunted Coward for the rest of his life to such an extent that he became sick of it. Everyone thereafter asked Coward to sing it, and in the end he would gallop through it so quickly in the attempt to get the thing over with, that Cole Porter once remarked he'd never before heard a complete number thrown off in a single breath.

During the Manchester try-out the musical director was taken ill and Coward himself, blithely ignorant of all technique, conducted the orchestra at two hours' notice. With Elsie April at his side hissing instructions – go on for thirty-two bars, switch to three four, keep going into six eight, two in a bar, dear – he beat his way manfully through the show, although he left the more complicated ballet scenes to Spike Hughes, the orchestrator. For two weeks he dominated the orchestra pit, relishing the sense of power and waving in elegant gestures the little white stick he had come to love. Cochran urgently engaged a professional replacement: Coward's monopoly of *Words and Music* was developing into a tyranny. Moreover, the revue was failing to attract audiences. Critics approved but the public did not, and after six months it had to come off. Cochran was proved right in his apprehensions, he lost money and, for the first time, a joint venture with Coward failed to make profits. Whereupon Coward asked him to revive *Hay Fever*. Cochran was still under his thrall and did so, although the time was not yet ripe. He regretted it as much as *Words and Music*.

Cochran was not the man to say 'I told you so' nor to revel in Coward's discomfiture. Coward knew this, although his awareness did nothing to make him any the easier as a collaborator. While he sincerely admired Cochran the showman, he remained suspicious of Cochran the businessman, and he never quite believed that he was getting fair treatment where credit and money were concerned. Their last work together, *Conversation Piece*, in 1934, began with a disagreement over detail which, though small, was typical. Cochran always said it was his idea that Coward should write a play for Yvonne Printemps. Coward, on the other hand, claimed the notion was his. Whoever thought of it first, the idea was an arresting one. Lately released after a noisy divorce from her husband Sacha Guitry, whom she had cuckolded with Pierre Fresnay in an intrigue recalling one of Sacha's own comedies, Yvonne Printemps was now a star fully-fledged. Her wide-open eyes, her snub nose and her pure singing voice had a magic which was hers alone. Her marriage to Sacha, the most jealous and possessive of husbands, had been a tedious existence in a gilded cage. She determined thereafter to be no man's slave. When, years later, she heard that Sacha was agonizing on his deathbed, she muttered: 'I hope he *suffers!*' Meanwhile she revenged herself on mankind by tyrannizing the gentle Fresnay who loved her with a humble devotion.

Conversation Piece, a tale of love set in Regency Brighton, was carefully tailored for Yvonne's gift. Since she had no English, she learned her rôle phonetically with the aid of Fresnay who knew the language. All the solo parts in the score were hers exclusively, and of course she sang the most famous number of them all, 'I'll Follow My Secret Heart', a melting tune which Coward had written in Ivor Novello style. Half-way through learning the rôle, she suddenly decided she could go on no

longer, she would never master it. A dramatic telegram revealed her decision. Cochran flew to Paris and argued that,
having learned so much of the script, the rest would come more
easily since many of the same words and phrases would recur.
She listened while he gently pointed out the logic of the case and
added that surely a great star like Mademoiselle Printemps, so
clever a linguist, so accomplished a mistress of beautiful sound,
could achieve this little task? He went back to London and sent
her a long letter. What a waste, he said, that Coward should
have written this lovely play entirely for her but to no purpose.
Of course, he concluded, he had not yet booked a theatre or
committed himself to buying scenery and costumes, so there
was still time to give up the idea completely. A week of silence
elapsed. Then Mademoiselle Printemps came to life. Yes, she
said, she could do it. Her Gallic accent proved a considerable
delight, not least when it gave birth to phrases like 'a clood has
pissed across the sun.'

Writing of her wayward charm, Agate observed: 'There is
probably more art behind this blob of heavenly nose than the
casual spectator might imagine, and this highly talented actress
has to thank Nature for yet another gift – that of self-caricature.
She can be more like Yvonne Printemps than Printemps has the
right to be, and it is then that her art attains the most
significance.' Another unusual name in the cast was that of
George Sanders among the four 'Regency Rakes'. This was one
of his earliest appearances on the road that led him to uneasy
stardom in Hollywood and five marriages. An attempt late in
life to make money from pig farming ended as disastrously as
his marriages, and, bored with life, he committed suicide. As the
Earl of Harringford in *Conversation Piece* he gave an early hint of
the world-weariness that marked his acting on the screen.

Coward himself played the hero, after Romney Brent had
done his best with the part and then thankfully relinquished it
to him. Here was another cause of dissent with Cochran who
did not think the author suitable for the leading rôle. He lacked
romance, Cochran thought, and his 'French' accent seemed
very English when compared with Yvonne Printemps'.
Cochran advised a number of last-minute changes to the play
which would, he felt, have improved it. Coward, too wrapped

up in his own performance, had no time for anything else and the improvements were never made. As the first night approached, Cochran sensed a feeling of estrangement. An indefinable chill hung over their meetings. It had always been his custom to give Coward a small souvenir of their first nights, and for *Conversation Piece* he found a Georgian snuff-box which might be used as a cigarette case. Upon it he had inscribed a legend which recognized that their partnership was dissolving: 'In memory of a not altogether unsuccessful association.'

Few people involved in a successful theatrical production are entirely satisfied with their due. The author, unworldly creature, suspects that he is being cheated of royalties by better business brains than his. The star is convinced that his percentage of the gross has been tampered with and, as always, that his billing does not do him justice. The designer feels he has by no means received the credit he deserves, and the supporting players, hardened by years of cynicism, take it for granted that recognition will be denied them. The impresario, who tries to co-ordinate all these unruly persons and, when he can, pays the bills, grows accustomed to the ingratitude that is his lot. For quite a long time Coward had been thinking of setting up his own production company. This was the only way, he thought, of ensuring that he obtained his fair share of profits which otherwise flowed into Cochran's pocket. He wrote a long and friendly letter to Cochran announcing his scheme. 'Particularly I want you to realize how deeply grateful I am for all the generosity and courage and friendship you have shown me over everything we have done together,' he was careful to emphasize, and Cochran would always be welcome to a share in any of his future enterprises. Theirs had been a 'tremendously happy and successful association,' and he had to say that 'without your encouragement and faith in me and my work it is unlikely that I should have ever reached the position I now hold in the theatre . . .' The letter, which had cost him so much thought and diplomacy, was duly posted. 'Dear Cocky' did not reply.

Days went by, then a week. Coward grew uneasy. One evening Cochran looked in at his dressing-room for a chat. He noticed that Coward seemed on edge and expected him to say something. At last the question surfaced. 'Did you get my long letter? I wanted you to get it before you saw me.' No, Cochran said, he had not received a letter. It had been addressed to him at his home and he immediately began a search. Eventually the letter was found, chewed up and crumpled, under his bed where his little dachshund Blake had made off with it for a game. It was Blake's playful habit to pounce on interesting items like this, and indeed he had once caused endless trouble by mangling a very important contract. At first annoyed by what he took to be a joke in poor taste, Coward was mollified when Cochran produced the tattered shreds of his letter as evidence. They laughed and spoke to each other as the best of friends.

Cochran was not surprised by the development as he had expected something of the sort to happen. He did not recriminate, described the situation as 'inevitable', and wished his collaborator the best of good fortune. Coward's decision was bad financial news for him, but, inured as he was to the vagaries of the theatre, he knew there would be other openings for him to exploit. Outwardly he was dignified and understanding and gave no sign of the resentment that might be simmering within. Had he been vindictive, though, he could, over the years, have taken a malicious pleasure in the fact that none of Coward's later musical shows ever succeeded as well as those he had produced in the grand days of their partnership. However great Coward's talent, without Cochran's flair and intuition an essential ingredient was missing. Did Coward realize this? If so, he never admitted it in public, and always believed until he died that Cochran had cheated him.

iii
'THE GREATEST DISAPPOINTMENT OF MY LIFE.'

'Life is sweet, however disgusting!'

A. P. HERBERT (*Helen!*)

Although Coward played a large part in Cochran's activities for nine years or so he was by no means the only important figure during that period. In 1930, year of *Private Lives*, the London Pavilion featured *Cochran's 1930 Revue*. Much of it was written by another clever young man, Beverley Nichols, whom Cochran for a time thought might be as gifted as Coward. Then thirty-four years old, he had already, at the age of twenty-five, written an autobiography which he entitled with endearing simplicity *Twenty-Five*. While still at Oxford he made a name for himself as President of the Union, and on graduating he very soon became a fluent journalist with stimulating opinions on such urgent matters as women's make-up, how to look after an old mother, and the place of male gallantry in modern life. He was full of thoughtful advice on creating dream gardens and getting to know your pet cat. Besides dispensing each week lavish amounts of counsel to the readers of women's magazines, he could also play the piano very nicely and compose music. He was to write plays (among them one based on the diva Nellie Melba whose secretary he had been), as well as novels and detective stories. Cochran swooped.

Nichols returned from 49 Old Bond Street ('I walked on air'), told his 'man' Gaskin the exciting news, and thereupon, at the piano, composed a tune which he called 'The Little Things You Do'. Cochran had emphasized to him the importance of the first act finale. You can go wrong, he said, in any other part of the revue, but if the first act finale doesn't hit the audience in the eye, you're sunk. Like every other revue writer, Nichols racked his brains and thought of crinolines, bustles, Vienna in waltz-time, Paris in the Spring, all of which had been done before. What about Heaven? That seemed to be about the only place no-one had yet put into a revue. 'An excellent idea,' chuckled Cochran. 'We'll send them all to Heaven.' Nichols saw everything in white: dresses, wigs, flowers, clouds. There would be famous characters from history who spoke their lines tricked out as moving statues. This scene, which Oliver Messel designed, was ultimately one of the most successful with its symphony of whites. 'Mr Messel,' said Agate, 'is a *blanchisseur* of riot.'

Another hit was the sketch called 'Madame Tussaud's in the year 1960,' where a group of tourists inspect various celebrities alive in 1930 and come across one made up like Bernard Shaw.

'How long has *he* been dead?' asks someone. The figure comes to life and exclaims: 'Dead? Not bloody likely!' At the first night Shaw came up to Nichols and said: 'That was the best thing in your revue – but then, of course, that line is absolutely fool-proof, always and everywhere. Its immortality is certain.'

Some of the music also was written by Nichols, and Cochran had at first thought of asking Ivor Novello to complete the score. He did not like what Ivor produced and thought of yet another bright young man, Vivian Ellis, who had just had his first success with *Mr Cinders* and that enchanting melody 'Spread A Little Happiness'. Cochran rang him up. 'This is Charles B. Cochran speaking,' he announced. Ellis thought it was an uncle of his who had the habit of playing practical jokes. 'And I'm Metro-Goldwyn-Mayer,' he riposted.*

Despite a violinist mother and a music scholarship to Chel-tenham, Ellis did not find the family sympathetic toward his musical ambition. After studying briefly with Myra Hess, he was forced to become a reluctant employee in his father's business. He soon left it and worked happily as a song-plugger at two pounds a week, having won the job on the strength of sight-reading Zez Confrey's 'Kitten On The Keys', a feat which can only be appreciated if you have tried to do the same thing yourself. Not long afterwards he was an established composer, and, now a sprightly octogenarian, for over sixty years has delighted the public with music both craftsmanlike and in-spired. Melody that is always fresh and inventive, harmonies that never fail to satisfy richly, are the features that characterize 'She's My Lovely' and 'Me And My Dog'. The nearest equiv-alent to him would be André Messager – not that Ellis is ever anything but original, the parallel being that he shares with the French composer an impeccable musicianship, an elegant melodic line and a stylishness that informs everything he composes. On the other hand, a long career in popular music has left him without illusions. For a Jack Hulbert film in the nineteen-thirties he was given the lyrics of 'The Flies Crawled Up The Window' and sought a tune 'that would please a

---

* When Noël Coward telephoned Lionel Bart for the first time he cheerily introduced himself: 'Noël here.' 'Noël 'oo?' enquired Bart. 'Noël Coward, you stupid Cockney cunt,' came the reply.

backward child of twelve,' he says. 'In as many minutes I'd jotted down a sixteen bar chorus containing a choice of two chords, two arpeggios and a five finger exercise. This was the era before Pop. "That," I jeered, "'is exactly what they want." It was. It sold a quarter of a million records and I never composed anything as easily again.'

His 'Wind In The Willows', sung by a chorus of Botticelli angels, was staged by George Balanchine, one of Diaghilev's choreographers. Hutch, then still in the London Pavilion orchestra, took it up as a solo performer and recorded it. Other Diaghilev survivors whom Cochran engaged included the dancers Alice Nikitina and Serge Lifar. He put them into a ballet called *Luna Park* by that most Gallic of English composers, Lord Berners. The various items were supposed to be danced by circus freaks, an idea of Boris Kochno, Diaghilev's former secretary, which profited from Berners' gift for quick, witty snatches tinged with melancholy on the lines of what he had already done for Diaghilev in *The Triumph of Neptune*. Indeed, the score of *Luna Park* might well have been a continuation of the earlier work: the small dimensions of the piece and the tart brevity of the motifs show that Berners excelled in the genre. Another ballet was commissioned from Henri Sauguet, then, like Berners, a young hopeful first promoted by Diaghilev (*La Chatte*), and a charmingly witty composer whose ascension in old age to the ranks of the French musical establishment has by no means curbed his youthful impishness. When you consider that the settings of the two ballets were, respectively, designed by Christopher Wood and Christian Bérard, you realize just how perceptive was Cochran's artistic eye. He may not have known much about music, he may not have been able to draw a line, but he knew enough, instinctively, to recognize the best talent and to encourage it by putting it to work. The *embarras de richesse* in this revue was completed by the joint talents of Oliver Messel, Doris Zinkeisen and Rex Whistler.

The usual tiresome problems of running order and the usual appalling dress rehearsal led up to *Cochran's 1930 Revue*. Chainsmoking, crushed by a lancinating head-ache, Beverley Nichols wandered around in the early hours of a Saturday morning and talked to the stage-hands. 'Those chaps are the most extraordinary of the lot,' he said to Cochran who sat patiently in his stall, bowler-hatted and hunched over his walking stick. 'The stage-hands?' replied Cochran. 'Yes. They're stage-struck, of course. No men could possibly stick it if they weren't.'

The Manchester opening was disastrous and next day Nichols, having sampled the atrocious reviews, prepared for the end of the world. Cochran appeared at his bedroom door resplendent in a crimson silk dressing gown. 'Cocky,' Nichols said, 'I can't begin to say how sorry . . .' Cochran waved him into silence. He had just prepared an announcement that Beverley Nichols and Vivian Ellis would be writing *Cochran's 1931 Revue*, such was his confidence in them. The gesture was not so quixotic as it might seem, for he knew he had a good property and was confident it would succeed in London. It did, and, even though the 1931 revue did not materialize, his generosity at a crucial moment was never forgotten by the young men to whom he had given their chance. *Cochran's 1930 Revue* opened to record bookings in London and would have run even longer than its two hundred and forty-five performances but for one of those acts of God which can unjustly doom the most successful shows. Very early in the run the popular American star Ada May was taken ill and had to drop out for a while. Since the London Pavilion held about a thousand spectators her ten performances had been seen by ten thousand people. Her absence lasted for thirty-two performances, by which time, Cochran estimated, there were thirty-two thosand people in London a little disappointed as against ten thousand who were fully satisfied. She came back too late, for word-of-mouth had already done the damage and *Cochran's 1930 Revue* did not pick up its early promise. Cochran now could add to heat waves, storms, national disaster and the competition of the cinema yet another reason for disappointment in the theatre.

Even before the revue began to waver he had been planning his next production, *Ever Green*, which he described as 'the best musical comedy I ever put on' with, as a bonus, his favourite song 'Dancing On The Ceiling'. It had music and lyrics by his old friends Rodgers and Hart and a book by Benn Levy, Socialist MP and playwright. Here was the big opportunity he had promised Jessie Matthews, although he foresaw an obstacle which might cloud her prospects. Evelyn Laye had just divorced Sonnie Hale and cited Jessie as co-respondent. Such an event would cause no surprise these days, but the judge had spoken disapprovingly of the co-respondent and, since Evelyn Laye was the greater star, public opinion blamed Jessie. Cochran invited Jessie and Sonnie Hale to a weekend at the country home he had taken for the summer. When Jessie arrived she noted, among her fellow guests, the vivacious Ada May and instantly prepared for war. On Sunday afternoon Cochran ushered her into the garden and showed off the roses to her. Then he took her to a secluded garden seat.

'With all this unpleasant publicity,' he began, 'don't you think it might be better if Sonnie did the show without you?'

'*Without me?*' she snapped while viciously decapitating a hybrid tea rose.

'Oh . . . I see . . . I suppose we could do it without Sonnie.'

She realized, now, that he thought of putting Ada May into *Ever Green* and she was determined not to let him. They argued all the weekend. He knew perfectly well that he had given her a contract for four shows. She would not retreat. When she returned to London he had promised to give her the lead with Sonnie Hale.

Yet at rehearsals he did little to encourage her by turning up with Ada May, in whom he had at the time an interest as personal as it was professional. Whereas he had in earlier shows let Jessie Matthews create her own interpretation, now he stood aside smiling enigmatically as others tried to impose their ideas upon her. The composer Richard Rodgers thought she was too coy. Benn Levy criticized her for not being coy enough. Frank Collins ordered her to put more feeling into her work. What, she thought angrily to herself, did those old men know about love? She swung into 'Dancing On The Ceiling':

> 'He dances overhead, on the ceiling near my bed,
> In my sight, throughout the night.
> I try to hide in vain, underneath my counterpane,
> There's my love, up above . . .'

She swooped, she pirouetted, she threw somersaults. All four men jumped to their feet and shouted at her. 'What the hell,' raved Cochran, 'do you think you're doing?' In the agitation his hat fell off and his cigar went out. Eventually she did as they told her, but she had made her point.

Ever Green offered an imbecilic plot involving a beautiful young revue star who has to disguise herself as her own sixty-year old mother. Even this, however, failed to detract from Benn Levy's witty lines or from the big number 'Dancing On The Ceiling' with its wry insinuating tune and immaculate lyric. Least of all did it affect the sumptuous trappings Cochran lavished upon the piece. He had lately taken the Adelphi Theatre under his management, done it up in opulent bronze and gold, and put in the elaborate revolving stage which so fascinated Noël Coward that he wanted it for *Cavalcade*. Once Jessie Matthews and the chorus became used to dancing in the opposite direction to the stage rotating under their feet they performed with a brio that made it all look deceptively easy. James Agate concluded that 'when you are tired of watching some of the loveliest colour and design that has ever been seen on the London stage, Mr Cochran gives you a faithful copy of that kind of ostrich-feathered, bediamonded and bepowder-puffed flamboyance which is the Folies Bergère. With this proviso, that every Folies-Bergère revue I have ever seen has looked dowdy in comparison with Mr Cochran's copy of it . . . Given the ingredients of this show, I know a dozen impresarios who could have successfully solved the Chinese puzzle of getting it on to Mr Cochran's stage. But I do not know any-body else to whom these notions as to what ought to be the ingredients would have occurred.'

Ever Green repaid Cochran with a long run and buoyant takings. Soon after the opening night, on a cold January day, he drove Jessie Matthews in his Rolls-Royce to Hampstead Town Hall where he was to give her away in marriage to Sonnie Hale. Her prospective husband was late. As the Registrar glanced at his watch, Cochran whispered to the would-be bride: 'Darling, I don't think this marriage is going to work. Why don't you call it off?' The minutes ticked by. 'Darling,' Cochran whispered again, 'if you want to walk out, I'm ready.' At last Sonnie Hale arrived. He had had, he explained, to send out his best man to buy a shirt. Cochran speedily adjusted to the rôle he had played so many times before, one he always enjoyed very much, that of the replacement father-figure handing over a beautiful protégée to her new husband. Jessie Matthews went on to make musical films of classic nineteen-thirties vintage, to marry for a third time, and to experience as many abrupt troughs in her career as she had known peaks. During the Indian summer of her life, her once pert beauty dissolved into matronly plumpness, she was to play for many years the role of a suburban doctor's wife in *Mrs Dale's Diary*, a radio soap opera of cosy but tenacious appeal.

When *Ever Green* showed signs of faltering, Cochran decided to replace it at the Adelphi with a new version of Offenbach's *La Belle Hélène*. He loved operetta and, although he never realized his ambition of producing Johann Strauss, with *La Belle Hélène* he reckoned that he had 'never more nearly realized my idea of theatrical perfection'. The original work needed a great deal done to it. Stuffed with contemporary allusions, puns and topical jokes comprehensible only to Paris audiences of the eighteen-sixties, the libretto would have to be entirely rewritten. Cochran chose as adaptor and lyricist A. P. Herbert, a writer whose name is little heard these days although in his time he was a very popular figure. His energy and versatility were limitless. Barrister, Independent Member of Parliament for Oxford University, sailor, poet, novelist, playwright, librettist and songwriter, he joyously diffused his talents over a breathless variety of activities. Partly this was because he depended on writing for every penny he earned, but also because his sheer *joie de vivre* insisted on permanent expression. One of his more serious achievements was an act of parliament which reformed the archaic marriage laws – he was to write a satirical novel about them called *Holy Deadlock* – and he was an early protagonist of public lending right for authors. His weapons in debate were humour and wit. Even his political enemies loved him, and he spent many happy hours watching cricket at Lords as the guest of Clement Attlee, head of a Socialist government which abolished Herbert's parliamentary seat and would have liked to do away with many of the other things he cherished.

'I've always wanted to meet you!' said Cochran, hand outstretched at his first encounter with Herbert. This was his usual ploy on such occasions. Flattery was a way of lubricating a new association, and few people could resist Cochran's insidious charm. He entertained Herbert at his house in Montagu Street. With a careless wave he indicated the Toulouse Lautrecs and Renoirs that lined the staircase. 'They're going tomorrow – most of them,' he remarked idly. The money was needed, he said, to finance the new Offenbach production. Which of the pictures were going? He did not even know. 'I told the dealer how much money I wanted, and to pick out the pictures he wanted.' This, thought Herbert, much impressed, sounded like a man who was keen on his work. Polite formality soon gave way to affectionate respect for his 'dear master', as Herbert called him. Later he disguised him as one of the characters in his novel *Holy Deadlock*.

His libretto for *Helen!*, as the new version was called, had grace and lightness. It prudently avoided the trap, one into which many current Offenbach adaptors fall, of overloading the text with modern gags. If, perhaps, it did not wholly capture the ominous undercurrent, the hint of future disaster which lies beneath the fevered merriment of the original, it certainly conveyed the bittersweet tone of the more romantic numbers. 'L'amour divin' comes out as:

'There's no life without love, and no love without pain
I have lived, I have loved – and I will not complain . . .'

The point-number about Leda and the swan is deliciously handled:

'For instance there was my poor mother
Who met a most attractive swan;
They fell in love with one another
(Though I don't quite know what went on) . . .
. . . Poor little waif!
Do you wonder she erred?
If it's not safe
To be nice to a bird,
No wonder some of us struggle and struggle in vain!'

The next collaborator to join the team was Oliver Messel who had been put in charge of designing the whole production. To Germany he went in the company of Herbert and Cochran. In Berlin they saw Max Reinhardt's revival of *La Belle Hélène* which had given Cochran the idea for his own show. They travelled on to Salzburg and up a hill to the castle where Reinhardt lived. It was a dark, stormy Sunday afternoon, and the English team sat around in deep armchairs toying with giant cigars while thunder rolled at a distance and Reinhardt, polite but daunting, heard out their plans. Herbert diffidently proposed his intention of adding a third act which should end before the walls of Troy. The idea was accepted and Reinhardt agreed to produce. The music was to be arranged and orchestrated by Erich Korngold, a name very familiar in later years to cinema-goers although at the time of *Helen!* he was still a promising young composer of symphonies and operas. His first work had been given at the Vienna Court Opera when he was only eleven years old, and by the age of nineteen he had written two successful operas. The rise of Hitler obliged him to leave his native city for refuge in Hollywood, where the eclecticism and extreme lushness of his music, earlier deplored by critics, became a positive advantage when writing incidental music to accompany the Technicolored exploits of Errol Flynn. He was the perfect musical chameleon and composed, when necessary, tunes for *Helen!* that were more Offenbachian than Offenbach. This, after all, was to be expected since Offenbach's music is so quintessentially French that only the German Jew Jakob Eberst could have written it. Korngold was especially proud of one pseudo-Offenbach air he produced that he would sit for hours at Herbert's piano bellowing to his own accompaniment:

'No vunder, Helena, ze fleets put oot to zay,
No vunder ze nations feet and dee fur zay.'

Cochran now had to control one of the most variegated production teams he ever assembled. A French play on a Greek theme in a German adaptation was to be supervised by an Austrian producer with an English cast and dances created by the Russian Massine. Each item in the jigsaw puzzle was weighed up and patiently slotted into position. At rehearsals Cochran never raised his voice more than was necessary for it to reach the stage. When crises arose and judgments of Solomon were required he made decisions that were often drastic but not impulsive. Squabbles, explosions of temperament did not shake his serenity. At four o'clock one morning during rehearsals for the Manchester try-out Herbert lost his temper and said hot things he afterwards much regretted. Cochran moved quietly away as if he had not heard them, and neither did he mention them later.

One of his biggest trials was Oliver Messel. The young designer had no idea of money, spent it profusely and, though not at all avaricious, demanded fees that were entirely disproportionate. Cochran offered him a thousand pounds for his work, a very generous sum in those days, and, when Messel objected, pointed out that Ernst Stern, the leading designer at the time, received no more than five hundred. Messel adopted a clever tactic. He constructed a three-dimensional model of the set and made of it so beautiful a thing that Cochran immediately gave way and conceded his terms. Yet the impresario had the last word. He was, he wrote, overjoyed at their eventual agreement and felt it a privilege to have introduced him to the English public. But: 'If I might offer a word of advice, it would be that you made a serious study of stage techniques, which will help you tremendously with your designing.'

The most ravishing stage picture Messel designed was Helen's bedroom, a vision all in white. White curtains and swags of white muslin draped the room. On each side of a dais leading up to the bed stood two white swans, a reference to Helen's parentage. Four white pillars supported the dome of a baldacchino, and white sheets were scattered over the bed. The 'white on white' theme was an inspired development of the 'Heaven' sequence designed for *Cochran's 1930 Revue*. Evelyn Laye, who played Helen, was given a white robe with a blue sash to wear as the face that launched a thousand ships. Gold was stranded through her false hair, and Messel himself worked on the belts he designed for her. Half mesmerised by the faun-like creature, Evelyn Laye remembers: 'I became rather like a doll in his hands. Something that he possessed in a way. I was not quite real to him. I was something he liked dressing up.'

Low comedy was represented by George Robey, the music-hall comedian who in his maturity had taken up 'legitimate' roles and was soon to play a memorable Falstaff. As Menelaus in *Helen!* he never flagged, thanks to a solid constitution and the gift of instant sleep which enabled him to drop off in a front-row stall while the orchestra banged away fortissimo at several inches' distance. Sometimes he grew impatient awaiting his turn in the wings as a complicated piece of business was rehearsed over and over again. At half-past six one morning he jollied on Mr Cochran's weary Young Ladies and told them jokes of such awfulness that they laughed despite their fatigue. 'Have you heard this one?' he enquired. 'What is it that comes out of Cow(e)s all hot and steaming – and goes plonk-plonk?' The girls giggled. 'A PADDLE STEAMER!' boomed George. An exasperated stage-manager hissed 'S'sh!' George turned aside and relieved his boredom with a sideways somersault.

Helen! opened to rapturous acclaim for its lovely settings and a bewitching performance by Evelyn Laye as the heroine. Reviews were good and box office returns promised well. Yet after only a few weeks receipts began to drop. A strange malaise affected some of the cast and they performed with increasing carelessness and lack of gusto. Several times Cochran assembled the whole company and berated them for their lack of team spirit. People who had seen *Helen!* in the early days and then towards the end of the run could scarcely recognize it, so lack-lustre had the thing become. Despite Cochran's exhortations he was powerless to stem the inevitable decline of a production which he once thought as near perfect as any he had ever mounted. 'It is hard enough to get success at any time,' he later observed. 'But it is doubly disheartening when, having achieved a measure of first-night success, the quality of the subsequent performances is dissipated by the players and the run of the play consequently shortened. It amazes me that so many actors and actresses receiving high salaries fail to realize the responsibility they carry on their shoulders. They are the controllers, not only of their own destinies, but of the manager's fortune and the livelihoods of all the people employed in the theatre.' *Helen!* was a burnt-out comet long before its proper time.

As a stop-gap he revived, against his better judgment, *The Miracle* which he had first produced in 1911. For years it had been touring Europe and America, most recently with Lady Diana Cooper in the role of the Madonna. Lady Diana was then, and remained until the end of her long life in 1986, a very famous person. Despite three volumes of autobiography and other memoirs devoted to her, it is hard to understand the reason for her celebrity. She was the wife of a minor politician who redeemed his failure to leave a mark on public affairs by writing what is the best biography, in French or English, of the diplomatist Talleyrand. Her own title to fame is much more slender. As the daughter of a duke – though even this is in doubt for there were arch references to her mother's lover, a handsome man of fashion – she caught the imagination of the newspaper-reading lower classes who in those days were more impressed than now by the aristocracy. Her talent lay in public relations, and gossip-columnists eagerly reported the 'outrageous' sallies with which she fed them and the adroitly calculated transgressions of polite behaviour which were passed off as loveable eccentricities. As a 'Bright Young Thing' of the nineteen-twenties she inspired Evelyn Waugh to create the formidable character of Julia Stitch. Above all she was noted as a society beauty, and although she had many rivals quite as lovely as herself they none of them possessed her unerring gift for self-advertisement. Cochran, himself a master of publicity, acknowledged her supreme talent in this direction and signed her up as the Madonna for his production at the Lyceum.

It was dressed, seven hundred and fifty costumes in all, and designed by Oliver Messel. The cavernous depths of Henry Irving's old theatre were filled with a cathedral setting imagined by the Viennese architect Oskar Strnad. To some it was 'large and magnificent', to others less respectful it appeared as 'Hollywood perpendicular'. Massine devised the choreography and Erich Korngold, released from *Helen!*, supervised the music. Tilly Losch played the important role of the Nun and did her best to upset Lady Diana with malicious practical jokes, such as tampering with her costume so that the Madonna's graceful descent from her niche was turned into a stumbling fall. It was no good complaining to Cochran, who was then at the height of his passion for Tilly. He had gone so far as to let her revise the concluding scene in a way that made nonsense of the Madonna's final appearance.

A spellbound first-night audience encouraged him to believe that he had scored a success both artistic and financial. He confidently booked his passage for a business trip to New York. By the third night, though, the box-office faltered. He cancelled his journey, launched a big press and poster campaign, and approached newspaper magnates among his personal friends with an appeal for their help. Bookings picked up and, when takings had doubled, Cochran set off for a necessary holiday in Marrakesh. Almost as soon as he arrived there news that the King and Queen intended to see *The Miracle* brought him rushing back. The royal visit stimulated business for a few days and then receipts fell again. Cochran gave up and announced the final weeks of the production. This, paradoxically, inspired an immediate rise at the box-office and he began to hope once more. Whereupon a sudden heat-wave reduced audiences yet again at the rate of a ten point fall in revenue for every degree the thermometer rose. The end, he decided, had really come. The fact that *The Miracle* played to capacity houses during the last week of its run did not console him for the seventeen thousand pounds he lost on it. 'Return visits are always risky,' he said philosophically, 'and to go back on one's tracks is to take a chance of disappointment.'

At the end of 1932 his accounts made dismal reading. The introduction of Entertainments Tax bit hugely into what profits he made, and outwardly successful shows like *Helen!* and *Ever Green* registered a loss. Until quite recently provincial tours had been a useful means of recouping losses made on London runs, but now, with touring companies reduced to more than a quarter of what they were in the previous year, even this outlet seemed closed to him. As usual in periods of financial crisis he published a book of memoirs. This time he called it *I Had Almost Forgotten* and brought up to date the story told in *Secrets Of A Showman* seven years previously. As A. P. Herbert remarked in a friendly preface, it told the reader very little about Charles B. Cochran himself. There was no advice on how the great man had reached his position, no handy tips on the art of success, no personal revelations. Instead, among much padding, the book offered polite memories of the famous, reminiscences of long-dead music-hall stars and meditations on the art and science of publicity. Still, *I Had Almost Forgotten* went into four printings and helped to preserve his remaining Impressionist canvases from the greedy hands of art dealers and the Inland Revenue.

'He is lovable and he is a leader,' wrote Herbert in his preface; 'he is calm and he is courageous; he is human and he is an artist; I think he is a great man, and I expect that he will die a poor one.' Herbert's next venture with Cochran did little to ensure that either of them died rich men. It was an adaptation of a German play, very successful in Europe, with music by Oskar Strauss, composer of *The Chocolate Soldier* and *A Waltz Dream*. Herbert called his witty version *Mother of Pearl* and Cochran planned it as a vehicle for Alice Delysia. She played a middle-aged actress whose lover is stolen by her own daughter. At the first night Herbert flouted tradition and visited the leading lady in her dressing-room. 'How are you feeling, Alice?' She slapped her chest and jubilated: 'I'm feeling fine. I'm going out there to show them what I can do.' This she did, and with great panache, but even her flamboyance was powerless to ensure a good run for *Mother Of Pearl* and Cochran was soon looking around for a new attraction. He found it in a novel which, ironically, his wife Evelyn gave him as a distraction to keep his mind off the theatre on a visit to Berlin. The book was called *Nymph Errant* and had been written by James Laver, then an assistant keeper at the Victoria and Albert Museum. The story told in a light-hearted manner of the adventures that befell a young girl as she travelled home from her finishing school in Switzerland. Cochran enjoyed it, as did many other readers, and as soon as he returned he invited Laver to 49, Old Bond Street and told him that he wanted to make a play out of it. There and then he offered the dazed author a handsome contract. 'I'd like to see some more of your work,' he added. 'Have you written anything since *Nymph Errant*?' The learned scholar paused. Then he replied: 'Yes. I've written a life of John Wesley.'

Nymph Errant represented only one side of Laver, the side that wrote poetry and imaginative novels. The other, erudite and precise, compiled histories of painting and costume. He became an authority on dress through the ages and evolved the theory that in different generations the 'erogenous zone' shifts over various parts of the body, so that at one period interest will focus on ankles, at another on bosoms, at yet another on legs, and so on. One cannot resist adding that he also contributed to a volume entitled *Memorable Balls of History*, although one sees what was meant.

Cochran rented a cottage for the summer of 1933 at Winkfield Green and there installed his collaborators on *Nymph Errant*. Romney Brent was to adapt the novel for the stage, and, since Cochran had decided it must have music, Cole Porter set to work on the score. What was Porter's address in Paris? Cochran asked. 'The Ritz bar,' said Porter. But what about letters or telegrams? 'The Ritz bar,' came the reply again. Porter had no bank account, and, when he needed money, called on Harry the barman, with whom he had deposited a permanent float. Laver thought Porter looked like 'an American college boy, a rather solemn college boy, as if he had something on his mind.' The impression Laver himself made on the new circle he entered as a shy museum curator, a circle of flippant and dashing stage folk, was no less intriguing. He was in Gertrude Lawrence's dressing-room when conversation turned to whether the government was right in spending a very large sum on the Sinai Codex. As an obvious authority his opinion was asked. 'I don't know anything about it,' he innocently replied. 'I am an iconographer not a palaeographer.' An awed silence fell.

At Winkfield Green the tiring work of adaptation was lightened by sessions of golf croquet at which Romney Brent showed himself to be a virtuoso player. Cochran, avuncular and hospitable, acted as a benign referee and Evelyn, adorable hostess, lavished kindnesses on her guests with particular attention to the younger and prettier women among them. Cole Porter wrenched himself away from Paris and gave the house-party a preview of the songs he had written. One of them was this gem, the lament of a cocotte faced with amateur competition:

'A busted, disgusted cocotte am I,
Undesired on my tired little bottom, I
Watch these fat *femmes du monde*,
With the men that once I owned,
Splash around like hell-bound hippopotami,

Since only dames with their names on their cheques appeal
To modern men, instead of sex, I now have ex-appeal.
What will Ma say to me when she learns I've turned out to be
An annoyed, unemployed cocotte?'

Once rehearsals began there were problems over a nudist scene in the play. How could it be presented without offending the Lord Chamberlain? Whatever ideas were suggested for discreet presentation, Frank Collins would champ on his pipe and mutter: 'It'll be seen from the side-boxes, Mr Cochran.' When, in desperation, they decided to leave it out altogether, Cochran insisted on keeping it in. Naturally the Lord Chamberlain was outraged. Cochran, as he had shrewdly planned all along, offered to withdraw the scene if the rest of the play, which contained other debatable material, were to be approved. So concerned was the Lord Chamberlain over nudity on the stage that he agreed, and Cochran got away with much more than he otherwise might have expected.

Oliver Messel was to have designed the sets but, having acquired a mysterious disease in North Africa where he claimed to have gone in search of local colour for a harem scene in the play, Doris Zinkeisen took on the commission at short notice. She, a woman of surpassing elegance, was also a keen member of the local hunt. A bad fall in which her mount crushed her pelvis did not cure her of the passion for riding to hounds, and afterwards she took a first prize with the same horse at an important show. Later she painted its portrait which hung at the Royal Academy. The sets of *Nymph Errant* were, for this dauntless female, an easy chore to be knocked off with the maximum of wit and grace. Cochran chose as his leading lady Gertrude Lawrence, an actress whose 'quality of dramatic radiance' he considered unique. An exotic addition to the cast was Elizabeth Welch, lately arrived from her home town of New York and already a much admired feature of the London stage and cabaret. In *Nymph Errant* she sang Cole Porter's 'Solomon' (not forgetting his thousand wives) with the power-house energy and voice like a melodious foghorn which have made the number her signature tune ever since.

Nymph Errant set off in a typical Cochran première, ablaze with orchids and white ties and tiaras in what newspapers used to call a 'brilliant' audience. Journalists noted the retiring figure of James Laver and asked him what he had to do with the show. 'Not much,' he replied. 'I merely wrote the book.' Cochran's generous terms helped to smooth the author's feelings. The royalties he was paid amounted to over ten times his museum salary, and when the film rights were bought he started to think of giving up his job and becoming a full-time author. He changed his mind in the following year when his income tax demand exceeded all the revenues he earned for the period.

Another collaborator with cause for disgruntlement, though in a different way, was Agnes de Mille. She provided the choreography for *Nymph Errant* and was not at all happy about Cochran's treatment of her. Having enticed her from America with the promise of two recitals at his theatre in addition to her work on the play, he overlooked, or conveniently forgot, his bargain. She suspected, moreover, dirty work at the box-office, was convinced that expense accounts had been doctored, and saw her fees dwindle to less than what was initially agreed. Like Noël Coward she was certain that Cochran had cheated her. He was, she complained, ruthless to failure and impatient with lack of success. When trouble arose he disappeared. If the unpleasant duty of sacking people became necessary he would leave it to his stage manager. For Agnes de Mille even his flair was in doubt: he relied, she said, on experts to make decisions for him, and he was quick to snap up talent which others discovered first.

A further grievance, though Miss de Mille sportingly did not lay it at Cochran's door, was that *Nymph Errant* failed to run long despite her own talents and those of Cole Porter, Gertrude Lawrence and Elizabeth Welch. Even while rehearsing it Cochran had been arranging his next play, a venture designed to benefit from the immense popularity of Margaret Kennedy's *The Constant Nymph* and from his discovery of a Viennese actress who he believed had the potential of greatness. With time to spare, waiting for a train on one of his German trips, he utilized it by looking in at a performance of Bernard Shaw's *Saint Joan*. The title rôle was played by a young woman called Elisabeth Bergner and she enthralled him. Whenever in Europe thereafter he made a point of going to see her act. Her range extended from Eugène O'Neill's *Strange Interlude* to Frederick Lonsdale's *The Last of Mrs.Cheyney*. The repertory of this versatile actress included Ophelia, Portia, and many other rôles in classic drama. Since he could speak no German he was chary of meeting her in person. He sent her, anonymously, a bouquet of flowers.

The hunt was up. When he learned that she knew English, he invited her to dinner in Montagu Street during one of her visits to Britain. The Nazi régime was gaining power in her native Austria and, being Jewish, she had begun to look elsewhere for career opportunities. She met Cochran the very day Hitler was appointed Chancellor. Henceforward she must act abroad, and for the next few years she lived in England where she finally took British citizenship. Slight, elfin, she had a girlish charm which veiled an inner pathos. She was also mischievous and wayward. At Malvern Festival with Bernard Shaw himself in the audience she found the matinée overlong and cut out one of her important speeches as St Joan. Afterwards Shaw came round and, she later told Sir John Gielgud, 'threw the book at her.' 'What did you do, Elisabeth?' Gielgud asked. 'Oh, I just threw it back', she beamed.

Although abroad her reputation was distinguished, in England she was unknown and Cochran searched anxiously for the right play which would introduce her to audiences here. One of her past successes had been the German version of that pertinacious best-seller *The Constant Nymph*. Why not, Cochran suggested, do a sequel to it? She agreed enthusiastically and the author, Margaret Kennedy, wrote *Escape Me Never* for her. More of a return than a sequel, *Escape Me Never* is the mixture as before and skilfully combines all the elements which had made the original a favourite novel, play and film. The hero is, again, a Bohemian composer called Sanger, and the heroine, yet again, a tragic waif-like creature. Pathos is added to the romantic situation when she has a baby which dies in hospital.

Cochran deliberately avoided any mention of Bergner as 'great' or 'famous' in advance publicity. Her name was printed on bills in the same size as that of the other players because he wanted to let audiences find out for themselves the quality of her acting. At the Manchester try-out his policy was justified.

The fall of the curtain, he afterwards said, was the most thrilling moment of his life. 'For what seemed a full minute, but was probably no more than twenty seconds, there was a dead silence all over the theatre. Then the storm of applause broke like a great wave . . . One hears of the house "rising" to a performance. It is a rare phenomenon. In the old days the house would "rise" to Irving and Ellen Terry when they were at the height of their fame. At Covent Garden the house would "rise" to Caruso and Melba. But one may be a theatre-goer for years without experiencing the curious thrill which follows that silent descent of a curtain – that gasp of amazement, a realization which heralds the frenzied acclamation of a great artist in a great moment of triumph.' That triumph was repeated at the London première in December, 1933, and the box-office telephone was permanently engaged. But Cochran's new star was a delicate plant. She suffered paroxysms of stage-fright and, at the end of the first act, lost her voice completely. Cochran found her in her dressing-room, shaking, with tears that poured down her face. He calmed her, got her to repair her make-up, and practically forced her on at her second act entrance. For weeks afterward all seats were sold out and standing room was full. She collapsed again from the strain in April and Cochran withdrew the play. When she recovered, a month later, he put it on once more to full houses. This time the hot weather discommoded her, and, since she did not favour long runs, Cochran reluctantly took off *Escape Me Never*. But for her frail health, he concluded, the piece would have lasted another year to capacity business. He comforted himself with the pleasure of having brought off an artistic triumph unique in his career and with having presented an actress whom everyone described as great – everyone, that is, except James Agate. He, who had been brought up on Bernhardt, Duse, Réjane and Mrs Kendal, refused to be gammoned. Miss Bergner, he conceded, had talent, a delightful quality of 'Germanness' and a miraculous felicity as the passionate waif. Yet *Escape Me Never*, an efficient though hardly major confection, gave little opportunity for greatness. One play alone was not enough to assess a performer's range, and claims of greatness were premature. It is a verdict with which posterity would generally agree.

During the run of *Escape Me Never* the young Peter Scott, son of the explorer Captain Scott, brought his godfather James Barrie to see the actress. One of the strangest characters in English literature, Sir James Barrie OM was also the most successful and richest playwright of the age. His adult life was haunted on the one hand by nostalgia for his boyhood and on the other by a desperate urge for paternity. When his own brief marriage failed ignominiously, for reasons which can only be surmised, he took a growing interest in the family of Sylvia Davies, Gerald du Maurier's sister. Her husband, who did not entirely welcome Barrie's absorption in his five sons, died young of a horrible and disfiguring malady, whereupon the dramatist became still more closely involved. At Sylvia's early death Barrie took over the boys completely. They were among the few human beings capable of rousing him from his dour silence. He paid for their education, lavished gifts upon them and took them for expensive holidays. Freudians would classify him as a pederast or a repressed homosexual. He was neither. His love for the boys was pure and innocent. His holiday adventures with them were to help inspire *Peter Pan*. When Elisabeth Bergner went to visit him in his dreary flat high up at Adelphi Terrace he was, inevitably, captivated by her androgynous charm and boyish figure. A pleasing legend, relayed by Bergner and the playwright's biographer, tells that he asked her what part she would like to act more than any other. 'The young David who slew Goliath,' she answered. Barrie gasped and his pipe clattered down on the brick hearth. Legend adds that he said: 'This is a historic moment.'

Within a few weeks Barrie had written the first act of *The Boy David* and read it to her in his gloomy home perched up among the London roof-tops. She was aflame to play it immediately. Cochran, however, had already bought an option on Giraudoux's *Amphitryon 38*, one of her European successes, which he intended for her next London appearance. He renewed the option and was to do so again several times over the coming months. Eventually he lost all the money he had paid out because Giraudoux could wait no longer and the play went to the Lunts. It was, he told himself, a small price for the honour of presenting Bergner in a new play by England's leading dramatist. When he read it he was delighted. The combination of Barrie and Bergner seemed irresistible. He would not, he said, have sold his rights in *The Boy David* for fifty thousand pounds.

His jubilation turned into anxiety when Miss Bergner announced that she first wanted to make a film of *Escape Me Never* directed by her husband Paul Czinner. Anxiety became frustration at the news that she then proposed to act in a screen version of Shaw's *St. Joan*. Only then would she be ready to appear in *The Boy David*. Barrie approved her plan and told Cochran that since he had written it for her she was free to do it only when she wished. Cochran opened negotiations with Shaw who started writing a scenario. Czinner upset everyone by calling in the dramatist James Bridie to collaborate on an adaptation. At this point Cochran's American backers grew nervous about the effect of Shaw on the powerful Roman Catholic community in the United States. Fortunately the project was dropped when Bergner played St Joan at the Malvern Festival on the occasion already mentioned and annoyed Shaw by cutting her part. 'I was tired,' she later told him. 'I know my performance was lousy, but I didn't know you were in the house.' He had already decided that tough women like Joan were not her forte. To Cochran's horror she embarked on a screen version of *As You Like It* with the infatuated Barrie in attendance to provide suggestions and ideas for the scenario.

Two years had passed since *The Boy David* was written, years in which Cochran was obliged to spend large sums of money for nothing and to stifle his impatience by reminding himself that Bergner was a great actress and well worth the trouble she was causing him. Even when preparations at last began they were almost immediately postponed because she fell ill and had to undergo a big operation. Barrie fussed over her and insisted she take a long rest in the country. From her cottage in Sussex she sweetly gave out the news that she intended to make another film.

Cochran, by now resigned to martyrdom, was also in trouble with Barrie. The latter wished to keep the nature and title of his play a close secret. Inevitably details about it had seeped out, various people read the script and gossip began. It was a biblical subject, rumour said, and the Bible, as everyone knew, was box-office poison. One morning the *Daily Mail* carried a full report of what the play was about. Barrie fumed with rage. He only allowed details of his new plays to be disclosed in *The Times* and *The Scotsman*, and then at a time of his own choosing.

Finally Cochran was able to announce a first performance of *The Boy David* at the King's Theatre, Edinburgh, in November 1936. He gave it a magnificent launch. Komisarjevsky was the producer, Augustus John designed the sets and William Walton composed the music. The full company, over a hundred including staff, set out from King's Cross for Edinburgh. Barrie accompanied them, seventy-six years old, very ill and in constant pain. Cochran's diplomacy, his tact and his patience were never more heroically deployed than in his handling of the morose and ageing dramatist. Barrie's biographer described him as 'the neat, pink-cheeked, blue-eyed and always slightly Corinthian Cochran,' a fair enough summary though he got the colour of the eyes wrong. At every false start over the past two years, at every occasion for annoyance, Cochran was at hand to soothe, to explain, to comfort. Embittered at having lost two of his beloved Davies boys, one in the 1914–18 war and the other in a swimming accident, Barrie suffered moods of black depression. Despite his wealth – in 1906 alone his royalties were over forty thousand pounds – despite his great popularity, he lived in a state of hopeless gloom, for he knew now that life would never give him what he really wanted, his own son and a return to his childhood. *The Boy David*, his last play, meant a great deal to him. The name David had a poignant resonance, for that was what his father had been called, and the young brother, too, who died in childhood. He laboured hard at the new play and did his homework industriously. The long stage directions with which, as usual, he indulged himself, contain much detailed information on the sort of clothes ancient people wore, the food they ate and the type of skins from which their tents were made. The story of David as told in the Book of Samuel is related deftly enough. The big scene where David kills Goliath is conveyed by the hero alone on stage discharging his sling at an invisible enemy and, later, dragging on the huge spear which belonged to the dead giant. The dialogue veers uneasily between formal English and biblical pastiche. Since everyone already knows the plot, dramatic impetus is lost and there is little room for the ingenious stagecraft which, in his other plays, had shown Barrie to be a master. As David, Elisabeth Bergner was fey and untameable. While crouched before Godfrey Tearle who played Saul and gazing raptly up at him, says Sir John Gielgud, she would pull hairs from his legs in an attempt to make him laugh.

The Edinburgh performance went very well except for an awkward passage involving Barrie, who, too ill to attend, stayed in his hotel room where he was accosted by a gate-crashing reporter. Once again Cochran patted his ruffled feathers and reassured him so expertly that, next day, he turned up for tea and gave a high-spirited imitation of Henry Irving.

Three weeks later *The Boy David* had its London première at His Majesty's. Cochran took every precaution to ensure a good atmosphere and even persuaded Marlene Dietrich, a prominent first-night guest, to make an unobserved entry by a side-door so that she should not steal la Bergner's thunder. All his toil went for nothing. The audience was bored and distinctly unmoved by the star's magnetism, Godfrey Tearle's spirituality as Saul and a barn-storming appearance as Samuel by Sir John Martin-Harvey. 'I shall never forget that first performance at His Majesty's,' Cochran remembered. 'There was a chill about it which sometimes returns to me in the form of a nightmare. Before the curtain had been up half an hour I knew the play was doomed.' *The Boy David* lost over a thousand pounds each week it played, and after fifty performances Cochran took it off. The usual happened: as soon as he announced its withdrawal bookings soared, every seat was taken and he found himself in the ironic position of refusing a demand for tickets which only recently he had been giving away to 'paper' the house.

The Boy David was Barrie's final variation on his lifelong theme of the boy who died in childhood, the pathetic lost boy who had inspired other books and plays he wrote. A few months later he himself died, thankful to quit an existence which had lavished upon him so much and yet so little. In his will he left Elisabeth Bergner two thousand pounds because, he wrote, she had achieved 'the best performance ever given in a play by me.' She afterwards concentrated on her screen career and, at the ourbreak of war, obtained an official permit to visit Canada and make *49th Parallel*, an anti-Nazi film approved by the British government. Once there she promptly gave up her rôle and stayed on in America until hostilities were over. This did not endear her to the admirers she left behind in blitz-torn London. She did, though, return some years later and end her life there at the age of eighty-eight, for by then the capital had become safe to die in.

As for Cochran, he was left with debts of many thousands of pounds and the rueful privilege of having produced Barrie's last play. He had known many disappointments, he confessed, but he did not think he was exaggerating when he said that *The Boy David* was the 'greatest disappointment of my life'. In books of reference he never listed it among his productions. His failure had been too absolute, too crushing for him to allow any mention of it.

Chapter Five

HIS FINAL BOW

'In my humble opinion, every man or woman
who sets out to entertain or instruct the public
ought to be a showman. Shakespeare was a
sublime poet and a resourceful dramatist – but it
is doubtful whether we should ever have heard of
him if he had not been a showman as well'.

Charles B. Cochran

---

i

UNHAPPY RETURNS

'You can have no possible conception of the pain that man is
suffering.'

COCHRAN'S DOCTOR

Cochran was a potent mixture of energy, determination and
uncrushable optimism. What his friends called strength of will
would have been rated by enemies as obstinacy, and if you
described him as resolute those who disliked him would have
preferred the epithet stubborn. All these qualities in his character, however you define them, were harshly tested during the
mid-nineteen-thirties. He was in his early sixties, a time when,
physically, things can start to go wrong. For years he had
suffered from arthritis in the hip. Every possible cure was tried:
massage, pills, numerous varieties of medical treatment, but all
in vain. The only relief he could find was in hot baths, and
these, when the water was heated to the farthest bearable limit,
encouraged the blood flow and, temporarily, eased the dull

heavy pain that accompanied every minute of his life. His limp became a hobble as he leaned on the friendly stick that kept him upright. He had thought, once, that the pain could not possibly get worse. He was wrong. It did.

In this extremity he eagerly seized on anything that offered hope. His doctor recommended a new type of crutch that eased the weight of the body and prevented it from resting on the top of the thigh bone. He took the crutch with him on a train journey to Glasgow where he was presenting, in association with Binkie Beaumont, a play called *The Old Maid* which had been very successful in America. The leading lady was Lillian Gish, famous Hollywood star, and the director was that formidable tyrant Leontine Sagan. The two of them did not get on. Gish remained unresponsive to Sagan's lesbian advances, and her director, infuriated by rejection, bullied her sadistically. Since the actress had no stage experience, she was soon reduced to a state of nervous humiliation and the play was wrecked. After a few performances *The Old Maid* closed and never reached London. At the first night Cochran sat in the stalls, his cherubic beam hiding not only apprehension over the fate of the play but also the burning agony of his arthritis. After the second act he could put up with it no more and, for the first time in his life, quitted a première before it had finished. He shuffled out of the theatre to the railway station and was offered an invalid chair. It horrified him and he waved it aside. His valet helped him into his sleeping car and took away the ineffectual crutch. Once more he crawled into bed knowing that a night of restless sleep tormented by pain lay ahead of him.

Professionally, too, he was under siege. At the time he was casting a new revue called *Streamline* which coincided with a move by Equity, the actor's union, to implement standard contracts. There were many employers who paid low wages for unfair hours and Equity was fighting to achieve better conditions. Cochran did not figure among the cheeseparers: he always gave his chorus and extras wages higher than the Equity minimum. What he objected to was the union's insistence on interfering with his right to bargain over what he paid his stars and featured players. A meeting chaired by Godfrey Tearle decided, after noisy scenes, that members should choose between Cochran and Equity and that they should not sign agreements with the impresario himself. Cochran was deeply hurt. While applauding an organization that stood up for the rights of the smaller people, he did not agree that it had any cause to be involved in negotiations with major names. He pointed out that in his experience he had always made more money by paying high salaries than by doing things on the cheap. The discourteous way Equity had conducted its campaign against him and the 'intimidation' of people he engaged for *Streamline* saddened him. Something that he prized above all, his independence, had been threatened, and he was tempted to leave the theatre. Indeed, 'my attitude at the moment is to avoid passing down any street in which there is a theatre,' he complained.

Another ordeal loomed in a complicated legal action brought over the touring and film rights of *Cavalcade*. The touring company claimed that, by allowing a film of *Cavalcade* to be issued before the tour ended, Cochran had damaged the good business they were doing and caused their audiences to dwindle. His fellow impresario Gilbert Miller gave evidence on his behalf. 'If a film of a play were bad – which most films are – the effect would be damaging,' he airily declared. 'The film of *Cavalcade* was excellent and therefore would be a good advertisement for the play.' After long disputation it was shown that Cochran, who had sold the film rights years before the touring agreement was drawn up, could not be accused of selling the same thing twice over. The plaintiffs claimed £60,000 in damages. They were awarded five thousand. Happily for Cochran, the compensation was paid by the Theatre Royal, Drury Lane, which had been his partner in assigning the right to tour *Cavalcade*.

After his battle with Equity and exhausting days in the witness box he set off on a business trip cum holiday to America. As Equity had cannily predicted, the lure of the theatre soon prevailed over his momentary disillusionment and he became as enthusiastic as ever in his search for new talent. The discovery of a mouth-organ player called Larry Adler was a highlight of his American visit. Cochran knew nothing of mouth-organ playing but was assured by Elsie April's small son that Adler was a good performer. On the strength of this recommendation he brought the nineteen-year-old American to England. Where, reporters asked him, would Adler be giving his English debut? Oh, murmured Cochran loftily, perhaps in the Albert Hall. Eventually he put him into *Streamline* and launched yet another star on its course. The excitement of discovery and of mounting another show eclipsed the unpleasantness with Equity. Cochran was back in all his old form, quick, enterprising, manipulative. He happened to be crossing Piccadilly Circus with Charles Graves, brother of the poet Robert and then a very well-known journalist who wrote three different gossip columns in weekly magazines and one in a national Sunday newspaper. Cochran asked him if he could think of a good name for the revue. 'I want a name that suggests those new-style streamlined American cars. Have you any suggestions?' Cochran said. He repeated: 'Smart new streamlined American cars.' Graves played the game and took the bait. 'What about *Streamline*?' he asked. 'My dear Charles,' said Cochran, 'that's brilliant. That is just what I'll call it.' There was no doubt that Cochran had long ago decided on the title and was only 'feeding' Graves. Yet both were happy. Graves could announce that he had given Cochran the title. He would also be more than usually interested in the progress of the revue, and so, by the same token, would the many thousands of people who read his four columns.

Most of the words for *Streamline* came from Alan Herbert and the music from Vivian Ellis. One of their best numbers was 'Other People's Babies', a poem Herbert had long ago written for *Punch*. Since a poem is not a lyric, Ellis turned it inside out, snipped it here and cut there until it was tailor-made for the warm fluent melody he provided. The song is a gentle lament by a nanny:

> 'Other people's babies,
> 'That's my life!
> 'Mother to dozens and nobody's wife.'

At once humorous and tinged with sadness, 'Other People's Babies' is a fine example of Ellis's craftsmanship. Even the introduction and the 'patter' interlude, which are so often no more than 'vamp till ready' passages, are written with the same skill and sympathy as the refrain. The Herbert/Ellis *pièce de résistance* was a full-blown parody of Gilbert and Sullivan billed as *Perseverance* by 'Turbot & Vulligan'. Within a short space are concentrated all the tricks of the two Savoyards: the patter song, the droopy female chorus, the portentous exclamations, the arch soprano, a hideously absurd plot and an unaccompanied madrigal. If, in his miniature libretto, Herbert deftly captured every quirk of Gilbert, in the music Ellis admirably hit off the Sullivan manner, especially in his way of leading up to a number. Less enjoyable for the two collaborators was the chore of concocting those brief items which were always needed in revues to fill the time when scenery was being changed and principals were getting out of one costume into another. What is more, they were always supposed to make Cochran laugh, not a very easy task, especially as they were usually tried out on him just after he had had a difficult meeting with his backers.

Streamline was Cochran's twenty-first revue and he celebrated with lavish settings designed by Rex Whistler and Doris Zinkeisen. Cecil Beaton also contributed. His earlier association with Cochran had been unfortunate. Some time previously the refined young man, as yet unused to life back-stage, had been introduced to Cochran and was disconcerted at the sight of '. . . a very ordinary little man . . . just like the provincial manager with cigar, whisky and soda and talking about pretty girls.' Cochran asked him to do some designs for bathing suits and warned him: 'They must be suitable for modern dancing, high kicks, cartwheels and splits!' Sighing 'How vulgar and commonplace,' Beaton quickly did some sketches. Months later they were rejected. At a subsequent Pavilion revue, however, Beaton noticed that some of his designs had in fact been used. Since he had no contract there was no redress. For *Streamline*, which included caricatures he drew of well-known society figures, he made sure a written agreement was prepared.

Although *Streamline* was doing 'wonderful business' Cochran never for a moment relaxed his vigilant oversight of performances. Members of the cast were peppered with notes that discreetly mingled praise and sorrowful reproach. He was 'dreadfully shocked', he told Florence Desmond, to find her 'giggling on the stage last night . . . We need 100% at every performance. Nothing annoys audiences more than to see an actress having a joke in which they are not "let-in" . . . Apart from the giggling, your performance in "Perseverance" is now too clownish . . . It wasn't a burlesque of Gilbert and Sullivan at all in the acting, but a rather bad burlesque of an amateur operatic society . . . I shall be seeing the play again in a night or so and would like to see "Perseverance" done as it was original-ly directed and played. You are brimful of talent, my dear Dessie, and have arrived at an important stage in your career. For your own sake as well as for that of the show, I beg you not to tamper with the high position you have gained.' He remained, 'with affectionate regards, Charles B. Cochran.'

Another, deeper cause of sorrow for him was the departure of Tilly Losch who, dancing as 'Harmonia Mobilis' to music by Rameau, made her last appearance in one of his revues. She had finally, as already mentioned, decided to marry the wealthy Edward James. Her choice had lain between James and the even richer Sonny Whitney. Maybe later on, after divorcing James, she could marry Whitney? She took the plunge with James, being careful meanwhile to engineer situations which, in subsequent proceedings, could be used as evidence of his homosexuality. His family, she reasoned, would be horrified at the publicity and ready to make a substantial settlement as the price of her silence. Events did not work out quite like that, and poor Tilly herself paid a high cost in the shape of four preg-nancies, all terminated, which quickly followed each other during her marriage to James. Still, she kept her figure, which was the paramount consideration. Cochran never forgot her. Neither did Evelyn, who admired her beauty as much as he did and who felt an emotional attachment to her almost as strong as her husband's.

Streamline was, said A. P. Herbert, 'one of the rare theatrical enterprises I had a hand in that actually made money.' Cochran used the profits from it to finance his next revue, *Follow The Sun*, which came out in February, 1936. He laid on the trimmings with a generous hand. Osbert Sitwell was commissioned to write the scenario of a ballet – it reads as idiotically as all ballet scenarios do and concerns an Edwardian shooting party, a dance of pheasants and the accidental death of a gentlewoman – with music by William Walton, sets and costumes by Cecil Beaton and choreography by Frederick Ashton. Another exotic feature was Ciro Romac and his Cuban band who introduced the conga and the carioca to London. Despite the labours of a Manchester try-out Señor Romac and his players decided to serenade Cochran one evening at his suite in the Midland Hotel. His daughter Carito wiggled a bare midriff enticingly. at the impresario who, unable to resist, gallantly partnered her in an impromptu dance that whirled them down three flights of stairs. Breathless and aglow, they burst into the hotel's Parisian room and were greeted with tremendous applause by the assembled diners. Once the exaltation had faded, Cochran's arthritic hip gave way and he retired miserably to bed. He lay there for the next two days, in torture and unable to move. His moment of impulsive jollity cost him dear and, ever after, made walking still more of an ordeal for him.

A new comedian he had seen at the Holborn Empire took the male lead in *Follow The Sun*. Viktor Oliver Samek, born in Austria, left his native country after serving as a cavalry officer, went on the stage and travelled America as part of a mediocre double act in which he was billed as 'The Continental Wizard' or 'The Piano-Playing Baron'. On his own he came to England, worked up a solo number as a comic violinist and called himself Vic Oliver. Cochran liked his excellent timing and the Austro-Hungarian accent that flavoured his jokes, and, although finding some of his material risqué, gave him his first opportunity in West End revue. While auditioning chorus girls Cochran also engaged a handsome young woman with flaming red-gold hair. She was Sarah Churchill, daughter of Winston. The distinguished family link by no means harmed her chances as one of the Young Ladies. At the same time she could dance well and showed signs of developing into a competent light actress. During the run of *Follow The Sun* she fell for the Viennese charm of Mr Samek and, before the show closed, had changed her name to Mrs Vic Oliver. This was the sort of incident that delighted Cochran who, besides playing the role of benevolent match-maker, harvested some useful publicity. The bridegroom's father-in-law was much less pleased, and Vic Oliver became yet another of the crosses Winston Churchill had to bear through the political wilderness he then inhabited.

The death of King George V postponed the show's London opening and only after an expensive delay was it able to start covering its production costs at the Adelphi. Cochran was already planning another attraction for 1937 which was to be Coronation Year, a time, he reckoned, when London would be full of visiting tourists ready to enjoy themselves at the theatre. His patriotic 'English' revue was called *Home and Beauty*. It had music by a Czechoslovakian composer, scenery by a French designer and featured the Hungarian soprano Gitta Alpar with her compatriots Rawicz and Landauer. (Did one of the latter pair come from Buda and the other from Pest? wondered Agate.) Only the words were English and they were supplied by that arch-Briton A. P. Herbert. He restored the national equilibrium by writing one of his best lyrics, 'A Nice Cup of Tea', though even this had music by an American:

> 'I like a nice cup of tea in the morning,
> For to start the day, you see,
> And at half-past eleven
> Well, my idea of heaven
> Is a nice cup of tea:
> I like a nice cup of tea with my dinner
> And a nice cup of tea with my tea,
> And when it's time for bed
> There's a lot to be said
> For a nice cup of tea.'

It was sung, with a teasing skittishness as her gramophone record proves, by Binnie Hale dressed as a maid. Years later the ditty was used for a television commercial by the Tea Council and brought Herbert a pleasant windfall. He was one of the very few people to benefit from *Home and Beauty*. Quite early on Gitta Alpar fell ill and disappointed audiences attracted by her European reputation. While *Home and Beauty* was still rehearsing, Edward VIII abdicated and cast a gloom over what should have been a time of public celebration. When the Coronation of George VI finally took place it was succeeded by a period of anti-climax in which the expected crowds at the box office did not materialize. On the night *Home and Beauty* closed five other London theatres also went dark.

Cochran's zest for showmanship remained undamped. Any opportunity to release it, even free of charge, was eagerly taken up, and he loved to exercise it in charity events such as the mammoth cabaret he organized at Grosvenor House for the Actors' Benevolent Fund. While on holiday in Morocco he had discovered a fifteen-year-old Berber girl from the Atlas Mountains, olive skinned, dark eyed, platinum haired and of exquisite loveliness. Throughout his career he was always coming across charmers like this and, on half a dozen occasions, he would launch them with skilful publicity as 'The Most Beautiful Girl In The World'. Her name was Abdaga, and he resolved to introduce her at Grosvenor House where she would be unveiled by all the most famous London actresses. Negotiations with the French authorities to bring Abdaga over here went on for two years and broke down at the very last minute when there was no opportunity of finding a substitute. Cochran laid contingency plans. In the meantime engineers protested to him that it was impossible to install both the stage and the three-ring circus he wanted at Grosvenor House because the roof was too low. 'Very well,' he said without a moment's pause, 'take the roof off!'

On the night a host of leading theatrical folk appeared in a glamorous show which continued non-stop for hours. The moment of Abdaga's entrance arrived. Amid a flurry of fanfares there appeared a gorgeous palanquin designed by Oliver Messel and bearing a veiled figure. Gertrude Lawrence stepped forward and removed the first veil. All the gentlemen in the audience leaned forward to catch a glimpse of the mysterious beauty. Tilly Losch flipped away the second veil and Claire Luce the third. When all the veils had been taken off, the figure skipped out of the palanquin to reveal the superbly made-up features of Duggie Byng in full drag. He then sang a parody of Cole Porter's 'You're The Top' which he entitled 'I'm The Bod'. Since the function was charitable, and since they had just seen a parade of stars which no commercial management would ever have been able to assemble, the audience accepted

Cochran's little hoax and cheered his favourite comedian with good grace.

Once the exhilaration of Grosvenor House died away Cochran was back in his office glooming over accounts which told a dismal story. He had lost heavily on *Follow The Sun* and *Home and Beauty*. *The Boy David*, object of his high hopes, engulfed many more thousands of pounds. A play starring what should have been the irresistible combination of Yvonne Arnaud and Ronald Squire proved an expensive disappointment. Whenever, in the past, Cochran met with failure, he usually found that his next production, or even the one following it, succeeded well enough to cover his losses and generate fresh capital for new ventures. It seemed now that his luck was running out. Had he lost his touch?

A startling gesture was called for, some imaginative ploy that would capture attention and intrigue the public. On one and the same day, therefore, he signed up Gracie Fields, the most popular and richest woman star in England, and Richard Tauber, the best known singer of the day. Their names had tremendous drawing power. All that remained was to arrange a suitable attraction in which these different but very bankable talents could shine. Soon afterwards, however, Gracie Fields became the lover of an Italian film director whom she eventually married. For once she allowed her private life to interfere with the magnificent career that up to then was hers, and Cochran had no alternative but to release her from the contract. He was left with Richard Tauber. Some years earlier Tauber filled Drury Lane with Lehár's *Land of Smiles*. The solution was obvious: put him into another Lehár piece and the mixture as before would draw full houses again.

Cochran bought the rights of Lehár's *Paganini* and commissioned A. P. Herbert to adapt the libretto. Herbert struggled manfully with an inferior 'book' yet, despite his best efforts, could not improve a defective third act. The only achievement he took any pride in was his version of the song he called 'Girls Were Made to Love and Kiss', a number which soon became one of the most popular in Tauber's repertory. Tauber, indeed, was a very fine singer and, in particular, a consummate Mozartian. As Paganini, it must be said, he was grotesque. It was impossible for audiences to see in that bland, portly figure the skeletal aspect of a violinist so macabre that during his lifetime he was suspected of being the devil incarnate. Tauber was, moreover, a poor actor who constantly disconcerted his partner Evelyn Laye with unpredictable behaviour. 'You never,' she recalls, 'knew what he was going to do.'

Although Cochran dressed *Paganini* with luxury and even, to enhance the effect of illusion, added a fake proscenium, it cost him only half of what he usually spent on his revues. With Tauber's fine singing and Evelyn Laye's charming presence he was sure his new production would succeed. If only . . . if only he could rely on six weeks' good business in the early days to get his costs back . . . if only London would recover from its mood of Coronation weariness . . . Neither of these things happened and he decided to end the run. Tauber offered to guarantee any deficit if *Paganini* were kept on, and, reluctantly, Cochran agreed, stipulating that no-one should know of the arrangement since, in the theatre, just as nothing succeeds like success, by the same token nothing fails like failure. To his annoyance the news of Tauber's move leaked out and *Paganini*'s failure became public knowledge. It closed after less than two months. 'To those of you who intend to become theatrical producers, let this be a lesson' Cochran wrote later. 'Never try to reprieve a play when the best of all critics – the box-office – tells you it won't do.'

Harassed by a string of disappointments and the ever-present agony of arthritis, he was taking large sleeping draughts at night. They were the only things that kept him under and blotted out the worry and the pain that dogged his waking hours. One morning he emerged from his stupefied sleep to hear from Evelyn that during the night Alice Delysia, now in America, had made an excited telephone call. He rang her back and she urged him to come over immediately. She told him she had business friends who could help him to earn £25,000 a year, if not more. There was a fortune awaiting him in America! He could make enough money to nurse his arthritis in the sunshine of southern France and Spain! He could solve all his problems and live grandly ever after! As she spoke, her husky voice crackled with emotion, her r's boomed and reverberated down the line. Cautious at first, he gradually came to share her euphoria. Why not? There was nothing in London for him at the moment.

He talked over the idea with Evelyn and with Elisabeth Bergner. They both advised him to go. On past trips to America he had always discovered something new, and anyway the atmosphere of the country stimulated him. He sailed the next day.

Cochran was not long in New York before he realized that Alice, kind, naïve, well-intentioned Alice, had brought him out on a wild goose-chase. No business-woman herself, she had been carried away by the grandiose talk of people she met and thought to repay Cochran for all he had done to help her career in the past. He was touched, thanked her prettily, and left New York for Chicago, scene of many adventures in his youth. There he toured night-clubs with his old acquaintances the Dolly Sisters and relived memories as a ringside spectator at boxing matches. From Chicago, he flew to Los Angeles and stayed as a guest in the mansions of film producers. There was discussion of his organizing a giant exhibition, of millions of dollars to be invested, of sites to be laid out and of halls to be built. Lolling beside blue-tinted swimming pools, glass of Coca-Cola in hand, he discussed with architects and entrepreneurs wonderful notions for the future. That these projects all evaporated in the hot sunny air did not really trouble him. He was feeling so much better. The thrill of juggling with ambitious projects once again and, most of all, the blessed sunshine and its comforting effect on his tortured arthritic leg, restored his confidence and made him the man he had been before. He sent a cable urging Evelyn to join him. What about the fare? Sell some more of his books and pictures, he told her.

When she arrived they sat about under the brilliant sunshine and wallowed in the hospitality of film tycoons. Hollywood celebrities came and went. Dazed by the sparkling atmosphere, he sought to fix up deals with Betty Grable and Ginger Rogers. The hours were filled with golden dreams and buoyed up with expansive talk about the great things he was to do in the future. His native optimism flourished and castles in Spain proliferated. Hollywood took him into its dangerous embrace and smothered him with hopes and expectations that could never be fulfilled. Far away from Europe and its political problems, he began to lose his sense of reality. Sometimes, though, despite the generosity he received from honey-tongued magnates, he still needed cash. This he raised by selling a few of his pictures to Edward G. Robinson, an actor whose villainous look concealed an aesthete with a passion for Degas and Lautrec.

The mirage of Hollywood gradually vanished and even Cochran wearied of the ebullient chatter which for the past few months had lulled him with comforting visions. He came back to London, Evelyn at his side, and looked around desperately for new ideas. There was nothing for him to fall back on. Unlike rival impresarios, the Tom Arnolds and the Jack Wallers, he had never invested his profits in the Stock Exchange or in bricks and mortar. Money was to be spent, to be enjoyed, to be used as a means of creating beautiful stage pictures. It was a philosophy he shared with his old competitor André Charlot who, by an ironic coincidence, was also about to suffer the Hollywood illusion and to end up as a pauper.

His Rolls-Royce was sold and went back to the dealers with his silver mascot of the crowing cock on the bonnet. Soon afterwards his manservant had to go, the faithful Rosling who had worked for him since the nineteen-twenties. After eighteen years of coping with his master's secret rages, of helping to preserve the public image of a man who rarely lost his temper, Rosling departed, not without relief, into the service of Princess Arthur of Connaught. Cochran, he said, was a good employer, 'but he kept me on the go'.

At his office in Old Bond Street Cochran held meeting after meeting. He called in Milton Rosmer, the well-known actor and producer, and asked if he would put on a play for him. 'Yes, indeed,' said Rosmer. 'I should be honoured. It is something I have always wanted to do.' 'Why?' asked Cochran, his curiosity piqued. 'Because there is a great deal of prestige in producing a play for Charles B. Cochran.' 'Once,' replied Cochran sadly, 'but not now . . . not now.'

Having seen Beatrice Lillie during his American visit he decided to present her in a London show which he called *Happy Returns*. Mr Cochran's Young Ladies paraded again in their lovely dresses and, as the programme noted, 'the Garters thrown in Act 2 are specially supplied for Miss Lillie by CHARNAUX.' Yet the old brilliance was not there, and the first act finale, keystone of the evening, turned out to be nothing more than a hodge-podge entitled 'Memories of Cochran Shows' that dished up past successes. The one stroke of novelty was his pairing of Beatrice Lillie with Flanagan and Allen. The comedians, 'looking like two overworked bookmakers' in Miss Lillie's words, had dreadful trouble learning their lines. Originally intended to open on Friday, 13 May, 1938, *Happy Returns* was postponed for a week after superstitious objections from the three stars. Perhaps it would have been better if Cochran had gone ahead with his first choice of the unlucky date which he had selected out of bravado. The postponement failed to save his last peace-time revue from disaster.

In April, 1939, he travelled with Evelyn to Albano in northern Italy. The mud baths there would, he hoped, improve his arthritis. He and his wife were the only English people in residence at the Hotel Trieste and Victoria. The rest of the clientèle were German, for rumours of war had sent home all other English folk. Slopping about in the mud baths, he found, had a pleasant effect on his aching leg but made no lasting impression. The Cochrans went on to Venice and Dubrovnik where they stayed with friends, old acquaintances who had appeared in past shows of his. They journeyed home via Paris and a champagne reunion with Yvonne Printemps. Cochran had little interest in politics or world affairs: the theatre was his domain and what happened beyond the stage-door concerned him only in so far as it touched the box-office. Yet even he could sense that an era was ending, that unknown horrors lay ahead. His stay in Paris took on a valedictory air. He went out to Joinville studios and watched Sacha Guitry making his new film *Ils Etaient Neuf Célibataires*. Also there was Bert Howell, Cockney, irrepressible, accomplished fixer, who once negotiated a contract with Sacha on Cochran's behalf and remained Guitry's impresario ever since. His gift for languages was miraculous. One Christmas Day, on a train going to Budapest, Howell said to Cochran: 'Now we start equal; they speak a language here which I know nothing about.' Twenty-four hours later he knew enough to ask the way. By evening he could sustain a basic conversation. Within a week there was little he did not understand or express. Howell didn't learn languages, said Cochran, he *absorbed* them. War came and the multilingual Bert vanished, probably into a concentration camp, never to be heard of again.

London was restive and anxious. Air raid shelters were dug in the parks and mounds of sandbags thrown up. Mr Chamberlain came and went. The Cochrans moved to a small flat in Westminster Gardens. Under the growing threat of hostilities the Trocadero shows had been cancelled – indeed, all theatre and places of entertainment were to be closed – and his only source of regular income dried up. On 3 September he heard the Prime Minister's broadcast announcing war. Minutes afterward an air raid siren blared its warning. The Cochran's neighbours at Westminster Gardens, Sarah Churchill and Vic Oliver, appeared at the door and helped the lame impresario down to a shelter at ground level. His leg dragged painfully behind him as he hobbled into the lift and sank back against the wall.

He wrote a letter to each of his Young Ladies thanking them for their loyalty and their cheerfulness. 'Of the many shattering blows inflicted upon this old impresario by this terrible war tragedy,' he told them, 'none touches my heart more deeply than the separation from my Young Ladies, and the break in the continuity (over fifteen years) of Trocadero shows. My fondest hope is that we may work together again before too long.'

That hope seemed a vain one. At the age of sixty-seven he had little he could look forward to and his career, faltering over the last few years, had come to a sudden halt. There must, he thought, be something he could do to help the war effort with all his great experience, his vast range of friendships, his organizing talent. A few half-hearted approaches from official bodies came to nothing. He sat and fretted alone in Westminster Gardens. At night friends occasionally looked in and stayed to dinner. A few hours after the meal Evelyn would go to bed, having first whispered to them: 'Stay and talk to him for a while . . .' Then he would come to life, sip his brandy with a new relish and speak of the great days, of Bernhardt and Duse, of Diaghilev and the Guitrys, of Irving and Guilbert, of Richard Mansfield and Houdini.

When the theatres opened once more he simply could not bear his inactivity. A summons went out to the Young Ladies: he was preparing a new revue and they must be ready to play the big provincial cities before coming into London. *Lights Up!* was what he optimistically called it, and he rummaged around in those days of scarcity to find materials on the cheap. Thrown together on a make-shift basis with costumes and scenery borrowed or hired from here and there, *Lights Up!* opened at the Manchester Opera House early in 1940. Since Cochran had sold his own piano he borrowed one from a collaborator on the revue. At the first night the piano's owner was astonished to see it being used on stage. It had, moreover, been painted white. When he protested Cochran helpfully replied: 'Oh, I thought you'd *like* it white. I always knew you had a soft spot for Edythe Baker,' a musician whose trademark was a white piano.

Lights Up! moved on to Glasgow and Edinburgh playing full houses. It arrived at the Savoy in February and instantly suffered comparison with George Black's much more lavish production of *Black Velvet*. It also, Cochran, realized, did not come up to the standard of his own pre-war revues, even though his old production team of Frank Collins, Elsie April and Cissie Sewell had used every bit of their formidable expertise to make the best of the threadbare materials given them. Yet *Lights Up!* had some good things, not least of which was Evelyn Laye singing Noel Gay's 'Only A Glass of Champagne'. In the role of Cora Pearl, the Second Empire's most notorious courtesan and mistress of Napoleon III, (as if this were not enough, Cora was also the sixteenth child of the man who composed 'Kathleen Mavourneen'), she put over with lilting mock solemnity the refrain:

> 'Only a glass of champagne,
> But it led a poor girl into sin,
> Only a glass of champagne,
> Was the door where the devil crept in . . .
> . . . Now all you young maidens
> Take warning by her,

> If you go out with a lord or a sir,
> See that you don't let the same thing occur,
> All through a glass of champagne.'

In a more straightforwardly sentimental mood she sang 'You've Done Something To My Heart', also by Noel Gay who here achieved one of his best songs, a melody full of tender appeal and graceful modulations. With dresses by Norman Hartnell, settings by Doris Zinkeisen and music by Geraldo's orchestra, *Lights Up!* brought gaiety and colour to a city oppressed by the ominous atmosphere of the 'phoney war'. But, even at the height of their enjoyment, audiences could not escape reminders of the world outside. A programme note on air raid precuations advised them: 'You will be notified from the stage if an air raid warning has been sounded during the performance – but that does not mean that an air raid will necessarily take place. If you wish to leave for home or an official air raid shelter you are at liberty to do so. All we ask is that – if you feel you must go – you will depart quietly and without excitement. WE RECOMMEND YOU TO REMAIN IN THE THEATRE.'

ii
ALL THAT EVER WENT WITH EVENING DRESS

> 'In the twilight, on a bucket upside down,
> Hear me babble what the weakest won't confess –
> I am Memory and Torment – I am Town!
> I am all that ever went with evening dress!'

KIPLING

While they were touring the provinces with *Lights Up!* the Cochrans had let their Westminster Gardens flat. On returning to London they were offered by the benevolent management of the Savoy a suite at the hotel and stayed there, over the shop as it were, for the rest of the run at the adjoining theatre. When *Lights Up!* closed, after a modest hundred and fourteen performances, they moved into a friend's apartment at Carrington

House. One of their early guests was James Agate with whom, over many years, Cochran maintained a warm friendship only occasionally blemished by artistic disagreements. Evelyn was in her wittiest form and spoke of a playwright who, she said innocently, had called on her that very afternoon 'and sweetly and kindly read me a very long play'.

At Carrington House the Cochrans lived through the blitz currently raining down on London. There were times when the whole building trembled and its steel frame seemed to rock back and forth under the blast of bombs. 'I felt,' said Cochran, 'like a cocktail being shaken.' No post, no milk, no newspapers were delivered. Their part of Mayfair, in peace-time very smart and respectable, had become a haunt of *belles de nuit*. On an expedition in search of exiguous rations one afternoon Evelyn told a shopkeeper that she would return and collect her purchases later. 'We close at 6.30', said the shopkeeper. 'I wish I could,' said a mournful whore in the queue.

Cochran heard that the passionate Greek actress Katina Paxinou was in London and anxious to play Ibsen's *Ghosts*. He called on her at the Savoy Hotel and found her coiled up serpent-like on a Louis XVI sofa, a flower in her mouth, diamond bracelets dripping along her arms. This, he said to himself, was not Ibsen's Mrs Alving and he had to tell her so frankly. She heard him without flinching. 'Come to tea at my flat tomorrow', she said. When he presented himself there the front door was opened by a hard-faced harridan, her hair flat and brushed back, her plain face glowering. 'I want to see Madame Paxinou,' he announced. 'I *am* Madame Paxinou *as* Mrs Alving,' replied the charmless creature. '*Now* do I play *Ghosts*?' There could be no argument and he put her on for a limited season at the Duchess Theatre.

This was his only excursion into the theatre for several years. In the meantime he had to content himself with organizing a radio series called, at A. P. Herbert's suggestion, *Cock-a-doodle-do*. At eight o'clock every Saturday night, a peak listening period, he introduced a programme for which he had himself chosen the artistes and the material. His career up to then had been entirely devoted to visual spectacle and the new medium of radio set him problems which were difficult to resolve. The sound of words and music had to be manipulated in such a way as to create an impression of beauty and excitement. He needed, besides, to track down singers, players and soloists who were scattered far and wide under wartime conditions. Life at home was not particularly easy, either. Kindhearted Evelyn acquired the habit of inviting women stranded by air raids to take shelter in their flat. In search of his sleeping draught he would get up from bed and walk to the sitting-room. On the way he would need to step carefully over the recumbent bodies of strange women that littered the corridor from end to end, piled up in the bathroom and lay scattered over the floor of every other room.

Carrington House became unbearable. Fortunately another Good Samaritan intervened and the Cochrans were invited to be the permanent guests of Barry Neame, eighteen-stone bon vivant, wine connoisseur and owner of the Hind's Head down at Bray. Neame cherished things of culture as well as of the table, and at Bray in the sunlit garden Cochran talked with his generous host of the theatre, of art, of literature. At a luncheon to publicize a new book on wine, he was confronted with oysters and champagne as a prelude followed by lobster mould, partridge, creamed mushrooms, toasted cheese, white wine and no less than six vintage wines in magnums. For a moment he was transported back to those dear dead pre-war days when he would take a cottage in the country and surround himself with collaborators on a new revue. All he could do now was to sit in an invalid chair and be wheeled along a towpath beside the Thames while he murmured to a sympathetic companion: 'No more theatre for me. Never again. I'm past it.'

Or was he? The friendship of a young actress and singer called Valerie Frazer helped to keep his theatrical interest alive. He had engaged her to begin with for his Trocadero shows where her obvious talent impressed him. One day, between rehearsals, she entertained the other girls with an imitation of her employer stumping along on his stick and muttering 'Good morning, m'dear. How are you, m'dear?' She did not notice that the girls' expressions suddenly froze. Absorbed in her skit she swung round, still limping, and saw Cochran himself watching in silence from the doorway. 'Very good m'dear,' was all he said. 'I always knew you were a good comedian.'

He did not take offence and soon afterwards put her into *Follow The Sun*. She became one of his principal Young Ladies and he started to groom her for larger roles. In *Lights Up!* he happened to notice that she was holding a rather awkward pose and he asked her what was the matter. Her reply startled him: her legs, she explained, were ever so slightly bandy and she was trying to conceal the fact. He exploded with laughter. He, the distinguished expert on women's figures, the international authority on feminine charms, had for once been misled. The revelation turned into a private joke between them and explains the ribald double meaning of the postcard he sent her from Albano: 'Be sure and keep them together.'

After the war started and he no longer had anything to offer her they kept in touch nonetheless. 'If I can help to make a star of you I shall be ever so glad,' he wrote. 'Of course, I can only give the opportunity and then it's up to you. I've given lots of girls the chance; some have grabbed it and been fitted; others have failed. You will remember I've believed in you for some time and if I can be of help to you I shall be so very glad.' At other times he was still more emphatic: 'I am going to make you a West End leading lady yet as I've made so many others. The war won't last for ever . . .' He ended as always, 'Love and kisses, C.B.C.'

Playfully he would refer to their little joke. 'I am glad the bandy legs are doing alright. Heavens above! Why shouldn't they? Legs can and do have personalities like people' And he would turn wistful: 'I want to see your bandy legs dancing again; they are very sweet.'

He gave her introductions, put work her way and told other producers about her. 'Your case is tough,' he told her, 'even in these days when everybody is up against it, as you were just about to get your chance . . . It would make me very happy if I could get you a nice job.' Good counsel flowed her way: 'The best advice I can give you is to be your own most severe critic; never leave off working on your singing or dancing, and your acting. Already you have one considerable asset in your diction, but it can still be improved upon. When an artist ceases going forward he or she always goes backward. Don't take too seriously praise you get from friends, but give the greatest attention to adverse criticism.' He returned, as always, to his obsession: 'Don't worry about the bandy legs – they're cute legs – legs with personality – and can be such an asset. I believe I see things about you that others don't.'

Then she married the playwright Archie Menzies and became a mother. 'My heartiest congratulation upon your new production,' Cochran wrote, 'with my best wishes for an unbroken run of prosperity.' Valerie reluctantly left the stage, although her gift was inherited by one of her sons, Lee Menzies, the West End impresario. Cochran's prediction of theatrical success for Valerie Frazer is being fulfilled at a distance of one generation.

Close on half the page he wrote to Valerie Frazer congratulating her on the birth of her son was taken up by a grandiose letter heading. Above a list of patrons both royal and noble stood the name 'TOC H', the well-known war charity, and below came an announcement that at the Albert Hall Charles B. Cochran would be presenting 'Seventy Years of Song' with Geraldo's Concert Orchestra, celebrity soloists and 'many famous stars'. Once more he was in action and life was filled with the delight of organizing a huge spectacular for charity on the lines of his pre-war Grosvenor House cabaret. This time he had the vast spaces of the Albert Hall to conjure with, a seventy-piece orchestra and a cast of, literally, thousands. When the treasurer of TOC H asked him to arrange a large-scale function, his first idea had been to mount a cavalcade of popular song over half a century. Since he kept discovering attractive tunes that fell outside the arbitrary limit of fifty years he extended the time scale and ended up with the more alliterative title 'Seventy Years of Song'.

His ambitious panorama opened with 'In The Gloamin'' and a twilit evocation of London street figures during the eighteen-seventies. With famous music-hall songs, ballads and popular ditties of every description he constructed a moving pageant which ended in a chorus of hundreds singing 'Land of Hope and Glory'. Elsie April came up from the farm to which she had retired and helped him out with the music arrangements. Cissie Sewell designed the costumes, and only Frank Collins of his usual team was unable to be there since his work with ENSA kept him abroad. The items varied from 'Our Lodger's Such A Nice Young Man' to Eva Turner singing 'One Fine Day', from Geraldo's orchestra banging out 'In The Mood' to Hutch playing 'Alexander's Ragtime Band'. Cochran, rejuvenated, had a euphoric time directing massed detachments from the Army, Navy and RAF, controlling their evolutions throughout the hall and guiding the endless columns as they moved from floor to stage and spread out in open order to form immaculate groupings.

Then, in a few hours, the event he had worked on for months was over and he retired to Bray, weary, deflated, empty. As a matter of principle, he would accept no fee where charity was concerned. The thrill of activity was enough for him. Now, though, the excitement had passed and he became aware more than ever that money was dangerously short. Early in the nineteen-thirties he had, like Gerald du Maurier and, later, Laurence Olivier, given his name to a commercial product. In their case it was a cigarette. In Cochran's it was a wine, and the 'C. B. Cochran Sherry' marketed by Gonzalez Byass brought him over the years a small but pleasantly regular income. This, in the nineteen-forties, dwindled to almost nothing. Barry Neame consoled him on his sixty-eighth birthday with a dinner for twelve guests and served Krug 1928 as an apéritif, a 1937 Moselle, magnums of Haut Brion 1920, Château Latour 1899 and a blissful Château d'Yquem 1921. He brightened up even further when he had the opportunity, which few people enjoy, of reading his obituary. A Turkish newspaper published trilingually in English, French and German, announced sorrowfully: 'It is now a full year since we have mourned the death of the grand Charles B. Cochran, and yet his place is still unfilled.' He was, said the newspaper, a Christian gentleman, a promotor of fox-hunting and bull-fighting, and an expert in *les jolies nues*. Out of curiosity he wrote to the editor asking how news of his death had been obtained. Much later a discreet reply arrived: 'Dear and Honoured Sir, Before this information we can furnish you with, we would ask you politely to inform us wherein lies your interest in this matter.'

The only source of making money left him was, yet again, to issue another volume of memoirs for which he borrowed the title of his radio programme *Cock-A-Doodle-Do*. Much of the ground he had travelled before, although the decade since 1932, year of his last autobiography, provided a quantity of new material. A. P. Herbert contributed a rhyming foreword:

'And what a fine mixed feast you had to show –
Ibsen and Coward, Shakespeare, Shaw and all,
Ballet and boxing, Robey and Rodeo,
Cowboy & Circus! – *and* the Albert Hall! . . .

. . . To men like you we pay no living wage,
And all their work is swept away like snow.
Yet you have left your footprints on the stage;
The world is the richer for the "Cochran Show".'

The poet's exuberant licence, and need for scansion, added two authors to the list whom Cochran had never produced, but Herbert, as everyone agreed, meant well.

Over a thousand people turned up at a Foyle's literary luncheon to salute the book and to celebrate his fifty years of showmanship. James Agate, red-faced like Cochran, bulky and booming, gave a speech because, he said, he had the maximum affection for 'C.B.' as a man and the maximum admiration of him as an artist. 'C.B. has failed only in the one thing that doesn't matter – money,' said Agate. 'In the less material world he has always been Colonel Up and not Mr Down. His artistic integrity has been whole and unimpeachable.' He quoted the Kipling verse which prefixes this chapter and observed that Cochran represented 'all that ever went with evening dress', for his genius consisted 'in giving the London theatre whatever great and respectworthy art of all kinds has had the most of dazzle and of chic.'

At lunch with Agate some time afterwards Cochran was mellow and philosophic, even about British cigars. They agreed in quoting the old French proverb: 'If you can't have what you like, you must like what you have.' That, thought Cochran to himself while Evelyn preened herself in a very smart new hat, applied to many things beside cigars. He summoned up all his energies and in 1942 put on what was to be his last

revue. *Big Top*, written by the witty Herbert Farjeon, opened in
Manchester on Easter Day and starred Beatrice Lillie. This
was the occasion when she introduced her inimitable turn
'Wind Round My Heart' –

> 'The night is black, and the icy rain
> 'Keeps beating against my window pane . . .'

– intermingled with a grotesque recitative which she was to
embellish with many inspired touches over the years. It ends:
'So now I wear this painted face to hide an aching heart. The
heart of a fool who loved you from the start. I've tried to laugh,
I've tried to cry. I don't know what to do. But every time I think
of you, there's gas – *wind* – round my heart.'

In the face of all superstition *Big Top* also included a skit on
what actors warily refer to as 'the Scottish play'. It was called
Mockbeth. Beatrice Lillie appeared as MacBreath. McBluff was
the corpulent Fred Emney, monocled, mountainous, beery-
voiced. Bea Lillie toyed outrageously with kilt and sporran
while reciting:

> 'Where shall we three meet again
> The Vic, the New or Drury Lane?
> What hags are those with their soup tureen?
> The middle one looks like Basil Dean!'

The Scottish play should not be mocked. Within a few days of
the opening the father of an actor in the cast had died. Before
the show even reached London a telegram arrived for Bea
Lillie whose adored son was on active service in the Navy.
'REGRET TO INFORM YOU . . . SON BELIEVED
MISSING,' it read. Her first reaction was to put on some
lipstick. Cochran immediately offered to close down *Big Top* for
as long as she needed. She refused. After all, her son was only
'missing' she argued, and for a hundred and thirty-nine performances she grimaced and fooled about on stage with perfect
light-heartedness. After the London first night she received
another Admiralty telegram: 'PRESUMED DEAD . . .' For a
very long time she could not believe it.

Big Top disappeared unhappily into oblivion. Apart from

Enid Bagnold's new play *Lottie Dundass*, which he produced in 1943, Cochran was to do nothing in the London theatre for another three years, until after the war. At Bray he had little to occupy himself but his memories. Arthritis never loosened its pitiless grip on him and one of his legs was now only too clearly shorter than the other. He found it hard to preserve his usual bland manner. Bitterness and ill temper would creep out despite his efforts to control them. For tactical reasons he had been obliged to sign up an actress he disliked for *Big Top*. At rehearsals, when she appeared wearing a tight and scanty costume, he, crouching painfully in his seat and bent over his walking stick, growled: 'I know every wrinkle of that famous old arse intimately!'

He was not a man given to introspection. Normally he lived in the future, not in the past, and if he had had his time over again he would probably have made all the same mistakes. Cochran was a Texan at heart, said the dramatist Benn Levy, 'and everything he did had to be gigantic, bigger and better.' He thought big and he acted big. A true gambler is not interested in money. He gambles for the thrill, for the love of the game, and that is what Cochran did. Money was only the means of startling, delighting and enthusing audiences with displays of beauty and lavishness. Such was his gambler's confidence that he rarely had trouble in raising money to finance his shows. He believed wholeheartedly in whatever he was doing, and that faith communicated itself to others and inspired them as much as it did himself. His leadership consisted in delegating specialist tasks to the people best qualified for the job – lighting, management, wardrobe, music, dance – and letting them get on with it under his supervision. In that way he never lost sight of the wood for the trees and was able to put his own personal mark on the shows he produced. His name was a by-word for polish.

This excellence was obtained by strict discipline. If one of his Young Ladies was a minute or two late for rehearsal she was fined on the spot. Other fines were exacted for the misdemeanour of creasing a costume by sitting down in it, or drinking alcohol while in the theatre, or indulging in dangerous sports. The Young Ladies and the chorus girls were forbidden to wear rings or watches or bracelets or anything that might harm the uniformity of their appearance. They were given costumes made of the finest materials available, and even their knickers, which no-one but they ever saw, were individually tailored in the best quality silk.

He could be very generous. When an actor he wanted was asked to name a salary and gave a figure double what he was then earning, Cochran had no hesitation in agreeing. If he thought someone worth the money he was willing to pay without question. A performer who pleased him was liable to receive a bonus or even a small percentage of the profits, although, as exasperated accountants later pointed out, Mr Cochran had no right to make such presents. Those who asked for a rise usually got it. On the other hand, Cochran could be petty. Duggie Byng remembered that he once refused him permission to appear in cabaret while doing one of the London Pavilion revues. Afterwards he relented, but only on condition that he took ten per cent of Byng's fee.

Cochran sometimes appeared at the Garrick and the Savage, but was not what would have been described as a clubman. He preferred to lunch and dine at the Savoy, where he set up his deals to an accompaniment of choice wines and cigar smoke. Independence was essential, and that was why he never formed himself into a limited company, as financial prudence would have indicated. He wanted to be in control of everything and detested interference from outside. From time to time he worked as a salaried manager but not for very long. If freedom meant bankruptcy, which it occasionally did, he was more than ready to take the risk. Only a passionate love of the theatre could have sustained him throughout the many disappoint-ments he knew, and only an unshakeable belief in his eventual success could have kept him going. The theatre, which had been his first love as a boy of seven, was also his last love as a cripple in his seventies.

He had flair and imagination. He could seize on possibilities and anticipate fashion. Inevitably he made mistakes, yet when he succeeded he did so on a vast scale. Failure was something he loathed. If one of his shows flopped he always had an expla-nation, often a justifiable one: weather that was too bad or too fine, the unexpected illness of a star, inadequate seating capacity, some public disaster beyond his control. Failure in others was not acceptable, and he could be unjust towards the less fortunate.

Away from the theatre he loved books, art, wine and women. At his death a cataloguer took a month to work through all the titles of the beautifully bound volumes, each with the cockerel bookmark, which made up his private library. They chiefly concerned the theatre, the ballet and the circus, and many were valuable presentation copies from famous writers. He enjoyed the appearance of an elegantly printed book, its fine typography and thick luxurious pages, much as he enjoyed the appearance of an attractive woman. The harvest of his young days in Paris included Impressionist pictures in abundance, Gauguins, Lautrecs, Renoirs, Utrillos and others which he had bought cheap when few people appreciated them. Over the years he sold off many of them to finance his theatrical productions, but enough remained to make up a private collection of rare value. His acquaintance with other arts was brief. Music he knew little about, although he liked a good 'tune'. The Russians appealed to him most, especially the composers of the Ballets Russes, and, of course, the Spaniards, who came from that country which was his favourite land after France.

His sense of humour was small and his taste in jokes primitive, as we have seen from his reception of Jessie Matthews when she came back from her first visit to America. Charm and flattery were his weapons, and he used them adroitly to get what he wanted. An awkward leading lady, dissatisfied with the size of her billing or the amount of her percentage, would be met with compliments – 'That shade of blue matches your eyes perfectly, m'dear . . . what lovely shoes, darling . . .' which deflected her anger and sent her away feeling even more attractive than she really was, the source of her annoyance temporarily forgotten in the warmth of his admiration. He knew how to handle actors and actresses, designers and directors, financiers and businessmen. His knowledge of human nature was deep and without illusion. Money and praise were what most people wanted, and he administered these things in doses skilfully adjusted to individual need. Though not tall of stature he had an authoritative manner which, according to the situation, could be commanding or paternal. When crises exploded, as they often did, he retained his coolness and diplomatically overlooked the angry insults which those around him were hurling at everyone. Only in the shelter of his home, with Evelyn and the domestics as sole witnesses, did he give way to the anger, the despair, the frustration that attacked him at various points of his career.

Wit and humour he left to Evelyn, whose tongue as the years went by sharpened in malice. He was content to listen and chuckle as she released her carefully polished barbs, although he did not enjoy being the target for them as, thanks to his frequent affairs elsewhere, he increasingly became. On occasion her resentment grew too violent to be decently clothed in epigram and she assailed him with acrid reproaches. Once, in the street outside the theatre at an important first night, they stood on the pavement shouting angrily at each other. In general, however, she was seen to be an ideal companion and hostess, the perfect adjunct to a famous public man. By upbringing they were Victorian and would never have contemplated the shame of divorce. So long as they were married they slept together in the same double bed. What did it matter that they both had transient infatuations with pretty girls? Their relationship endured and they still needed each other for different reasons. As Cochran once remarked with heartless male complacency, 'Blondes may come and blondes may go, but Evelyn goes on for ever.'

In the hurly burly of the theatre feelings are bound to get hurt and injustice cannot help but flourish. There were those who found Cochran ruthless and unforgiving. Many more discovered in him a man of great sympathy and encouragement whose acts of kindness outnumbered the times when he was cruel or inequitable. He himself rarely complained of the treatment fate reserved for him, and, even though he might have many explanations for the failure of a particular show, he never cursed the public for rejecting what he offered it, unfair though the circumstances might have seemed.

Although he has his place in theatrical history as a master of revue, he by no means confined himself to the lighter side of the

stage, and while his showmanship embraced rodeos, performing fleas, circuses and roller skating, his cultural taste was
broad and informed. The very first production he undertook
was Ibsen's *John Gabriel Borkman* in 1897, not a very well-known
Ibsen piece even today, and at the time, when the Norwegian
playwright was thought hopelessly avant-garde, a venture of
considerable daring. In later years he was to present the
Guitrys, Brieux, Rostand, Sarah Bernhardt, Eleanora Duse,
Pirandello, Pitoëff, Moissi, Eugene O'Neill, Diaghilev and
Sean O'Casey. Among the artists and designers he commissioned were people like Augustus John, Léon Bakst, Oliver
Messel and Cecil Beaton. His choreographers included
Massine and Frederick Ashton. His composers were, on the one
hand, Cole Porter, Noël Coward and Vivian Ellis, and, on the
other, William Walton, Henri Sauguet, Lord Berners and
Martin Shaw. He might have said, with Oscar Wilde, that his
taste was simple: nothing but the best. If he thought something
was good of its kind and it pleased him, he wanted other people
to share his enjoyment. However obvious the formula, Cochran
applied it in a way that ensured a standard of excellence which
is legendary.

iii
SWEET VOICES

'I may here take occasion to remark upon what, in my own
estimate of my judgment in management, I have always
thought the most valuable quality – *courage*. I mean chiefly with
respect to the strength of will necessary to withdraw a play while
it was still very remunerative . . .'

SIR SQUIRE BANCROFT

To kill the boring hours of idleness and, more urgent still, to
earn money, Cochran dictated yet another book of reminiscences which he published in 1945 as *Showman Looks On*. A
réchauffé of earlier writings eked out with tales of Hollywood and
wartime experiences, the book did well and a second edition

was needed. An excellent piece of luck befell when the Rank Organization paid him what was then the large sum of ten thousand pounds for the film rights to all the volumes of memoirs he had brought out over the years. Cochran stipulated that he should have the option of choosing the actor who was to play him and began to explore the unfamiliar world of cinema. No film was ever made, though in a BBC television programme after his death he was impersonated by Frank Lawton, husband, appropriately enough, of his dear friend Evelyn Laye.

The windfall stimulated plans he was already making for a return to the theatre. When the war ended in 1945 he was seventy-three and full of ideas. *Seventy Years of Song* had proved that he could still organize on the grand scale and work for long hours at a stretch. He looked out for an experienced but younger man with whom he could go into partnership as 'Cochran and Blank' or 'Blank and Cochran'. Thanks to sub-lets there were premises available rent-free and now he had the necessary finance. He found the partner he wanted in Lord Tony Vivian. They lunched at the Savoy Grill and talked over the details of their association. If it did not work, said Cochran, there must be something else they could do together outside the theatre. 'This, for example,' he said, indicating the Savoy with a broad gesture. 'A restaurant. We should need a first class chef. But you know about wine, Tony. And I understand cigars . . .'

They discussed many projects and, with hindsight, made the usual number of mistakes. When Tony Vivian showed Cochran the script of *Seagulls over Sorrento* he turned it down out of hand, rather as Frank Collins had wanted to reject *The Better 'Ole*. The play became one of the biggest post-war successes and ran for over fifteen hundred performances. They thought of presenting the famous Indian dancer Ram Gopal but lacked funds. Gopal owned a number of valuable Indian carpets worth several times more than the cost of production and suggested they be used to raise the money. 'Tony,' said Cochran to his partner, 'we're not in the carpet business.' A New York agent who proposed a musical version of *Pygmalion* was met with derision. 'I can think of nothing more frightful, Tony, than G.B.S. to music,' exclaimed Cochran. *The Chocolate Soldier* had obviously escaped his memory and he could not have been expected to foresee *My Fair Lady*.

No, what he wanted was something from his old friend A. P. Herbert whom he asked for 'a thoroughly English play, with the past, present and future of our people specifically in mind.' As composer he thought of William Walton who had already written for him in *Follow The Sun*. Or what about Eric Coates? The final choice, and the happiest, was Vivian Ellis. Herbert supplied him with *Big Ben*, a libretto which told of a Socialist heroine elected to Parliament who falls in love with a rich Conservative M.P. By an amusing coincidence, Ellis had, in 1926, composed a *Big Ben* revue which, starting out from Swansea, came no nearer the West End than Finsbury Park Empire. This time he was luckier. Despite a pre-London tour marred by temperamental clashes – 'I wouldn't have remained in the business all these years if I didn't feel capable of coping with them,' said Cochran – *Big Ben* arrived safely in London at the Adelphi Theatre and opened on the 17 July, 1946. The audience included Princess Elizabeth, a rather sleepy Winston Churchill, Field-Marshal Montgomery and the Prime Minister Clement Attlee. It looked as if all the old pre-war glamour of a Cochran first night had been magically restored, except, alas, for the absence of the prime architect: Cochran himself was too ill for it.

At the dress rehearsal he surrendered to the kidney trouble which for several months had been paining him. The agony and discomfort of it all overcame him and he spent the first night of *Big Ben* miserably in his St James's Court flat. Vivian Ellis went there after the final curtain to report the triumph and found him slouched in a brightly coloured dressing gown which contrasted with his grey shrunken features. Very soon afterwards Evelyn took him to the London Clinic where one of his kidneys was removed after a long and exhausting operation. He fretted about what should become of her. 'She has lived through a nightmare and wrings my heart whenever I see her,' he told Herbert. 'It is tragic that a woman should centre her life in the being of one man and such a man! My only ambition now is to give her some happiness and peace for the rest of her life. I can't see the road clear.' The blondes were forgotten. Only Evelyn remained. Touched by his solicitude for her, Ellis and Herbert conceded some of the performing rights in *Big Ben* and other works to Cochran as 'a little pension', a personal gift which ensured that Evelyn would benefit from them after his death.*

It looked for a time as if *Big Ben* would indeed, like *Bitter Sweet*, prove to be an old age pension for both Cochran and his wife. Unfortunately running costs were high and, once the initial excitement evaporated, *Big Ben* closed after a hundred and seventy-two performances. That it was not quite good enough is due to Herbert's libretto which, given the author's fascination with parliamentary lore, is sometimes a little too specialized in its wit for the ordinary playgoer. The sub-Gilbertian echoes tend also to distract, which is curious given Herbert's often expressed dislike for the author of *Iolanthe*. There was, however, nothing wrong with a score that contains the nonchalantly romantic 'Let Us Go Down To The River' and the vigorous 'I Want To See The People Happy'. Cochran, certainly, did not lose his faith in the Herbert/Ellis partnership. While still on his sick-bed and recovering from the grim operation, he told them he was 'dead keen' on the 'Victorian light opera' he wanted them to write for him next.

Bless The Bride was inspired by Herbert's browsing in old volumes of *Punch* and has for its heroine a well-brought up Victorian Miss engaged to a stolid English gentleman. She, on her wedding day, elopes with a dashing French actor. After adventures in Europe she believes, encouraged by a jealous woman friend, that her French lover has been killed and resigns herself to marriage with her original betrothed, whereupon the hero suddenly comes back very much alive and claims her for a second time. The tenuous plot was embellished with pleasantly humorous dialogue and a generous allowance of hit numbers by Vivian Ellis. The artful simplicity of 'I Was Never Kissed Before' is as well found as the delightfully complacent gavotte tempo of 'Thomas T.', that is to say, 'Thomas Trout', the

---

* Their kindly gesture led to unfortunate complications after Cochran died. The new owners of his production company claimed that the rights belonged to them and there were protracted legal arguments. Having paid £36,000 in tax and surtax over a period of six years Herbert was naturally aggrieved that his generosity should be rewarded in such a way.

heroine's very Anglo-Saxon fiancé. The score has many charms, among them a Victorian polka, 'Oh, What Will Mother Say', replete with the subtle harmonies characteristic of Ellis. Moods are skilfully created, as witness the breezy exhilaration of 'Ma Belle Marguerite' and the wistful romanticism of 'This Is My Lovely Day'. The latter gave Ellis a great deal of trouble at first. Herbert wrote him three different lyrics before settling on the final version which was originally called 'I Shall Remember This'. Ellis did not like the title and begged for another one. 'How about "This Is My Lovely Day"?' said his collaborator on the spur of the moment. The composer sat down at the piano and found a tune emerging instantly. This may help to explain why *Bless The Bride* has such spontaneity. 'My enthusiasm mounts hourly,' Cochran told Ellis when he heard the music. 'I have a terrific hunch.'

The hunch was correct. *Bless The Bride* opened in April, 1947, and ran for well over two years despite competition from *Oklahoma* and *Annie Get Your Gun* which started around the same time. A strong cast was led by Georges Guétary whom Cochran and Vivian Ellis had found on a trip to Paris in search of a French hero. He was, of course, Greek, but learned English as competently as he had mastered French, and his accent impressed London audiences as the real thing. After a hesitant start *Bless The Bride* settled in comfortably at the Adelphi. Everyone made money out of it. Herbert, for example, in the financial year 1949/50 paid £8,383 in tax alone, and Cochran was able to exult in the achievement of having, at the age of seventy-five, produced his most successful musical show yet. His judgment, and the public's, has been confirmed by the passage of time. Forty years afterward *Bless The Bride* was professionally revived at the Northcott Theatre in Exeter, its charm and humour undimmed by the years.

With money coming in at last Cochran decided it was time to make his will. On the 25 March, 1948, his solicitor drew up for him a simple document two paragraphs long. In it he devised and bequeathed all he possessed to the long-suffering Evelyn. That same year the Honours list mentioned his name for 'services to the theatre'. Arrayed in silk hat and morning dress he drove with Evelyn to Buckingham Palace where the Band of the Coldstream Guards played a selection from *Bless The Bride* while he limped over red carpets and knelt, unsteadily, to receive the accolade. That evening at the Comedy Theatre, home of the satirical revue *Slings and Arrows*, Hermione Gingold and the company sang:

> 'And we were delighted
> When Father was knighted
> So Bless The Show!'

At the end of 1949 he showed what Sir Squire Bancroft described as managerial 'courage' by ending the run of *Bless The Bride* while at its peak. Or was it foolhardiness? Audiences were still flocking to the Adelphi and bookings extended healthily into the months ahead. Partly his decision came from restlessness. Boredom quickly set in with Cochran, and once he had created the perfect thing he could not wait before moving on to the next challenge. He was, moreover, confident that in A. P. Herbert and Vivian Ellis he had a partnership that rivalled Gilbert and Sullivan. At his command they wrote another piece, *Tough At The Top*, and he set out on a tour of Europe and the USA, just as in the good old days, to find the best singers the world could offer him. In Paris he recruited a beautiful soprano called Maria D'Attili. In New York he signed up the American baritone George Tozzi. The settings were designed, lushly, by Oliver Messel.

Tough At The Top proved an unhappily prophetic title. Having reached a peak with *Bless The Bride*, Cochran was to plunge way below with its successor. His new production, which opened in July, 1949, had to close after four months of public indifference. All the customary excuses were offered: the leading roles were not strong enough, the show opened in the middle of a long heat-wave . . . In fact the plot and the libretto were inadequate. *Tough At The Top*, the romantic story of a Princess who fell in love with an American boxer and then renounced him to marry the aristocrat chosen by her family, was the sort of thing that only Ivor Novello could get away with in his Ruritanian operettas. At the first night Cochran sat out front with Evelyn. Before it was over he knew he had an expensive flop on his hands. 'I shall not make a speech,' he

whispered to Vivian Ellis who was also beside him. He discreetly waved his handkerchief as a signal for the final curtain. It was
the last time he ever did this.

In 1950 a small consolation for the failure of *Tough At The Top*
arrived in the shape of a French honour. This was the ribbon of
Chevalier de la Légion d'Honneur for his work in introducing
French plays and artists to English audiences. No-one could
have deserved it more. He and Evelyn spent that Christmas
with Vivian Ellis at his home in Somerset. A burst boiler
deprived them of heat in their St James's Court flat and they
moved out for a time to the Hyde Park Hotel. Repairs were
done and they went back to Chesham Street and the flat. Vivian
Ellis called to see them one January Sunday in 1951. He chatted
affectionately with them and admired the pictures, still quite
numerous, which Cochran had not yet sold to finance his
shows. With an innocence which later events showed to be
appalling, Cochran remarked on how blissfully hot the water
was again.

A few days later he rose early to take the warm bath which
helped ease his arthritis. Evelyn usually ran it for him and
checked the temperature, but she had slept badly that night
and he did not care to disturb her. He went into the bathroom,
locked the door and switched on both hot and cold taps. Since
the heat was only tepid he turned off the cold tap and lay full
length in the bath. The hot water continued its flow and he
reached to turn it off as well. He found that he could not. His
arthritic hip immobilized him in a helpless position. The hot
current went on running amid a cloud of thickening steam and
the temperature rose ominously. He shouted for help but his
screams were muffled by the din of a vacuum cleaner which the
maid had just begun to operate. Still the hot water gushed and
the unbearable heat reddened his body, tormented every nerve,
flayed his skin. Evelyn awoke and, hearing his shouts at last,
went to the window suspecting a disturbance in the street. Then
she realized where the noise was coming from. The porter was
called and, with the help of neighbours, broke down the
bathroom door. Cochran's tortured body was lifted out. As they
slid him into the ambulance he murmured to Tony Vivian:
'Look after the show, Tony. Look after the show.'

He was taken to Westminster Hospital. Long periods of conciousness and suffering were broken by moments of delirium. On the fourth day Evelyn nerved herself to see him and was overcome by the ghastly sight. The scalding water had made him almost unrecognizable. She was told that if he recovered he would never move beyond an invalid chair. Why, she asked, did they not let him die? It was, they told her, their duty to preserve life.

Except for Evelyn, Lord Vivian and their old friend Dorothy Dickson, no-one saw the dying man. On the ninth day the hospital summoned her to visit him for the last time. She took special care with her make-up and chose one of her prettiest dresses. 'She was almost like a Cochran Young Lady', Tony Vivian recalled.

They entered his room and she bent over his pillow.

'Cockie,' she whispered, 'do you know what happened to you?'

'No . . .'

'Well, you must close your eyes. You've had that operation . . . you remember the doctor in Lisbon? . . . Now you are cured. Close your eyes and when you open them you'll never feel any pain again.'

He lay, immobile, and gazed blankly at the ceiling. Death released Sir Charles B. Cochran on the 31 January, 1951. Three days later he was cremated at Golders Green in a coffin draped with a black Spanish shawl. Although he had expressly asked that no memorial service be held for him, there was a small ceremony at the little 'actors' church' of St Paul's in Covent Garden. A tablet was put up bearing a quotation from *Coriolanus*:

'I thank you for your voices: thank you:
Your most sweet voices.'

Noël Coward's tribute was briefer. 'Poor old Cochran died after his horrible accident,' he noted laconically in his diary. He had still not forgiven his one-time partner.

What little estate Cochran left was cleared up and shown to be worth £22,921. 10s. 5d., a derisory sum for a man who had made today's equivalent of millions – although, of course, he had also lost them. As he often said, 'Any fool can save money. It takes a wise man to know how to spend it.'

Later that year Valerie Frazer organized a nostalgic gathering at the Adelphi Theatre which had been so closely associated with Cochran. From all over the country and from abroad as well came more than sixty of Mr Cochran's Young Ladies. Most of them now were wives and mothers, golden girls married to chaps with steady jobs in banking and insurance. Their talk was of homes and children rather than of first nights and chorus lines. Yet when Anna Neagle unveiled Peter Lambda's bust of Sir Charles B. Cochran with its uncanny likeness, piercing eye, commanding tilt of the head, they suddenly felt again the presence of their old boss and were silent.

Evelyn moved from the flat in St James's Court and left its tragic memories for a new apartment at Ashley Gardens near Victoria Station. She survived her husband by nine years and was able to live, as he had hoped, in modest comfort on royalties from his estate. When she died on the 19 November, 1960, she left £8,028. 7s. 7d. The press cuttings and books compiled by her husband were bequeathed to James Laver. Her pictures went to Mrs Henry Sherek, wife of the impresario. The royalty income was left on trust for Dorothy Dickson to administer, and to the King George's Pension Fund for Actors and Actresses. Evelyn was cremated and her ashes, with those of her husband which had been stored until her death, were buried at her side in her mother's grave at Hanwell Cemetery. The blondes had come, the blondes had gone, and Evelyn had Charles to herself for ever.

In 1966 the survivors of Mr Cochran's Young Ladies met again at the Adelphi Theatre beside his bust, and, rallied by Anna Neagle, went over to the Savoy for a tea party. They pitched in to smoked salmon sandwiches and blackcurrant tarts as they waited for Jessie Matthews to join them from a late recording session of 'Mrs Dale's Diary'. She finally arrived to be greeted by Anna Neagle throwing her arms round her neck and exclaiming 'Jessie darling!' Said one of the Young Ladies ecstatically: 'Now we can really begin!'

Six years later Sir Peter Saunders mounted his own tribute at the Vaudeville Theatre with a show entitled *Cockie!* It included all the famous musical numbers from productions by Sir Charles B. Cochran. Once more the ghosts of Alice Delysia and Noël Coward flitted across the stage for a brief moment in evenings electric with memories. A flesh-and-blood presence from the nineteen-twenties was the indestructible Max Wall who could date his association with Cochran back to *One Dam' Thing After Another*. Since then he had appeared in every branch of entertainment except for Shakespeare and the circus. Few performers could equal a record which also included a *White Horse Inn* on ice.

More recently an unknown vandal tipped over Cochran's bust in the foyer of the Adelphi Theatre and defaced the memorial plaque. Valerie Frazer and a cohort of the Young Ladies, now sadly reduced to little more than thirty in number, met together there in September, 1986. A new tablet had been prepared and the image of Cochran removed to a position safe from impious hands. Sir Peter Saunders gave an address and Evelyn Laye performed the unveiling. The 'sweet voices' from *Coriolanus* were heard again. Over the years they echo still.

BIBLIOGRAPHY

Agate, James. The Contemporary Theatre, 1926. Chapman and
  Hall, 1927.
Agate, James. My Theatre Talks. Arthur Barker, 1933.
Agate, James. First Nights. Ivor Nicholson and Watson, 1934.
Agate, James. More First Nights. Gollancz, 1937.
Agate, James. Ego 5. Harrap, 1942.
Agate, James. Ego 6. Harrap, 1944.
Agate, James. Red Letter Nights. Jonathan Cape, 1944.
Agate, James. Ego 7. Harrap, 1945.
Agate, James. Immoment Toys. Jonathan Cape, 1945.
Baddeley, Hermione. The Unsinkable Hermione Baddeley. Collins,
  1984.
Byng, Douglas. As You Were. Duckworth, 1970.
Castle, Charles. Oliver Messel. Thames and Hudson, 1986.
Cleugh, James. Charles B. Cochran. Pallas Publishing Ltd, n.d.
Cochran, Charles B. Secrets of A Showman. Heinemann, 1925.
Cochran, Charles B. I Had Almost Forgotten . . . Hutchinson, 1932.
Cochran, Charles B. Cock-A-Doodle-Doo. J. M. Dent, 1941.
Cochran, Charles B. Showman Looks On. J. M. Dent, 1945.
Cochran, Charles B. Various prefaces to books on the theatre, etc.
Coward, Noël. Collected Sketches and Lyrics. Hutchinson, n.d.
Coward, Noël. The Noël Coward Diaries. Edited by Graham Payne
  and Sheridan Morley. Weidenfeld and Nicolson, 1982.
Coward, Noël. The Essential Noël Coward Song Book. Omnibus
  Press, 1980.
Coward, Noël. Autobiography. Methuen, 1986.
Curtis, Anthony (Editor). The Rise and Fall of The Matinée Idol.
  Weidenfeld and Nicolson, 1974.
Desmond, Florence. Florence Desmond By Herself. Harrap, 1953.
Ellis, Vivian. I'm On A See-Saw. Michael Joseph, 1953.
Ellis, Vivian. A Composer's Jubilee. Chappell Music Ltd., 1982.
Finck, Herman. My Melodious Memories. Hutchinson, 1937.
Gänzl, Kurt. The British Musical Theatre, Vol. 2, 1915–1984.
  Macmillan, 1986.
Graham, Sheila. The Late Lily Shiel. W. H. Allen, 1979.

Graves, Charles. The Cochran Story. W. H. Allen, n.d.

Harding, James. Sacha Guitry, The Last Boulevardier. Methuen, 1968.

Heppner, Sam. 'Cockie'. Leslie Frewin, 1969.

Herbert, A. P. A.P.H. His Life and Times. Heinemann, 1970.

Howard, Denise. London Theatres and Music Halls, 1850–1950. The Library Association, 1970.

Huggett, Richard. The Curse of Macbeth. Picton Publishing, 1981.

Huggett, Richard. 'When failure was a dirty word.' *The Stage and Television Today*, 18 Sept., 1986.

James, Edward. Swans Reflecting Elephants. (Edited by George Melly). Weidenfeld and Nicolson, 1982.

Laver, James. Museum Piece. André Deutsch, 1963.

Laye, Evelyn. Boo To My Friends. Hurst and Blackett, 1958.

Lesley, Cole. The Life of Noël Coward. Jonathan Cape, 1976.

Lillie, Beatrice. Every Other Inch A Lady. W. A. Allen, 1973.

Mander, R., and Mitchenson, J. Revue. A Story In Pictures. Peter Davies, 1971.

Mander, R., and Mitchenson, J. The Theatres of London. New English Library, 1975.

Matthews, Jessie. Over My Shoulder. (As Told to Muriel Burgess). W. H. Allen, 1974.

Mills, John. Up In The Clouds, Gentlemen Please. Weidenfeld and Nicolson, 1980.

Milton, Billy. Milton's Paradise Mislaid. Jupiter, 1976.

Morley, Sheridan. A Talent To Amuse. Heinemann, 1969, revised 1984.

Morley, Sheridan. Spread A Little Happiness. Thames and Hudson, 1987.

Neagle, Anna. There's Always Tomorrow. W. H. Allen, 1974.

Nichols, Beverley. Are They The Same At Home? Jonathan Cape, 1927.

Nichols, Beverley. All I Could Never Be. The Right Book Club, n.d.

O'Casey, Sean. The Letters of Sean O'Casey. (Edited by David Krause), Vol. 1, 1910–1941. Cassell, 1975.

Parker, John. Who's Who In The Theatre. 4th, 5th, 7th, 9th, 10th, 11th and 13th editions. Pitman, various dates.

Play Pictorial, The. Special issues featuring Cochran productions.

Pound, Reginald. A. P. Herbert. A Biography. Michael Joseph, 1976.

Reader, Ralph. It's Been Terrific. T. Werner Laurie, 1953.

Saunders, Sir Peter. The Mousetrap Man. Collins, 1972.

Sebba, Anne. Enid Bagnold. A Biography. Weidenfeld and
   Nicholson, 1986.
Stage, The (and Television Today). Various issues during
   Cochran's lifetime.
Stage Yearbook, The. Various editions.
Theatre World. Special supplements featuring Cochran
   productions.
Traubner, Richard. Operetta. Gollancz, 1984.
Vickers, Hugo. Cecil Beaton. Weidenfeld and Nicolson, 1985.
Wall, Max (with Peter Ford). The Fool On The Hill. Quartet
   Books, 1975.
Williams, Emlyn. Emlyn. Bodley Head, 1973.
Ziegler, Philip. Diana Cooper. Hamish Hamilton, 1981.

THE MAJOR THEATRICAL PRODUCTIONS
OF CHARLES B. COCHRAN

At one time or another in his career Cochran was licensee, lessee or manager of the theatres listed below. There were occasions when he ran half a dozen of them simultaneously. He was also manager for a period of The Royal Albert Hall.

Adelphi, Aldwych, Ambassadors, Apollo, Comedy, Empire Leicester Square, Garrick, London Pavilion, New Oxford, Palace, Phoenix, Princes, St Martin's.

1897   John Gabriel Borkman. Ibsen. New York

1902   Sporting Simpson. Royalty Theatre.
Lyre and Lancet. F. Anstey. Royalty Theatre.

1911   The Miracle. Volmller/Humperdinck. Olympia.

1914   Odds and Ends. Grattan/Jones. Ambassadors.

1915   Watch Your Step. Irving Berlin. Empire.
More. Grattan/Jones. Ambassadors.

1916   Half Past Eight. Paul Rubens. Comedy.
Pell Mell. Nat D. Ayer, etc. Comedy.
Houp-La. Nat D. Ayer, etc. St Martin's.

1917   Damaged Goods. Brieux. St Martin's.
The Man Who Married A Dumb Wife. Anatole France.
   Ambassadors.
The Hundred and Fifty Pounds Revue. St Martin's.
The Three Daughters of Monsieur Dupont. Brieux.
   Ambassadors.
The Better 'Ole. Bairnsfather. Oxford.
Carminetta. Hoffe/Finck, etc. Prince of Wales.
Wonder Tales. Fagan. Ambassadors.

1918 As You Were. Wimperis. London Pavilion.
Jolly Jack Tar. Hicks, etc. Princes.
In The Night Watch. Morton. Oxford.

1919 Sleeping Partners. Guitry/Hicks. St Martin's.
Cyrano de Bergerac. Rostand. Garrick, Drury Lane.
A Certain Liveliness. Hastings. St Martin's.
Afgar. Thompson. London Pavilion.
Maggie. Thompson/Maltby. Oxford.
The Eclipse. Thompson/Oppenheim. Garrick.

1920 Pretty Peggy. Rose/Austin/Adams. Princes.
The Man Who Came Back. Goodman. Oxford.
One Night In Rome. Manners. Garrick.
Sacha Guitry Season. Aldwych.
Anna Pavlova Season. Prince's.
London, Paris and New York. Wimperis/Darewski.
    London Pavilion.
Her Dancing Man. Armont/Bousquet. Garrick.
Cherry. Knoblock/Gideon. Apollo.

1921 League of Notions. Anderson/Barratt. New Oxford.
Sarah Bernhardt Season. Prince's.
Diaghilev Russian Ballet Season. Prince's.
Les Chauve-Souris. London Pavilion.
Fun of The Fayre. Turner/Barratt. London Pavilion.
Babes In The Wood. New Oxford.

1922 The Man In Dress Clothes. Hicks. Garrick.
Mayfair and Montmartre. Turner. New Oxford.
Chuckles of 1922. Archer/Cook. New Oxford.
Sacha Guitry Season. Prince's.
Phi-Phi. Christiné. London Pavilion.
Battling Butler. Melford/Furber. New Oxford, Adelphi.

1923 Partners Again. Glass/Goodman. Garrick.
Anna Christie. O'Neill. Strand.
Sacha Guitry Season. New Oxford.
Eleanora Duse Season. New Oxford.
Comédie Française Season.
Music Box Revue. Irving Berlin. Palace.
Dover Street to Dixie. Harvey/Simpson, etc. Palace.
Little Nellie Kelly. Cohan. New Oxford.

1924 Old Vic Season. New Oxford.

1925   On With The Dance. Coward. London Pavilion.
        Still Dancing. Wimperis/Jeans. London Pavilion.

1926   Turned Up. Rigby. New Oxford.
        Pirandello Season. New Oxford.
        Le Miroir Juif. London Pavilion.
        Cochran's Revue. Jeans. London Pavilion.
        Sacha Guitry Season. Gaiety.
        Black Birds. Meyer. London Pavilion, Strand.

1927   One Dam' Thing After Another. Jeans/Rodgers and Hart.
            London Pavilion.

1928   This Year of Grace. Coward. London Pavilion.
        The Road To Rome. Sherwood. Strand.

1929   Wake Up and Dream. Turner/Cole Porter. London Pavilion.
        Porgy. Du Bose and Heyward. His Majesty's.
        Sacha Guitry Season. His Majesty's.
        Caprice. Sil-Vara. St James's.
        Paris Bound. Lyric.
        Bitter Sweet. Coward. His Majesty's.
        Castles In The Air. Wenrich/Peck. London Pavilion.
        The Silver Tassie. O'Casey. Apollo.

1930   Alexander Moissi Season. Globe.
        Pitoëff Season. Globe.
        Japanese Players' Season. Globe.
        Cochran's 1930 Revue. Nichols/Ellis. London Pavilion.
        Private Lives. Coward. Phoenix.
        Ever Green. Levy/Rodgers and Hart. Adelphi.

1931   Strictly Dishonourable. Sturges. Phoenix.
        Cochran's 1931 Revue. Coward. London Pavilion.
        1931 Varieties. Palladium.
        Marx Brothers Season. Palace.
        Grand Hotel. Baum/Knoblock. Adelphi.
        Cavalcade. Coward. Drury Lane.

1932   Helen! Offenbach/Herbert. Adelphi.
        The Cat and The Fiddle. Harbach/Kern. Palace.
        The Miracle (revival). Lyceum.
        Words and Music. Coward. Adelphi.
        Sacha Guitry Season. Cambridge.

1933 Mother of Pearl. Straus/Herbert. Gaiety.
Wild Decembers. Dane. Apollo.
Music In The Air. Hammerstein/Kern. His Majesty's.
Nymph Errant. Laver/Brent/Cole Porter. Adelphi.
Escape Me Never. Kennedy. Apollo.

1934 Conversation Piece. Coward. His Majesty's.
Magnolia Street. Golding/Rawlinson. Adelphi.
Why Not Tonight? Palace.
Streamline. Herbert/Ellis. Palace.

1935 Mesmer. Nichols. King's Theatre, Glasgow.
Anything Goes. Bolton/Wodehouse/Cole Porter. Palace.
The Black Eye. Bridie. Shaftesbury.

1936 Follow The Sun. Jeans/Turner, etc. Adelphi.
The Old Maid. (With Binkie Beaumont). King's Theatre,
   Glasgow.
Blackbirds of 1936. Mercer. Gaiety.
The Boy David. Barrie. His Majesty's.

1937 Home and Beauty. Herbert/Brodsky, etc. Adelphi.
Paganini. Lehár. Lyceum.
Laughter In Court. Miller. Shaftesbury.

1938 Happy Returns. Adelphi.
Flashbacks. Palace.

1940 Lights Up. Jeans/Gay. Savoy.
Ghosts. Ibsen. Duchess.

1942 Big Top. Farjeon/Brodsky, etc. His Majesty's.

1943 Lottie Dundass. Bagnold. Vaudeville.

1946 Big Ben. Herbert/Ellis. Adelphi.

1947 Bless The Bride. Herbert/Ellis. Adelphi.

1949 Tough At The Top. Herbert/Ellis. Adelphi.
The Ivory Tower. Templeton. Vaudeville.

INDEX